FREAK OR UNIQUE?
The Chris Evans Story

David Jones began his journalistic career on his home town newspaper, the *Morecambe Guardian*, in 1976. Six years later, via Preston and Manchester, he arrived in Fleet Street. There he has won two awards and held many posts, including United States Correspondent, Environment Editor, News Editor and Associate Editor. He is currently freelance, writing principally for the *Daily Mail*.

Born in 1956, Jones has been married for twenty-one years. He and his wife Angela live with their two sons, two daughters, a dog and two cats in Surrey. Passionate about sport, he is the ageing player-manager of a Sunday football team and a wicket-keeper-batsman of modest ability. His other enthusiasms include cooking, fishing and travel.

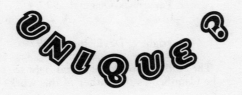

THE CHRIS EVANS STORY

DAVID JONES

HarperCollins*Publishers*

HarperCollins*Publishers*
77–85 Fulham Palace Road,
Hammersmith, London W6 8JB

A Paperback Original 1997
1 3 5 7 9 8 6 4 2

A catalogue record for this book is
available from the British Library

ISBN 0 00 653017 6

Set in Sabon by
Rowland Phototypesetting Ltd,
Bury St Edmunds, Suffolk

Printed and bound in Great Britain by
Caledonian International Book Manufacturing Ltd, Glasgow

The summer of 1992 is drawing to a close and for brilliant young radio and television presenter Christopher Evans, the future appears to be filled with treasures. He is about to exchange his modest studio flat for a spacious detached house in a secluded lane overlooking London's Hampstead Heath. To remind himself of the rarefied circle in which he now moves, he need only stroll a few metres from his door. The leafy streets are lined with top-of-the-range Mercedes and sporty BMWs; the shops are beyond the price range of ordinary people; his neighbours are writers and artists who wander down to the village brasseries for lunch al fresco, where the talk is of film scripts, parties and big-money deals.

Even amidst this glittering firmament, Chris Evans is already attracting sidelong glances, and not only because of his technicolour clothing, Eric Morecambe glasses and carrot-coloured hair. Having arrived in London barely four years ago as a penniless nonentity from Warrington, in the heart of the industrial North West, he has hurtled from the backrooms of local radio to become the cult hero of national television, seemingly without drawing breath. Michael Grade and the 'suits' at Channel 4, where he is now the zany frontman on *The Big Breakfast*, adore him. Almost every major station would break the bank to sign him. And yet, just at this moment, when all his boyhood dreams are becoming reality, Chris Evans feels lonelier and more wretchedly miserable than he ever has in the eventful first twenty-five years of his life.

The rapidly-accruing wealth, the celebrity status, the glowing newspaper articles – all have a hollow ring. How can it be otherwise when Evans is prone to dark depressions and increasingly violent mood-swings? Barely a working day passes without him flying into a rage, often over the smallest hitch. A camera angle need only be fractionally wrong or a cue-card innocently misplaced, for him to lambaste the offending colleague with such foul-mouthed ferocity that tears and even resignations follow. And when he leaves the Docklands studio, his misery deepens. Tormented by chronic hypochondria since his teens, his fears have plumbed such morbid depths that he imagines the most minor ailment to be terminal. Meanwhile, his marriage to broadcasting production manager Carol McGiffin, cemented barely twelve months ago, already appears doomed. When they argue – which is often – their rows invariably escalate into a cacophony of shattered ornaments and splintered glass.

Today, as we observe Evans in the throes of his latest despair, he and Carol have clashed yet again. Helplessly confused as to the source of his perpetual anger, his gaze falls upon the Yellow Pages directory for North West London lying beside the phone. He has made it a steadfast rule never to discuss his past, much less dwell upon it. But now, as if on auto-pilot, he picks up the book and thumbs through until he reaches the Psychotherapy and Analysis listings. At random, he selects the name of a local practitioner, Claire Chappell, and tentatively dials her number.

The intensity of the ensuing Friday evening therapy sessions, each lasting two hours, is so great that Evans can bear to attend for only ten weeks. Under Claire's guidance, he is transported back to a time so painful that he has locked it away in the least accessible corner of his mind for thirteen years, hoping, no doubt, that he will never have cause to search for the key.

It is 1979 in Greenwood Crescent, a council estate in the

grim Warrington suburb of Orford, where Chris and his family live. One day he and his father, Martin, are giggling over a game of miniature snooker in his untidy, toy-strewn bedroom, while his mother, Minnie, contentedly prepares supper downstairs. The next, an air of sadness has descended on the house, and the parents are talking in hushed tones. In the weeks that follow, Chris watches his beloved father – a proud, thick-set, rapier-witted man – deteriorate, in physique, if not in spirit, almost by the day.

He remembers how his father's clothes began to hang off his withering frame. He remembers the wheelchair, and the red-checked blanket, and how he and his mother would take turns to push Martin around the block, trying always to remain cheerful and optimistic, and never showing him their tears.

He remembers, as if it were only yesterday, 25 April 1979, the day he returned home from school to find all the curtains in the house drawn. And how he was taken aside and told that the man he admired and trusted above all others had died.

The thought that Minnie, who lived for her husband and family, would now be left to face life alone was more terrible even than his own grief. His father was only fifty-seven and his mother fifty-three, and if any couple had deserved to live happily together, long into retirement, it was them. In a neighbourhood with more than its fair proportion of dysfunctional families, theirs had been a beacon: music from the piano, laughter, days out at the Blackpool coast, homework done communally by the fire.

The flames of Evans's inner rage were to be fanned by further trials and indignities, but with the death of his father the fuse had been lit.

CHAPTER ONE

Ever the diplomat, Chris Evans gave an honest answer when asked by an interviewer whether he missed his home town of Warrington.

'Yeah,' he replied, deadpan, 'I try to miss it every time I go past on the motorway.'

As his wealth and fame have grown, such wounding insults have been served up at regular intervals, deepening the division between Evans and his old Warrington friends and neighbours, many of whom now passionately despise him for turning his back on his roots. Were he foolish enough to venture into the Greenwood pub – the bunker-like grey concrete alehouse that sits diagonally opposite his mother Minnie's house on the council estate of Orford – he would be lucky to leave with his teeth.

'We've no problem with Minnie,' said one of the local hard lads who while away the afternoons downing strong lager and arguing over football. 'She's the salt of the earth. But that lad of 'ers, it's gone to 'is 'ead. Worra bloody wanker.'

Though the language is diluted in the more affluent southern suburbs of Warrington, such as Appleton, Thelwall and Stockton Heath, these sentiments are echoed throughout the town. If they were brutally honest, however, the Warringtonians might concede that – as is often the case – their prodigal son has touched a raw nerve. For, commercially successful as its new-tech industries have made it in recent years, even the most loyal townsfolk would be hard-pressed to make a case for modern-day Warrington's elegance.

Originally built into the only fordable elbow of the River Mersey between Manchester and Liverpool, the solid Victorian villas and thriving redbrick factories that lent the town an air of Northern grandeur and prosperity after the Industrial Revolution are today either dilapidated or gone. From their ashes, a hotchpotch of ugly and incongruous shopping malls, fast-food drive-throughs, inter-linking walkways, low-rent flats, houses and business units has arisen. Surrounding this garish urban hub, sprawling out to the confusion of motorways that has attracted such modern-day industrial giants as IKEA, Fiat and British Nuclear Fuels, stand the strangely muted and alien communities that promised working families like the Evanses a bright new dawn: the New Town.

These days, as Minnie Evans sits in her favourite armchair beside the window that looks out on to the pub and the residential care home where Chris's Uncle Billy is housed, one cannot help but wonder whether she yearns for times gone by.

Bostock Street, within shouting distance of the town centre and at the heart of the Bank Quay area, was where Minnie Evans's family – the Beardsalls – were rooted, and where they lived until 16 March 1970. Then the council's Compulsory Purchase Order came into effect, emptying two-thirds of its houses in readiness for the bulldozers that arrived the following May. Minnie and her husband, Martin, tried gamely to remain cheerful and optimistic about their enforced move. They reassured their eldest son, David, then aged sixteen, daughter Diane, who was six, and little Christopher, two weeks away from his fourth birthday, that it was all for the best, and that a move offered the chance of a new start. But in reality, as they packed their belongings in readiness for the two-mile move to the council home in Capesthorne Road, their hearts were heavy. Bank Quay, with its red-brick houses, cobbled streets and gas lamps, was all they had known.

Bostock Street ran parallel to the main thoroughfare of Lovely Lane – so called because, in centuries gone by, it led to Bewsey, the most exclusive local village, inhabited by lords of the manor. Long, narrow, and almost arrow straight, it was identical to countless more Coronation Street style developments that gridded the north western townscape after the Industrial Revolution.

Warrington's sons and daughters tended to marry their near-neighbours. They rarely moved far away. They would gain a basic education at church schools like St Barnabas, which stood at the top end of Bostock Street, leave at fifteen and find a job. Work was readily available at dozens of thriving factories a short walk away: White Cross Wire, which supplied wire rope for Swiss cable cars; the Alliance Box Company, a cardboard manufacturer; the United Velvet Cutting Shop, Broadbents leather tannery; the pin factory; Lancashire Steel, and Bennetts Bakery, which filled the air with a tempting aroma from dawn till dusk.

Many of the women were known as 'Cotton Queens' because they were machinists at the local cotton mill. Minnie's parents, Alfred Beardsall and Emily Sheldon, moved into 19 Bostock Street after their marriage in 1913. He was a labourer in an aluminium rolling mill, and they produced three children: Alfred (who took his middle-name, Ronnie), Vera and Minnie, born 17 September 1925.

According to Betty Mather, one of Minnie's friends at St Barnabas school, she was 'a quiet, nice, polite girl', quite shy and academically 'nothing special'. She was employed in the soapery department at Crosfields, one of the nation's biggest soap and detergent producers before being taken over by Unilever, where she packed the tablets into wrapping paper and boxes. Palls of yellowy-grey smoke from its imposing chimney still belch out over the town centre today. By the end of the Second World War, however, when Minnie was nineteen, she had evidently begun to blossom and to develop the innate talents which were handed down to her children and undoubtedly played a major part in Chris's future development.

Ernest Beardsall, who is no relation, became friendly with Minnie in 1944 and provides a valuable insight into her character. They met at the YMCA in Sankey Street, where, displaying the money-making drive that characterizes both the Beardsalls and the Evanses, she then worked part-time in the kitchen to supplement her soap factory income.

'She was very pretty, with long, red curly hair like Chris's, and the thing I most remember is how outgoing she was,' recalls Ernest.

'At that time Warrington was full of Yankie servicemen from the nearby airbases and they used to go into the YMCA. You had to be quick-witted and give them as good as they gave, and Minnie certainly could. She was very popular, and a keen dancer.'

A natural performer, Minnie developed her talents later in life. Her last job before retirement was as a care assistant in the now-closed Orford Hall, where the shows she arranged and performed for the residents have passed into local folk-lore. Her *pièce de résistance* was playing the Chief Fairy in the chorus line of 'Fairies Over Forty'. Breathing in deeply, she and her fellow fairies would squeeze into colourful leo-tards, fasten on wings and funny headgear, and prance around the day-room waggling their wands and singing until tears rolled down the residents' cheeks.

During Chris's early career as a Tarzan-o-gram, one of the devices that set him apart from his rivals was an ability to pen witty lyrics that homed in unerringly on his victim's most notable physical, personal or circumstantial trait. This he undoubtedly learned from his mother.

'Minnie and I did a lot of concerts together and she was very good at putting words down. She called them her ditties,' says Pat Daley, a long-time colleague at Orford Hall whose DJ son Ian became, for a brief period of debauched lunacy, Chris's best friend. 'She would make up all kinds of funny rhymes and songs – I remember one was about the nit-nurse, who used to come to school and check kids' hair for lice – but she always read them, or sang them, with a deadly serious stone-face.'

Although Minnie Evans now claims to be baffled as to the cause of her son's outspokenness and extremes of extroversion, he appears to have inherited these traits from her. Pat Daley's photograph album reveals how, well into her sixties, Minnie clowned her way around Newquay during a holiday with friends as though she were still an adolescent. One picture shows her standing in a crowded market-hall with a pair of knickers, plucked from one of the stalls, pulled down over her head.

'Minnie is still a big kid and when you see her you understand where Chris gets his sense of fun,' laughs Pat.

Evans's verbal elasticity and razor-sharp humour can be attributed to his mother, but Martin Evans handed down important characteristics, too. It is from his father that Chris learned not only to utilize his wits, but to live profitably from them. It was from Martin, as much as from Minnie, that he learned that flair was only an advantage if it was harnessed to hard graft. And it was from him that he garnered the priceless ability to rub shoulders with all classes and creeds, without ever feeling inferior or over-awed. Martin is remembered as a clever man, quite intellectual and able to converse on many different subjects.

Four years Minnie's senior, Chris's father was born 12 November 1921, the son of William Evans, an oiler and greaser at an iron and steel rolling mill and his wife, Annie, née Patton. Martin is survived by two brothers: Harry, who wears the same thick-rimmed spectacles as Chris and who some say he most closely resembles; and the tragic Billy, whose learning disabilities meant that he never married, and who began living in care while still in middle-age.

Shorter and stockier than Chris, who stands over six feet tall, Martin Evans developed a penchant for snappy suits and overcoats early in life. But his clothes were not all that set him apart from his neighbours. He possessed a lightening-fast brain, particularly for mental arithmetic, and was determined to use this gift to avoid donning boots and an overall and following his father and contemporaries on to the production line. By the time he had finished his National Service, he had found the ideal vehicle for his remarkable calculating powers: bookmaking.

During the forties and fifties Warrington was developing as a lucrative centre for backstreet bookmakers. It was not until 1961 that off-course betting was legalized, paving the way for household names such as Ladbrokes and William Hill to appear in the high street. Nonetheless, the wire-workers and tanners, the soap packers and steel rollers – not to mention the thousands of bored and high-rolling American servicemen stationed at nearby Burtonwood airbase – were intent on gambling somehow. It was here that the legendary Tommy Drew, king of the backstreet bookies, and his imitators came into their own.

Operating from garden-sheds and workshops, kitchens, living-rooms – anywhere capacious enough to house a ticker-tape machine and a makeshift betting counter – literally dozens of bookmaking operations began to mushroom. Many of them were controlled by the Pimpernel-like Drew, of whom everyone had heard but few ever saw in the flesh. Bets were sometimes placed personally, but those who could not sneak away from the factory or base for long enough to reach the bookmaker's personally employed the service of a runner, with whom they entrusted their stake. As the results came through on the ticker-tape machine notice of the first, second and third placed horses would be posted outside in the yard, and pay-outs were made immediately.

According to Tony Hayes, whose father was one of these bookies and who later became friendly with Martin Evans when he ran his local newsagent's in Orford, any type of organized betting away from the racecourse was against the law. But the police largely turned a blind eye.

'Every now and then we'd get a call from the local police station saying they were coming for us, but they never did. It wasn't legal, but it was accepted. They knew if your dad, or such a person, was a bookie. They knew all the bookies and what they were. This went until the sixties, when above-board betting shops came in, and there were heavy licence fees and the Customs and Excise were involved. A lot of them went out of business then, because they were little one man bands. Suddenly, it became organized and legal, and they didn't want to know.'

For obvious reasons, perhaps, Chris Evans has never spoken about his father's participation in this industry. In interviews he has described him only as a hospital wages clerk, the position he held for the final years of his life. It is difficult to be precise about Martin Evans's progression in this field, but it appears that he quickly rose through the ranks. On 26 July 1952, his wedding day, he coyly described himself as a clerk, and when their first son, David, was born in October the following year he wrote on the birth certificate 'Clerk, turf accountants'. When his daughter, Diane, was born, in May 1963, he grandly described himself as a Commission Agent, which meant he was running his own book.

At the same time, he was helping Minnie to run a corner shop which they had taken over at 39 Bostock Street from Jane Spilsbury in October 1954, and kept until it was demolished by the council.

'Martin must have had a very sharp brain because the bookie's clerk needed to think very fast,' says Tony Hayes. 'His job was to work out the odds. You might have, for example, someone who had placed a treble on three horses, and they'd all won. One's, say, 100–8; one's 9–2; one's 13–4, and you've got to work out fairly quickly how much is to be paid out because the guy's waiting for his money and there's a line of punters behind him, and maybe two or three hundred bets to work out. There were no calculators or anything in those days, and they had a way of doing it like lightning. They had to be very quick and spot on, because it was your money or your gaffer's money you were losing if you got it wrong.'

Martin was thirty when he and Minnie married, and she was twenty-six, which made theirs a comparatively late union. Both were intent on bettering themselves and offering their children the most advantageous upbringing that their modest means would support. They saved hard and leaped at the opportunity to move from their two-up, two-down terraced house in Glazebrook Street to the shop, at the junction of Bostock and Selby Streets, near Sankey Green. Dorothy Verdon, who then lived a few doors away, recalls how Martin and Minnie, always smartly dressed behind the counter, maximized its potential by staying open from 9 a.m. until 9 p.m. Meanwhile, she says, Martin continued to take bets round the back.

Another former neighbour, Mike Cullen, remembers how the bookmaking side of the Evans family enterprise worked.

'There was a wooden garage in Selby Street and it had a cubby-hole. Martin took bets from there.'

The house had an outside toilet and no central-heating, like that of their neighbours, but Martin's entrepreneurial skills placed them slightly above the norm.

'Martin would turn his hand to anything he could think of – he would just do it,' adds Mike Cullen's brother. 'At one point he had a black Morris Minor and he ran it as a taxi. He had the shop, the bookies; he would do anything that didn't require putting overalls on. I admired him. He wanted to have a good life, and he would try anything.'

The Cullen brothers are certain that, at least for some of the time, Martin was employed by the elusive Tommy Drew himself.

'He had three or four agents around our area and Martin was one. You had to be honest to work for Tommy, and Martin was honest as the day is long. Tommy trusted him.'

For all their desire to 'do well', as the local folk termed it, Martin and Minnie somehow found time to punctuate their feverish activity with relaxation. Clearly devoted to one another, they would take the Morris Minor for runs in the surrounding Cheshire countryside, listen to music on the gramophone or radio and play games. Minnie went dancing at Fletchers works club and the Liberal Club, while Martin was a keen snooker and billiards player. Their siblings and parents, who lived close by, were frequent visitors. It was into this close, warm, decent, industrious and quintessentially Northern post-war working-class family that Chris Evans was born. The date – almost inevitably, his mother would later sigh – was 1 April, the year 1966.

In that year, Labour had just regained power with Harold Wilson as the new, Beatle-loving, technologically-friendly Prime Minister. Australian troops had been airlifted to fight in Vietnam, an American H-bomb had been carelessly lost on the Atlantic sea bed and, as the Cold War raged, a much-feared but little-known hard-liner named Leonid Brezhnev had taken an iron grip on the Kremlin. Away from these menacing uncertainties, in the world of popular culture, sex siren Sophia Loren was madly in love once more and about to marry mega-rich Carlo Ponti, *The Sound of Music* had been voted the year's best film, *The Walker Brothers* were topping the charts with 'The Sun Ain't Gonna Shine Any More' and *The Hollies* were at number two with 'I Can't Let Go'.

No one inside the family is prepared to say whether Minnie intended to fall pregnant with her third child when she was almost forty and her husband almost forty-five. Accident or planned afterthought, however, when Chris arrived his parents already considered themselves blessed with the perfect son and daughter. David, by now a tall and solidly-built twelve-year-old, had proved himself an exception by passing his eleven-plus exam and taking his place among the 'nobs' and 'boffins' at the Boteler Grammar School. Diane, though not yet three, was also clearly of above-average intelligence, and would soon begin to show her gift for music. Perhaps because their age difference was so marked, David Evans immediately took to baby Chris and neighbours remember him pushing his infant brother in his pram. Even in early childhood, however, Chris and Diane would squabble incessantly. During their teens the rift widened to the point where, for long periods, there was no communication between them at all. Neither was invited to the other's wedding. Friends are baffled by the reasons for their mutual disdain and, when asked to describe the relationship, strong phraseology is used.

'He hated her and she couldn't stand him,' said one source. 'Whenever I was in the house they didn't even acknowledge each other, let alone have a conversation. I just don't think they have anything in common.'

This state of war reached its nadir when Diane, by this time a teacher, married an import and export manager named Paul McAlinden, who lives across the road from Minnie. In view of Chris's well-publicized love affair with alcohol in recent years, it seems somewhat ironic that he disapproved of the boozy circles in which Mr McAlinden moved. Yet, according to regulars in the Greenwood pub, one of McAlinden's favourite haunts, that was the case.

'He was specially pissed off by what happened on Paul's stag do,' chuckled one of McAlinden's drinking pals. 'We stripped Paul naked and tied him to the pub sign outside, in full view of Minnie Evans's house.'

Chris, Gazza, Danny Baker and the rest of Evans's current drinking chums couldn't have dreamed up a more hilarious prank. But this was family and on his own doorstep. This was different.

As a small boy, Chris's parents held him over one shoulder while serving groceries. He would toddle around safely on the largely traffic-free street outside the shop. The neighbours all fussed over his lovely bright-red curls and his cornflake freckles. There was little crime in Bank Quay then, and certainly no mugging, drugs or gratuitous street violence. To a man, the street's former residents will swear today that it was a 'smashing' place to grow up.

Then, when Chris was about to celebrate his fourth birthday, came the first in a series of unwanted upheavals over which he had no control, and which were to shape his character.

As if leaving the shop, with its endless supply of sweets and its sheer extraordinariness were not bad enough, Chris found himself transplanted into an alien world at 113 Capesthorne Road, Orford. On the up side, there was a garden and gas-fired central-heating and their new semi-detached house had more space, but there was an unmistakable air of abandonment about the area. Tentative efforts had been made by the local council to keep the diaspora from Bank Quay's condemned streets close to one another in their new communities. But this plan was only a limited success and Chris's new neighbourhood was largely made up of strangers whose safe lives had been buried beneath the rubble and dust of their torn-down redbrick terraces.

According to Phil Hazell, who lived next door, Martin and Minnie attempted to ease Chris's passage by spending some of the cash they received for the shop on an array of new toys.

'He had the best bike, best games, best clothes, everything,' says Phil, who is several years older than Evans, his envy evident almost a quarter of a century on. 'He wasn't a mingler. He was shy. He seemed more spoilt, if anything.'

Relations were not helped when Phil's mentally handicapped sister Elaine pushed Chris into a nearby stream, called Granny's Brook. Luckily it was running only knee-deep that day, and he was able to clamber up the bank and run home, sodden and crying to his mother. Although this act was perpetrated in innocence by a little girl, it proved to be a portent of the pain, terror and ritual humiliation that were to be routinely heaped upon Chris Evans for years to come.

Once he had been singled out as a soft touch – a scrawny, freckly, red-haired 'mard-arse', to use the local terminology – there would be nowhere to hide from the merciless young sadists who ruled the new urban jungle of Orford.

CHAPTER TWO

Barely three years after leaving Bostock Street, the Evans family was on the move again. Unable to settle in Capesthorne Road, they applied to the council for a house-swap and found willing participants in James and Kathleen Smith. The Smiths lived around the corner, opposite a fish and chip shop, newsagent's and pub, at 319 Greenwood Crescent.

The two houses were of similar dimensions but they were very different in character; and, although they were only a few hundred metres apart, to the parochial folk of Orford they stood in markedly separate territories. Newer and built from light-grey concrete as opposed to dark red brick, the Greenwood estate – as the avenue and its surrounding offshoots are locally known – arose from the old Padgate RAF site in the early and mid-sixties. In its thirty-odd years of existence, it has seen such a remarkable fluctuation in character that it can be regarded as a barometer of urban social change. The mood of optimism that permeated its clean, safe, graffiti- and litter-free new streets and green verges in the sixties was replaced in the seventies by a sense of menace, as gangs of mods and skinheads began to roam. By the mid-eighties an under-class of hard drug addicts, criminals and impoverished 'problem tenants' had been dumped there, making the estate a virtual no-go area for the old and vulnerable, particularly after dark. At one point the Greenwood pub was even firebombed.

Today, a measure of equilibrium has been restored. Many of the residents have bought their homes from the council and given them an individual identity. There are brightly coloured doors, crazy stripes across pastel pebble-dashing, neatly manicured lawns and, at Minnie Evans's house, extended windows and distinctive, multi-shaded stone cladding. Yet even as late as December 1993, Minnie returned from a short visit to see Chris in London to find that thieves had broken in and stolen £20, the only cash she had left behind. Concerned, her son offered to buy her a new home somewhere safer but his mother values familiarity and likes her neighbours. A bright yellow burglar alarm was fitted, and she has resolutely stayed put.

It was into Seventies Model Greenwood that six-year-old Chris arrived. A dangerous enough place for any outsider, but particularly one who, by his very appearance, stood out from the crowd. Evans didn't help his own cause. Unwilling or simply unable to curb his acid tongue, he frequently talked his way into a thumping while pals who kept quiet escaped. If someone shouted an insult from across the road, he couldn't resist making an impudent response – and with his gangling gait he was never the fastest of runners. To make matters worse, he was always immaculately turned out. 'Worra mardarse' indeed.

The bullying began at St Margaret's Church of England Infants School, and gathered pace when he entered the Juniors. The children were of widely differing academic ability, but from the outset it was clear that Chris was among the very brightest; another factor that counted against him as far as his aggressors were concerned.

'He was very nice – not like he is now at all,' says Ethel Jones, who taught him when he was six. 'He was gorgeous because he was very extrovert, always with a big smile and a lovely mop of red hair. He was a little child you would take to. Always laughing, very cheerful.'

Mary Smith, one of his junior school teachers, was equally enamoured with the young Chris.

'I was quite fond of Chris; he had a lot about him. I've read articles describing him as a misfit, but I didn't think of him as a misfit then. There were two streams, A and B, and Chris was in the A stream, which sat the eleven plus exam.'

Academically, his was a good year. Seventeen children passed examinations to enter the grammar school out of thirty-nine. Chris was up near the top.

'He was effervescent, full of beans and always seemed to be happy. You could smack children in those days, and there were a few I did smack, but not him. We used to do school assemblies, each class took a turn on a Wednesday morning. I remember doing one about talents, and pupils came and performed what they hoped to do when they got older. Chris must have fancied himself as a comedian or poet because he did Pam Ayres, and he was very funny.'

Tellingly, Mrs Smith added: 'I remember his mother saying to me that Chris was very different from others in the family because the others were so quiet and he was so boisterous, but we liked him. I have watched him on television, and his originality was typical of the Chris I knew then.'

Evans's headmaster in the Juniors, Don Antrobus, also has fond memories of him.

'He was a very bright pupil. I can see him now, peering over those spectacles as he does on TV. Even then he bent his head down and looked over the top with that quizzical, mischievous grin. He was bright as a button, always quick-witted, and ready for fun, just as he is now. I'm sure he took a prominent part in all the dramatic productions and pageants, and he was also quite good at cricket. We didn't have a team then, but one of the teachers took him and some other lads for coaching after school.'

None of his teachers can recall Chris being picked on. But many years were to pass before schools began to operate anti-bullying campaigns and the suffering of victims frequently went undetected. According to his contemporaries at St Margaret's, Chris was the classic case. One of his early tormentors, his friends attest, was a scowling, tousle-haired boy named Anthony Vanes, who was frequently in trouble and has since become embroiled in petty crime.

'There used to be netting to climb up against the wall in the school yard,' recalls Chris's one-time best pal, Trevor Palin. 'Vanes would wait until we were half way up, then start hitting us and frightening us half to death.'

Determined not to become the school whipping boy, the diminutive Palin took up boxing at a very early age and became a local champion. Devoid of either the muscle or the conviction to defend himself, however, for Chris the misery grew worse. Another loyal friend, Glynn Povey, saved Chris from Vanes's clutches on more than one occasion.

'Me and this other lad were regarded as cocks of the school and Anthony Vanes reckoned he was Bruce Lee, a karate expert,' he said. 'He kept bullying Chris, among others, and one day I stuck one on him and he never came back again.'

'He got into trouble because of the way he looked. He was weedy-looking,' says Dave Hinchliffe, who sat next to him in class.

Trevor Palin added: 'I wouldn't say I protected him but I could see the bullying and stuff like that going on, and I didn't agree with it, even at that age. But, in a way, Chris kind of asked for it. He didn't provoke, but he would retaliate in a way that would be insulting. Plus, he could do his sums and they couldn't. You ask yourself whether that is why he is so hard with people now.'

Somewhat paradoxically, Palin says that he regarded Chris as 'definitely a leader', a boy to be looked up to.

'He could make great models out of wood and canvas, and he had a record-player in his bedroom, which was unusual round there when we were kids. I remember one day he was changing the needle because he had just bought a diamond-tipped one. They had just come on the market, and he was really excited.'

Chris always seemed to have a bit more money to spend than the other lads, too. Palin stops short of describing him as mean, but says he was unusually interested in amassing cash, even then.

'I would spend mine but he would keep his and I'm sure he always had savings. Whereas we always bought tons of sweets, Chris would definitely not. Knowing Chris, he probably had a TSB account or something.'

Later, in their teens, Chris's reluctance to open his wallet would bring the two friends to blows.

In those days of gang violence, life in Orford was perilous.

'The estate was the equivalent of, say, Hulme or Moss Side in Manchester,' said Palin. 'It was new at the time, it was staking out your territory, it was fighting, it was gangs. If you weren't in one, even at an early age, you were in trouble. Me and my brother Jason actually got tied up once. They were building the Greenwood pub, and some guys trussed us up and hung us by the arms from the beams. Then they beat ten tons of shit out of us. We were only little kids and God knows what we were supposed to have done. You couldn't walk across the estate then without getting hit or chased or something like that.'

Glynn, whose family remains close to Minnie Evans, recalls an episode which illustrates the fragility of Chris's psyche.

'When we were nine or ten we had a paper aeroplane contest at school and the whole class entered. The teacher told us that whoever built the most aerodynamic plane would win because theirs would fly furthest. Chris thought he was an ace at making paper planes and he took it deadly seriously. But I came first and he came third, and he was so upset he started skriking [crying] like a baby. He hated losing at anything.'

Kenny Maudsley, sinewy, tough, hard-drinking and currently in prison for a drugs offence, appears to have adopted a dual role when Chris was around. On one occasion he remembers keeping Chris out of trouble after he had kicked a ball through a neighbour's window and the police were called.

'He was a mummy's boy and I was a ruffian, so I took the flak.'

On the other hand he claims he made the nervous Evans – who had no wish to be involved in dishonesty – 'keep nicks' while he and another lad went on sweet-stealing expeditions.

'You always get a nob-head in the bunch and it was Chris,' Maudsley sneers disdainfully.

Maudsley's powers of recall may be somewhat addled, but, speaking a few days before he was jailed, he distinctly remembered how Chris was again attacked, this time on a trip to the Isle of Man. It happened, he says, when the two boys – then aged about twelve – were members of the Woodcraft Folk, an alternative to the Cubs and Boy Scouts, with a philosophy based on non-competition, peace and co-operation. Why, one might ask, would it attract the likes of Kenny Maudsley?

'Because it wasn't just for lads,' he grins. 'Girls could go as well, and we thought we'd have a better chance of getting off with them if we joined.'

Meetings were held in the old Co-operative Hall, on Orford Lane which, despite its name, was an 11p bus-ride away from Orford itself. Those who could afford it handed the leader, John Bacon, a 10p weekly levy, and the really well-off completed the evening with a tray of chips and gravy. One evening Mr Bacon announced a forthcoming adventure: for £25 the Warrington Woodcraft Folk could take a ferry to Douglas and spend a few days camping. For Maudsley this was an unimaginable sum. But necessity being the mother of invention, a few days later his pockets were bulging with three times that amount, pinched, he says, from a purse in a car. The Evans family being considerably better off, Chris had only to ask Minnie for the money.

'It was boring at first, being away from Warrington, so we decided to make some fun,' said Kenny. 'The tents were pitched about two or three miles outside Douglas but one night we walked to town and went to a disco for a laugh and some pop. Anyway, Chris and me went to the toilets and this big bloke started asking us what we were looking at. I was frightened. I thought he was queer or something. Chris never said anything but the bloke just decided to punch him. I ran to get help from one of the supervisors, but the bloke just disappeared.'

Had Chris cried?

'He was always fucking crying. He was a mard-arse. You know, you don't tell your mam, do you? But he always did.'

Maudsley relates this sordid little tale over Friday night beers and throbbing disco music in the Coach-house Hotel. At its conclusion, others weighed in with their own Chris Evans stories. A short, heavily-built, pug-faced local doorman and ex-boxer named John Haybyrne was among them.

'I chinned Evans once myself,' he says matter-of-factly. 'In Orford Youth Centre, it was. He was mouthing off like he always did and I just hit him. He went down like a sack of spuds. His nose was splattered and he was squealing like a stuck pig.'

Haybyrne takes a draught of his lager and smiles at the memory.

Given that he suffered such traumas, it becomes easier to understand why, today, Evans's own childhood recollections veer so wildly from one extreme to another. In February 1994, in an interview timed to coincide with the first episode of *Don't Forget Your Toothbrush*, he confessed to Andy Coulson of *The Sun*: 'Being a ginger kid was hell on earth. I was picked on and got into a lot of fights but didn't win a single one. When I was ten it was decided that I needed glasses and that only made things worse. Being a red-haired, skinny four-eyes does you very few favours at school. I may be smiling in the pictures [carried with the article] but I wasn't the cheeky chappy you might think.'

Yet by the following November, when he spoke at length to Robert Crampton for an article published in *The Times Magazine*, he had apparently blanked out these bleak memories altogether. Questioned about his school days, he stated flatly that he 'was never bullied'. Evidently having forgotten his Pam Ayres take-off, he also insisted that he had never told jokes, much less performed publicly, during his school days.

In the opinion of Dr Bryan Tully, a respected chartered

and forensic psychologist who frequently acts as an expert witness for the police and the Official Solicitor, the tendency to mythologize key events in early life is not uncommon among adults who were bullied in their youth.

'There is a phenomenon called state-dependent learning,' he says. 'It means your emotional state at the time you experienced and learned something has an effect on how you remember it in the future. This is particularly marked, for example, among depressed people who actually remember the miserable times in their life more than others.

'Under certain conditions, the former victim might feel a reason to give a kind of heroic story-line to a sad tale. How I made it from rags to riches despite all the odds, that type of thing. If you have a personality which is fragile, or even unstable, then there is a constant rewriting of history. There can be an element of self-protection and justification because some of the implications of past memories are very painful.'

If, indeed, Evans's apparent mental block is a result of state-dependent learning, then he may remember the good times rather more reliably than the bad. And, for all his trials, good times there were. If he were to stage a reunion with Trevor Palin – highly improbable, given his almost pathological habit of cutting old friends and acquaintances out of his life – he would be reminded of the Beano Club. Its principal members were Chris, Trevor and two other school chums, David Massey and Joanne Hinds.

'We all used to get the *Beano* comic and one day we just came together and formed this club,' Trevor smiles. 'We called it the Beano Club, which I think would have been Chris's idea, and we would go and do all different games on the wasteland.'

According to Trevor, Chris's first crush was directed towards the pretty Joanne, and she was his first childhood girlfriend. But another of the chums, Johnny Hoyles, remembers differently.

'At junior school he had a bit of a thing about a girl called Jane Pucill. I recall standing outside her house and Chris was shouting at the top of his voice, "I want to see you, Jane!"

It just so happened that her Dad was on nights and trying to get some sleep. Putting it mildly, we were told to leave.'

Now happily married with a two-year-old son and living in Hertfordshire, Jane Kapoor confirms the story. 'I was his girlfriend for a while when we were nine,' she says, with a wistful laugh. 'I think we kissed, but it was a long time ago.

'He was very self-contained. Trevor was the extrovert. It was Trevor who told me that Chris really liked me, so we started going out. He used to come round to my house and my older sister would give him pop and crisps. He didn't talk a lot and at first I thought he was shy. But one day he really surprised me. We went on a school coach trip and he sat on the back seat and did a rendition of Tommy Steel's song 'Little White Bull' in front of everyone. He knew all the words and I was very impressed.'

Such early displays of individuality, or even eccentricity, would continue to pay dividends when it came to attracting the opposite sex. From his mid-teens Evans dated an enviable string of sought-after girls. His romantic prowess both mystified and frustrated his conventionally better-looking friends. They couldn't comprehend why any girl would fancy this bespectacled ginger-topped geek above them. But his method was perfectly straightforward: always use original chat-up lines and keep making them laugh.

It was a formula that would help him to win early girlfriends like Tamara Davies (now Bradshaw), Tina Yardley – the first real love of his life – and many others. After Tina came Heather From Over The Road, Alison Ward, who was to bear his illegitimate daughter, and Dawn The Barmaid From Bolton. In Manchester, while working for Piccadilly Radio, Evans was envied by just about every single man on the station when he began dating the petite, sophisticated young newsreader, Sara Green. Sara was briefly succeeded by Holly Samos (later famous as Holly Hotlips on his Radio One Breakfast Show), Carol McGiffin, to whom marriage was to prove so ill-fated, and a string of long-legged blondes including Rachel Tatton-Brown, Kim Wilde and his current partner Suzi Aplin. Sometimes he was seeing more than one woman at once, and even then he somehow found room for a stream of fleeting sexual encounters. These ranged from conventional one-night stands to impromptu orgies and even an escapade with a German prostitute. But that was later.

But during the early years, Chris's favourite companion was his father. Soon after the move from Orford, Martin Evans had put his head for figures to a different use, taking a job as a wages administrator at nearby Winwick Hospital. After his mother collected him from St Margaret's, Chris would wait patiently by the window for his father's return, and then the fun would start. Martin didn't run around after footballs; he was getting a bit too old for that. But Chris then supported Liverpool (to his old pals' annoyance he has since switched allegiance to trendier Manchester United), and he was interested in Warrington's rugby league team, so they would hold animated conversations about sport. They played less strenuous games, however, but often went on for hours on end. A favourite was miniature snooker on the scaled-down six by three-foot table in Chris's bedroom. Under his father's tutelage, Chris also became adept at making models; and on fine summer evenings they walked through the fields behind the house with Max, the family's much-loved pet Alsatian.

'Chris's dad always reminded me of Winston Churchill,' says Glynn Povey. 'He was a very solid man and he seemed very big to us then. He was usually in a black blazer and tie, even in the day time, and on the surface he seemed quite strict. But he was very close to Chris.'

Family summer holidays were an especially treasured experience, one of the most popular destinations being Blackpool, only forty-five minutes' ride north, with its Golden Mile and end-of-the pier variety shows.

Chris has fragmented memories of one incident that took place there – though here again it is interesting to note how confused he has become over times and dates.

'It was the day the lights were being turned on and Dad and I went for a walk along the sea front,' he told Andy Coulson. 'Red Rum was supposed to be performing the big ceremony that year but we found this fella hidden away in a shed surrounded by electrical equipment. He was the man who was actually going to flick the switch, not Red Rum, and he let me do it. I can remember walking back to the hotel with my dad, prouder than I'd ever been.

'We were a great family. Dad never raised a hand to us and he gave us whatever he could. We had great times on holidays and day trips but I'll never forget that summer we spent in Blackpool.'

A touching anecdote, lovingly retold. The one puzzling factor is that Coulson, presumably guided by his subject, wrote that it happened when Evans was 'just a toddler'. In fact Red Rum switched on Blackpool's Illuminations in August 1977, by which time Chris was eleven years-old and already in his first year at Boteler Grammar School.

It appears the past was so poignant that Evans's only method of dealing with it was by having his memory play tricks on him. The same thing would recur over and over again after the single most cataclysmic event of his life. It happened barely two years after he flooded the Blackpool sea front with fluorescent colour, and it snuffed out a light inside him for ever.

CHAPTER THREE

'And where I, the saide Sir Thomas, have delyvered by indenture tripartite into the custody and kepynge of the right reverend father in God John th' abbot of Whalley that now is 500 markes of gold, savelie to be kept to myn use and to be disposed at my pleasure, it is my full will and mynde that myn executors shall have the dispocion and orderinge of the saide summe of 500 markes to purchase and obteyne lands and tenements or rents to the yerelie value of ten pounds above all chardges, or as much thereof as shall be unprovided and unpurchased by me the said Sir Thomas, and therwith to founde a free grammar scolle in Weryngton to endure forever . . .'

Extract from the last will and testament of Sir Thomas Boteler, founder of the Boteler Grammar School, dated 1520

Late in September 1979, Chris began his first day at the Thomas Boteler Grammar School. He felt hideously drowned by his pristine black blazer and crisply-pressed flannels, and his sky-blue and navy diagonally-striped tie hung down over his belt like a spaniel's tongue. But his mother assured him that he would soon grow into these strange new clothes and, knowing how proud she was that he had been accepted for the only boys' grammar in town – indeed, the most prestigious school for many miles around – he put on a brave face and gave Minnie a cheery wave as he made his way to the bus stop. The three-mile journey to Latchford, way beyond the busy Manchester Road, was an ordeal in itself. Each time the bus stopped he was confronted with a group of scowling new faces and, although he was accompanied by a couple of old pals from St Margaret's, they all appeared to be glaring at him. But it was not until he walked through the school's imposing, stone-pillared memorial gates that he fully awoke to the new dangers that awaited him.

Whereas the teachers at St Margaret's had smiled at him and spoken in soft tones, here, they seemed stern and remote. Some still wore black gowns and mortar-boards and, should their pupils have failed to grasp the relative lowliness of their status, lessons were often delivered from raised lecterns. At junior school Chris's witty ripostes and japes had been accepted as part of his zest and intelligence, but now they were no longer tolerated. Yet the teachers were only one half of the problem; the pupils were the other.

Founded by Sir Thomas Boteler, a medieval Lord of the Manor, the school may have been justifiably proud of its traditions. By the late seventies, however, it was a very different school from the one David Evans had attended twelve years earlier. Its values were being eroded by small pockets of trouble-makers – thugs and bullies – and, according to pupils who attended at that time, Boteler had developed a reputation for turning out its fair share of hard-cases as well as Oxbridge undergraduates.

'I got expelled in the third year for hitting a teacher and I went to Orford Secondary School, which was supposed to be the toughest school in town, but Boteler was a hundred times tougher,' says one of Chris's contemporaries.

'There was quite a lot of bullying,' agrees Shaun Chadwick, one of Chris's friends. 'I was one of those who got bullied. With me it was mainly name-calling, but the odd person got his head pushed down the toilet – the royal flush. There wasn't much you could do. There were about five or six lads who used to go around doing it all the time. They were always covering up for each other.'

Strolling around the playground at break-times, innocently strumming his favourite tune, 'Mull of Kintyre' by *Wings*, on an acoustic guitar, Chris Evans was as defenceless as a wildebeest lost among lions. *Deus Spes Nostra* – 'God Is Our Hope' – the school's motto ran. If ever anyone needed a little divine intervention, Chris Evans needed it now.

Academically, he had no difficulties whatsoever, for even when placed among the brightest boys in the borough he was in the top echelon. Each year had a three-form entry, but although the pupils were rigorously streamed, attempts were made to camouflage the system. So instead of having A, B and C forms, there were B, G and S – the initials of Boteler Grammar School – and each year the letter used for the top stream was altered. In Chris's year it was S, and not only was he among the elite, but class-mates reckoned him to be among the five cleverest of its thirty-odd boys.

'He was the top man in two or three different subjects out of about ten,' says Mark Rutter, who also made the leap from St Margaret's and became Chris's closest ally at Boteler. Although Evans insists he has read just a handful of books, most of them standard school texts, Rutter added: 'He was pretty good at English, history as well – I was second, he was first.'

Shaun Chadwick, another fellow pupil, describes him as 'a bit of a swot. One of the brainy ones, in most of the top sets'.

Early end-of-term reports confirm this assessment. 'Enthusiasm and ability in a broad range of subjects . . . excellent,' reads one. Records show that he also turned out for the school cricket team and played for the Crosfields Cricket Club Colts XI, and that during his second year he appeared in the school play, *Androcles*. So much for his claim that he never participated in school activities.

Chris started to misbehave in the second year, according to one former teacher, who says, 'He was actually quite a naughty boy on occasions', but declined to elaborate. His form teacher, Elizabeth Lord, now a headmistress else-where, was also diplomatic in her assessment. She describes him as 'very bright and lively', but added caustically: 'Let me say to you, I'm not surprised he's in the job he has, because he always had a ready quip. If someone was going to say something that others wouldn't, he would have said it.'

Did that mean he sometimes got into trouble?

'Yes,' she says, adding hastily: 'No one got into serious trouble. It was a boys' grammar school and terribly strict.'

Johnny Hoyles, another who attended both St Margaret's and Boteler with him, recalls 'a few run-ins' with the teachers. Now employed in a senior position with British Nuclear Fuels, he says that Chris had a particular clash of personalities with a chemistry teacher.

'One incident I remember distinctly was Chris writing something on the desk lid and he got caught. I think he wrote that this master was gay or something, because he really didn't get on with him. I remember him getting punched around the room for that.'

Literally punched?

'Yeah, well, you know, pushed around the room. I know there was a lot of argy-bargy and it carried on outside the classroom. It went straight to the headmaster, this one, I think. It was the straw that broke the camel's back, I imagine. You know Chris, he pushed things a little, didn't he? That's how I'd put it. His personality was a little bit too large for some of them. Even from junior school he'd got this desire to be famous, and he really pushed it.'

A third classmate, Barry Melton, took an altogether harsher view of Evans – one that was shared by many.

'He was a weirdo. He used to go round the corridors singing and playing a guitar which he borrowed from the music teacher, and we would hear him while we were having a fag in the corridors. I think he was highly-strung and a bit of a dick. I didn't like him then and I don't like him now. He was a fucking weirdo. He didn't fit in with anyone.'

The role of Evans's tormentor and humiliator fell to a

stocky, aggressive boy named Rob Carey and his tall, powerful sidekick. Carey, who was expelled at fourteen, admits he made Chris's life a misery, and a source in the class describes how he did it.

'We had a form room and all our books were kept there, in desks with lift-up lids. We had about five minutes between lessons to go back and get the books we needed. Carey and this other lad, who was the hardest in the year, used to nick Chris's books for a laugh. He would go back to the form room and they weren't there. So he would get into trouble, and he daren't tell or he'd get it.

'Another thing they'd do was make him put his head inside the desk, then shut the lid over his head and fuck off to the next lesson. They would say, don't pull your head out of the desk or you've had it, and he was too scared to move. Chris would be ten minutes late for the next lesson. Then he would get bollocked. They did that a few times and they were very heavy, those desk-lids. He had to take it because the other lad with Carey was six foot two tall and he ran the year. That was in the second year.'

The source shook his head and added: 'I can't imagine Chris being happy at Boteler. There were scores of lads who weren't happy there because it was run by bullies.'

If he wasn't happy at school, at least Chris's home life was reassuringly solid and secure. Returning to Greenwood Crescent at 4 p.m. after another nerve-racking day at Boteler, he was immediately consoled by the comforting aroma of his mother's cooking and the sloppy affections of Max the Alsatian. By this time he was also becoming something of an addict to popular radio and television shows. They didn't have to be racy, nor even necessarily aimed at people of his age-group. He admired good ideas, slickly presented. During the week he particularly enjoyed the BBC early-evening magazine programme *Nationwide*, which many young people might have found heavy going. Saturday afternoons were invariably reserved for *Grandstand*, not because he was addicted to sport but because, with Frank Bough in the chair, it was, as he later put it, 'a fucking good watch'. Bough, he proclaimed, was 'the master of rhythm in more ways than one'.

But the best viewing time of all was Saturday morning. While his friends were out playing soccer or hanging around the streets, at nine-thirty he would switch on the television and flick between the two programmes that were guaranteed to hold him spellbound: ATV's *Tiswas* and *Multicoloured Swap Shop* on BBC1. At the end of the seventies and early eighties, these ground-breaking marathon compendiums were locked in a fierce ratings war and there was heated debate over their influence on their impressionable young audience. *Swap Shop*, fronted by the smooth Noel Edmonds, assisted by Keith Chegwin and Maggie Philbin overseeing its on-screen exchanges of toys, records and games, was the less controversial of the two shows. At least the pop music and cartoons were punctuated by animal films and travelogues. But Evans says he thought it 'dead cool'. He was impressed, he said, by the way Edmonds organized it. 'The way he was at the centre of everything.'

By contrast, *Tiswas*, presented and produced by Chris Tarrant, with Sally James as his co-star and a youthful Lenny Henry cracking the gags, took the same type of format and made it anarchic. Edward Barnes, then Head of Children's TV at the BBC, dismissed it as 'indigestible candy-floss without any intellectual grit'. Maybe he was right, but it suited Chris Evans's palate. Esteemed guests like Sir Geoffrey Howe and Princess Anne were unceremoniously hosed down with water, the heavyweight comedian Bernard Manning was placed on an exploding weighing machine and no one was spared by the Phantom Flan Flinger. Moreover, anything remotely educational was re-packaged as fun and given a catchy label. The animal slot, for example, became the Creature Feature. Freak or Unique, the slot on Evans's current Channel 4 programme *TFI Friday*, in which guests perform a garish array of hideous anatomical party-pieces, would have been perfectly placed on *Tiswas*.

The seeds of a highly fertile imagination were sown.

A similar osmotic process was beginning when he listened

to the radio. Evans would either tune in to 261 on the medium wave, the frequency used by the fledgling local independent station, Manchester's Piccadilly, or 275 and 285 – national Radio One. He relished the rapid-fire patter of DJs like the chirpy and mischievous Dave Lee Travis, who had taken over Radio One's breakfast show from Noel Edmonds in 1978, and followed in a tradition that stretched back to Kenny Everett, Stuart Henry and Tony Blackburn.

'I thought the breakfast show was the ultimate,' he has enthused, when harking back to this period. 'It was the golden years of Radio One.'

Later he also became an avid listener of Piccadilly's motor-mouthed 'man of the people' Mike Sweeney. In an era when most mainstream broadcasters were still striving to sound accentless, Sweeney and, to a lesser extent Derbyshire-born DLT, not only stayed true to their broad northern brogue, but turned it into a virtue. Another reason he found them more exciting than 'serious' music jocks such as Andy Peebles and John Peel was because they mixed pithy, one-line gags with pertinent observations on humdrum everyday occurrences. In this way they were trading on the sort of humorous banter that had always filled his own house, led by Martin and Minnie. Imagine doing that and getting paid for it!

'His parents were both funny and cheerful in their own way,' says Tony Hayes, the Greenwood Crescent newsagent. 'I can picture them in the shop together, like a double-act, laughing and joking. Martin didn't tell jokes in the term of a made-up story with a funny ending, but certainly he was very witty and sharp and he could pull your leg.'

Away from his tormentors at school and with his redoubtable dad at his side to guide him, twelve-year-old Chris no longer saw himself as a picked-upon playground freak. He felt confident, loved, special.

But then, with what seemed to Chris like indecent abruptness, the cheerful and optimistic atmosphere at home took on a bleak, doom-laden air. Troubled by recurring abdominal pain and bowel problems, Martin Evans had finally decided to make an appointment with his local GP. Concerned by his symptoms, the doctor referred him to a specialist, who told him exploratory surgery would be necessary.

'I won't be seeing you, Tony, for a week or so,' Martin told Mr Hayes when he popped in for his *Daily Mail* the following morning. Typically stoical and upbeat, he added with a wink, 'I'm going into dock so they can have a look at my engine.'

When he next saw Martin, Tony Hayes remembers how his smile was still fixed in place, even though it was all too evident that something was terribly wrong.

'Before he went into hospital I think he thought he just had tummy trouble and they were going to sort him out,' he says. 'But when he came out he was walking with a stick. He had already lost weight and he was certainly a different person. The lady who had the fruit shop next door, Dot King, knew them well, and she came into the shop and asked me if I had heard the news. She told me he had cancer and was terminally ill.'

When the surgeon had examined Martin Evans, his worst fears had been confirmed: the cancer that had developed in his colon was already so well advanced that little more could be done. In Britain, cancer of the colon is the second-most common form of the disease, but since the late seventies considerable strides have been made in its treatment. Had he been living today, Martin's life might have been prolonged by chemotherapy, perhaps administered intravenously from a continuously-operating pump. But twenty years ago there was little that could be done but manage the pain. Over the winter of 1978–9 Martin's neighbours watched sadly and averted their gaze as he deteriorated, almost on a daily basis. He grew painfully thin and his complexion became jaundiced.

'Everybody on the estate knew about his cancer but we didn't know the details,' said Mrs Patricia Tranter, who lived three doors away from the Evanses. 'I remember Minnie, David, Diane and Chris used to take turns at pushing him in the wheelchair. They were a very close family and you couldn't help but feel for them.'

From Mr Hayes's recollection, Martin lasted only a few months but he never once moaned about his fate.

'Minnie used to bring him to the shop and she used to put him so that he could lean over and shout in, "Hey, Hayesy! Hey Hayesey!" "Yeah, hang on, Martin." And I'd go out and talk to him.'

Martin Evans was only fifty-seven years of age when he died on Wednesday 25 April 1979 at Warrington General Hospital. Cause 1(a) on his death certificate states 'carcinomatosis', which indicates that the cancer had spread throughout his body. Cause 1(b) is given as carcinoma of the colon. His brief obituary, published as is customary in the Warrington *Guardian* on Friday 11 May, read as follows: 'Lived in the Bank Quay area for many years and worked for ten years as a clerical officer at a local hospital. In his earlier days he was a keen billiards and snooker player. Before moving to Orford was a proprietor of a shop in the Bank Quay area. He leaves two sons and a daughter.'

Chris's pal Glynn Povey must have been one of the first to visit the Evans household after the death.

He says, 'I can still smell the house and feel the heaviness. The rooms were all dark, the curtains were drawn and everything was very quiet. We must have been playing out and I went in wearing my school uniform, and Chris just turned round and said, "My Dad is dead" and he burst into tears, and I went home.'

David Evans, who qualified as a nurse and is now a mental health lecturer in New Zealand, where he lives with his wife and two teenage children, had already moved away from home when his father died. But he was the rock upon which his mother and his younger brother and sister leaned, and it was he who took care of formalities like registering the death and arranging the service. Meanwhile, Minnie began uttering a phrase which she has used repeatedly when attempting to describe the effect of her loss: 'I just feel cheated,' she told well-wishers, by which she meant that she had been robbed of her best friend and soul-mate and left to face the advancing years alone. She was still using the same, stark expression a couple of years ago when she sat next to Tony Hayes at the local Residents' Association Christmas meal.

'Cheated,' she said, 'I still feel cheated.'

How had Chris coped in the days preceding and following the death?

'I knew that something was wrong but I had no idea just how serious it was,' he told Andy Coulson. 'Mum bore the brunt of Dad's illness. She shielded me from it all. She was incredible.'

By all accounts, he dealt with his torn emotions by attempting to shut the tragedy out of his mind and escaping into a world of his own. This might explain why, on the few occasions when he has spoken in interviews about Martin, he has always stated that he was fourteen when his father died. In fact he had turned thirteen less than a month previously. It might also explain why he could not bring himself to be present at the funeral, at the Walton Lea Crematorium, where the vicar of St Margaret's and Orford, the Canon Eric Wilkes, led the prayers. But his absence served to deepen the psychological scar, adding a feeling of guilt to his sense of abandonment. For years afterwards, well into adulthood, it meant he was incapable of discussing the loss of his father, even superficially with those closest to him.

Alison Ward, who bore his daughter and lived with him when both were in their late teens, says he told her his father had died 'and said no more than that, really'. Carol McGiffin looks perplexed when asked what her husband told her about Martin. Then comes the strange realization that in all their years together, he spoke about his father 'briefly, maybe twice'. But Michael Gates, who became a close confidant when Chris was in his teens and lodged in his parents' house, was entrusted with a rare insight into his inner feelings.

'He really liked my late father, Bill. He spent a lot of time with him and was always asking him how to fix things, like his radio. He never spoke about his own father but he was obviously affected enormously by his death. You got the impression that that is why he wanted to put his time to the best possible use. Because he thought that he could die any time, and he had to live for every moment. One day he said to me, right out of the blue: "Make sure you spend a lot of time with your dad."

'He didn't say any more, but the way he looked said everything. I think that the chief factor in his development is his father dying. Everything he has done since stems from that.'

If Martin Evans had not been struck down by cancer when Chris was thirteen, who knows what his son might have become? His former masters and classmates at Boteler are convinced he was destined for Oxford or Cambridge, where his originality and tangental thinking would have made him a candidate for glittering academic prizes. But his father's premature death set him on a markedly different course. He became so disenchanted with school, particularly the lessons that he found boring, that, according to classmates, he was disruptive and difficult to control. The vivacity which had always been part of his make-up took on a hyperactive, manic edge.

The positive side to this was that, at an age when most teenagers have no idea what they want to do with their lives, Chris identified a goal and worked towards it with a single-mindedness that became obsessive. His target was to become the Radio One breakfast show DJ, and once he had fixed it in his sights, nothing and nobody would be allowed to obscure it from view.

'Even at junior school he'd got this desire to be famous, but I don't know if he knew what he would be,' says his friend Johnny Hoyles. 'But later on [when he found his goal] he really pushed it. He was very clever, and he used situations to better himself and always made sure he was in the right place at the right time.'

According to psychologist Dr Bryan Tully, children react differently to tragic events. Some are 'resistant' and all turns out well, no matter what; while others who live through the same circumstances may become neurotic or depressed by them.

However, he adds, 'There is quite a bit of evidence that the loss of a parent at an age like this can be a spur to some people. On the surface you couldn't get two more different characters than John Major, who lost his father early in life, and Chris Evans. But both are high achievers. The determination to show the world might make one more ruthless, which is a component to achievement, particularly among males. It means he would deal with the world in an aggressive way. A person such as this has a strong sense of entitlement: they have suffered greatly and now they will do as they please and have the rewards they deserve. They seek it aggressively and may deal punitively with anyone who doesn't fully accede to their specialness and their rightful deserve.'

Assuming that Chris Evans's behaviour followed this broad pattern, his sense of 'specialness' was soon being demonstrated to his teachers. By nature something of an exhibitionist, he developed an aberrant tendency which has, in adult life, become one of his habitual eccentricities: publicly exposing his nakedness.

'It's another breaking of the rules,' says Dr Tully. 'It shows that rules are not important to a man such as this . . . he is a man (or at this stage boy) to be reckoned with, and so much himself that he doesn't meet ordinary standards. He's a one-off and he expects to be treated that way. Other people have to meet standards. Not him.'

The first known occurrence of Chris's little habit came in a geography lesson at Boteler, and if Johnny Hoyles's recollection of time is correct it would have happened within a few months of his father's death. Whether seen as amusing or disturbing, the event may be regarded as indicative of Chris's tangled emotions.

'I think we were in the third year and Chris had got a bit bored so he got his todger out,' chuckles Hoyles. 'I started laughing. I sat next to him and it was just under the desk. The teacher said: 'Hoyles, what are you laughing at?'

'I can't really tell you, Sir.'

'You tell me what you're laughing at, boy, or there'll be trouble.'

'I'm laughing at him, Sir,' replied Hoyles, reluctantly, giving a sideways nod to Chris.

'Right, Evans, stand up!'

And without batting an eyelid, much less replacing his penis and zipping up his trousers, Chris Evans obeyed his teacher's command.

'I can't honestly remember what happened after that, but the whole classroom just erupted,' adds Hoyles, still incredulous more than fifteen years later. 'But I do remember Chris standing there, very matter-of-fact about it, just hanging out of his zip.'

Was he seriously punished?

'I imagine so. I mean, stuff like that would have been dealt with outside of the classroom.'

And had this incident typified his general behaviour at that age?

'Yeah, he had become eccentric.'

Nevertheless, there was a spin-off that made whatever punishment he received well worth taking. After almost two years of being the form's whipping boy, now – for the first time, though certainly not the last – Chris's controversial behaviour had turned him into something of a cult figure. Boys like Carey who had picked on him and attempted to guillotine him with his own desk lid now held him in grudging admiration. Evans might not have been much of a fighter and he might have looked like something of a freak, but they had to concede that he had some bottle and that, maybe, that mardarse Evans wasn't such a dickhead after all.

If that was the word now spreading around the corridors of Boteler Grammar School, then sadly it was still not always heard by the intellectually less fortunate inhabitants of the seamier side of Orford. There he continued to run the gauntlet almost every time his unmistakable ginger head surfaced above the parapet. Perhaps his most debasing indignity was perpetrated by a raw-boned, bare-scalped ex-borstal boy, whose street fighting has made him infamous throughout the locality: Steve 'Shaver' Browne.

The setting was again Granny's Brook Bridge – just along from where Phil Hazell's sister had pushed Chris in the stream – and Shaver clearly feels a degree of pride as he takes up the story. Now a steamroller driver with 'HATE' tattooed on his knuckles, he says: 'I reckon I was about fourteen and he was a couple of years younger. I was with a group of lads but he never knocked around with us. He was a bobbo when he was a kid. A nerd. He never had no mates. You'd see him on his own, walking to school. Everybody called him carrot-head and ginger nut, all that . . . But he was a bit of a loud-mouth, always had something to say. He was bullied, you know, got a bit of stick.

'Anyway, this day he must have said something to me – or, then again, maybe he didn't and I was just picking on him – and I gave him a slap. Well, a few cracks. He fell over in a heap and lay there. I think he was crying or mard-arsing, so I got my dick out and pissed on his head. Soaked him wet through. I don't really know why I did it, it just seemed like the right thing to do at the time. Everybody just started laughing.'

Hadn't his intention had been to humiliate Chris utterly, to ruin his name in the locality and break his spirit?

Shaver takes a more simplistic view. 'He didn't have a reputation so it didn't affect him. It was a bit of fun, that's all. It was on my behalf, anyway. That's my claim to fame now he's on TV. One of my mates at work, his party-piece is, "My mate pissed on Chris Evans's head." '

Dare anyone suggest that Shaver is exaggerating the incident, there are witnesses who will confirm that it happened. Occurring shortly before the onset of his father's illness, one can only wonder at the psychological damage that it caused. Yet at least Chris was beginning to win popularity with the opposite sex. During lunch-breaks at Boteler he and his mates would wander down to Devil's Dyke, a small copse at the bottom of the playing fields, and chat up the lasses from nearby Warrington High School for Girls. Chris was forever trying to entice one or the other of them deeper into the woods for some exploratory sexual adventure, but while they were content to talk and joke around, the best-looking ones usually had older, more mature boyfriends. Dating boys of their own age was virtually out of the question, and with his cherub-like face, freckles and red hair, Chris wasn't even in the picture.

This state of affairs played on his mind, until finally he thought he had hit upon a solution.

'He decided that all the sixteen-year-old lads who were going out with nice girls had spots, and that this must be the secret of their success,' says Hoyles. 'So we used to do daft things like rub our chins with matchboxes so it looked like we had spots. We thought it was really big.'

According to Hoyles, the matchbox tactic was an abject failure with the girls from Warrington High. Nonetheless, something must have worked, for it was in Devil's Dyke, with one of the 'grammar lasses', that Evans may well have lost his virginity. An anonymous classmate who claims to have had sex in the grass at the same time with the girl's friend just a few feet away, paints the following graphic description of the big event.

'It was like a double-date but we weren't really going out with the girls. We just knew them because they went to the girls' high school over the back, and boys like us, from Boteler, and lasses from there were always getting off with each other. I remember us meeting them at lunch-time, then getting together again after school. Chris's was quite good looking, with very dark hair. They were in their uniforms, blue skirts and blazers and blue and purple ties, and we were in our black ones. We had a bit of a kiss and a cuddle down in the woods and things progressed from there . . .'

If Chris's friend's memory serves him correctly, the relationship began and ended the same day.

'It may well have been Chris's first time but I'm not one hundred per cent certain. People tell lies don't they?'

Exposing himself in class, insulting the teachers, scrawling on desks and now having sexual intercourse while wearing the famous old school colours. Though the acting headmaster around this turbulent period, Mr Eric Percival, has no memory of taking any severe measures against Chris, and is certain that the ultimate deterrent of corporal punishment was not used, it was clear to everyone that matters could not continue as they were. Indeed, they did not.

Today, when staff at the now-comprehensive Sir Thomas Boteler High School delve back into Chris's personal file, they find that his third year record is blank. Why this should be, when the records of all his contemporaries are there, they are at a loss to explain. It is believed that as the end of his third year approached, Minnie and senior masters held crisis talks. It was decided that it would be better for Chris, and for Boteler, if he continued his education elsewhere. The newly-opened Padgate High School – only a few hundred metres from his home and academically less exacting – was the obvious choice

Neither Hoyles, nor Mark Rutter, nor any of his old friends was offered any explanation for the sudden transfer. Neither did he tell his new classmates at Padgate High why he had arrived. Several years later, however, he would brazenly attempt to glamorize what, from the outside, must have been viewed as a retrograde step. Dave Whittaker, who did not attend school with him but became a close friend when both were in their late teens, once asked his pal why he hadn't stuck it out at the grammar school, and remembers the response.

'He wouldn't tell me at first,' he says. 'He kept saying he'd tell me another time. I pestered him and eventually he told me he got expelled for smashing a teacher with a wooden stool, a tall one like you have in science labs. And he told me that this came about because there was a particular teacher who hated him. Chris used to say that the teacher hated him because it was as if Chris knew more than him.

'On one particular occasion the teacher asked a question, Chris put his hand up to answer before he had finished asking it ... and the teacher, in anger, came at Chris and started prodding him in the chest, you know, the way that annoys you. And he said he just snapped: turned round, grabbed one of these tall wooden stools and just laid into him with it. Smashed it over his head. He said he made a mess of him, obviously. Had to be restrained by the rest of the class, or whatever. And he had to be expelled. He told me that the teacher didn't press any charges. I think it was just sort of hushed up. Chris got expelled and that was it.

'The picture I have built up in my mind now is that it was pushed under the carpet and all the other teachers sort of said, well done, because they knew what this teacher was like and they were pleased. That's how Chris told it, anyway. He was obviously very angry at the time, with his dad dying.'

Alison Ward says Chris told her categorically that he had been expelled from Boteler, because he and an unidentified accomplice had 'tied a science teacher to a tree'. However, neither Mr Percival, nor anyone who taught him has any memory of the incident, or of his 'expulsion', and it appears the truth may be somewhat less dramatic.

'There is nothing on his record to indicate that he was expelled and the only member of staff who was here at that time says it isn't true,' said the current head of Sir Thomas Boteler High School, Mr John Higgins. 'He moved schools for family reasons, it would appear . . . but then as his record is blank the expulsion story could be true. It is all a bit of a mystery.'

Mark Rutter's mother, Mrs Sue Rutter, may provide the most accurate picture.

'After Chris lost his dad I just don't think he felt that he could cope at Boteler. The workload was a lot heavier than at Padgate High . . . Chris opted out and didn't get the education he might have had. His dad's death was a big blow to him, definitely. He was very close to his dad and after he died I just don't think he had the heart for it any more.'

Her son agrees. The science teacher story, he said, sounded 'a lot of rubbish. I just think that once his father died he wanted to be closer to his mum.'

Not for the first time, Chris's own recollection of past

events has altered. On the one occasion since he became a celebrity that Chris has spoken about his school switch, he said only that he had left around the time of Martin's death because he 'just wanted to be around' for his mother. Perhaps there is some veracity in both explanations. In Johnny Hoyles's view 'the teachers had probably had enough of him', and the general feeling might have been 'it may be better if you move to a different school.'

He added, 'I wouldn't be surprised if that were the case but I never knew the real reason. He just said, "I'm going to another school from now on", and that's it. He seemed happy to go.'

A light-brick New Town establishment, as modern in appearance as in outlook, Padgate High was light years removed from stuffy Boteler Grammar. His grief now submerged, though not washed away, by the passage of time, Chris found genuine happiness there. Instead of being addressed as 'boy' the teachers appeared happy to accept that he actually had a Christian name, and for the most part his individuality was welcomed.

Far more importantly, from his viewpoint, the school was co-educational. For the first time since reaching puberty he was in regular close contact with girls. Unsurprisingly, given the way he had been mistreated by boys, he generally preferred their company, and he certainly trusted them more. They, in turn, were seduced by his total lack of machismo. With their frilly, brightly-coloured post-punk and New Romantic clothes and dandified hairstyles, the other lads preened and postured in a manner some girls found off-putting, even threatening. But Chris seemed blissfully unconcerned by the vagaries of fashion, dressing and behaving as the mood took him. At the same time, he had an eclectic taste in music, and, of course, an infectious sense of humour. Inevitably, therefore, it was at Padgate High School that his romantic star began to rise. Though its arc could hardly be described as smooth, it has been soaring ever since.

His first real relationship quickly ended in disappointment, however. He fell for a pretty fifteen-year-old, Tamara

Bradshaw, and when he asked her out she agreed. But when their relationship was in its infancy, Tamara says, she finished with him.

'We were best friends for a lot longer than that, and people thought something was going on when there wasn't,' the now married Tamara Davies recalls. 'As soon as there was something in it, we decided it wasn't right. We separated on not a particularly pleasant note. He wanted to carry on going out. It was my decision to put an end to it.'

She refuses to elaborate, adding only, 'He was always a star, even when he wasn't. He always had a captive audience, even as a schoolboy.'

In a brief interview with *The People* newspaper, she reportedly described Chris as 'a real nutter at school, who loved an audience. But when it came to romance I don't remember very much. We never got past the kissing stage. Chris was too obsessed with music and besotted with John Lennon.'

A far more durable relationship followed. It was formed with another strikingly attractive girl at Padgate High, a slim, long-legged fourteen-year-old with dyed red hair called Tina Yardley. She may have been more than a year his junior, but they soon discovered that their mutual attraction extended beyond the physical, and during his final year at school, when he was preparing to sit his O-Levels, there was rarely an evening when they weren't cuddling on the sofa in one of their homes.

'She was absolutely gorgeous,' he has said. 'We were inseparable for well over a year. I loved her totally and absolutely, but things fell apart once we left school. Tina was special, though, really special.'

One of the things that drew them together was a shared passion for drama, and their bond grew stronger when they stayed behind after school to rehearse a music hall-style variety show. They subsequently performed it as a Christmas special in nearby old people's homes, including the one where Minnie was working. Chris's mother must have felt she was watching herself perform as Chris kitted himself out as a soldier to sing a military number, then joined in a rousing chorus of 'Down At The Old Bull And Bush'.

'Chris and I really loved doing that show, and it went down really well with the residents,' smiles Tina, now an English teacher at Cowley High School in St Helen's. I think we got on so well because we were quite different. I'm the sensible type, very easy-going, and I don't like to do too many things or take chances. I'm always thinking, "What if . . . ?" Chris is the total opposite. I would be the one who kept him down to earth and pulled him up if he was getting anything wrong.'

She stops and adds, only partially tongue-in-cheek, 'And, of course, he was so desperately in love with me.'

Tina is convinced that Chris was content with life then. He shared his innermost feelings with her above anyone else. Of course she was aware that his father had died, but he was 'quite close' about the subject and didn't dwell on it.

That one taboo apart, she says, 'There was one hundred per cent trust between us then, total loyalty, which is something he rarely gets now. That is what he likes, but it has to be unconditional. He wasn't tied or pestered when I was with him: I was there when he needed me to be. I was around. We went out for well over a year, and we split up, then got back together again. He was my first and only love.'

Discovering his natural aptitude for showmanship, it was while he was dating Tina that Chris began working for the local hospital radio station. For a youth of his age this was no mean achievement. The patients evidently loved his breezy, fresh style, which contrasted so sharply with that of the older, less adventurous amateurs who had volunteered to raise spirits on the wards. Yet with the fuse of ambition inside him now beginning to fizz and crackle, the airwaves of Warrington General quickly lost their allure. In keeping with the pattern he has followed throughout his career, no sooner had he achieved his immediate aim than he needed something more. Something bigger and better. He wanted to work on a real radio station. This ambition turned into a burning obsession after he won a competition and landed a day-trip to

Piccadilly Radio's Manchester studios to watch how the shows were put together.

'I'm going to be working there myself pretty soon,' he informed his mother and friends with absolute certainty.

In rare moments of public self-analysis, Evans has attempted to explain the motivation behind his relentless march onward. Referring to his father, he has said: 'When you lose someone that close, you just don't want to stop to think about it and I was hell-bent on making a success of myself. As a result I was living life so quickly because I was running away from the tragedy.'

On another occasion, he described his father's death as 'the shotgun that started the race'. He attributed his determination to carry through his convictions to his mother, Minnie, who had 'shown me how much strength it is possible for a person to have. I was a fourteen-year-old who was suddenly forced into dealing with the realities of the world. In a way, that's when my life started. I grabbed every moment of every day. I still have that attitude.'

The race had started, but during the opening laps Chris Evans skidded all over the track like a Formula One driver veering out of control at maximum speed. Desperate to earn money to supplement the family income – and equally intent on shutting out his emotions by filling every second of his time – he hurled himself into such a variety of jobs and quick-earning scams that his daily schedule would have taxed the most resilient adult, never mind an adolescent. He once calculated that he worked for twenty-one different bosses before leaving the North West for London in 1988. Some of the jobs lasted a few weeks, others a few hours.

Close acquaintances barely retained his loyalty for longer. A mesmerising variety of people became caught up in his slipstream. Male and female, old and young, his phenomenal energy and exuberance made them feel as though their mundane lives had been transformed by his presence. Invariably, however, the crazy, high-octane journey was over before it had really begun. The moment an apparently life-long friendship had been forged, or a brilliant new idea had been embarked upon, Evans simply lost interest and zoomed off elsewhere. The old bangers he screeched around in were changed at a similar rate. Friends remember several Minis, an MG, a Wartburg, a Skoda, a camper-van, a Talbot

Horizon and a gruesome old chocolate-brown Romanian contraption called a Dacia.

Alison Ward, who lived with Chris between summer 1985 and winter 1987, summed up his teenage years succinctly.

'He fitted more into a day than other people fit into a week. He flitted and changed and tried all different things. One minute he was mad keen to do one thing, the next minute he had decided to do something else completely, only he had forgotten to tell you about it. If he looks back now he probably hasn't got a clue himself about what he did or when he did it.'

Recording these busy teenage years chronologically is difficult, sometimes impossible to do. One certainty is that Chris was first employed at fourteen, delivering papers for Meachin's newsagent's, on Poplars Avenue in Orford. At around 5.30 a.m., when other Padgate High School pupils were sleeping, Chris would creep out of bed, drag on the nearest old clothes he could find, and traipse off to the shop, a short walk away. His work would be done just in time for him to yawn his way through morning assembly and, by the time he was in the Lower Sixth, he was burning the candle at both ends.

His latest hero at Piccadilly was an impossibly mad character who made Chris Tarrant and his *Tiswas* team seem positively straight-laced. He was a hyperactive five foot four inch loon whose standard dress, even though his audience could not see him, was a pair of gigantic colourfully-framed glasses, Bermuda shorts and outlandish suits. His name was Timmy Mallett, and his ridiculous appearance belied a brilliantly inventive mind. A Warwick University history graduate who had started out on a local station in Oxford before moving to Manchester, Cheshire-born Mallett was pushing back the boundaries of independent radio.

The other disc jockeys were genial, easy-listening types whose between-record chatter was not unlike the most banal office clerk having a conversation with himself. They told you where they had been the night before, commented jokily on the latest news titbits and made supposedly witty observations which invariably began, 'I don't know if this happens to you . . .', or, 'Have you ever noticed how . . .' If Timmy Mallett ever listened to these shows he might have belched out his trademark expression of revulsion: 'Bleugh!' On his own late evening slot, Timmy On The Tranny, the music was merely incidental and the emphasis was on fun of the most basic kind. His listeners were invited to abandon their grown-up world and join him in a wonderfully simple land where phrases and situations were invented as if by children lost in a fantasy game.

To create this world he needed a cast of characters to back him, so he enlisted young volunteer helpers. Their task might be to go out in the streets of Manchester and interview a manhole cover about its day. If anyone doubted his – or their own – sanity, Mallett reassured them that stunts like this were 'utterly brilliant'. Soon he would achieve wider recognition, when his *Wide Awake Club* replaced Roland Rat as the children's hook on TV-am. Later still he topped the charts with a version of 'Itsy Witsy Teeny Weeny Yellow Polka Dot Bikini' (re-worked by Sir Andrew Lloyd-Webber). But now he needed a new assistant and Chris Evans was among those who answered the call.

The tale of how Chris employed a carp fisherman's stealth to land the job has passed into newspaper folklore. Legend has it that he bowled up to the studios unannounced, waited for Mallett to emerge, followed him back to his house and pretended he wanted to interview him for hospital radio. There may be elements of truth in this, but like so many old stories about Evans, it has become exaggerated and distorted in the telling. Tina Yardley, still his girlfriend at this time, and Mike Gates, who became his closest confidant at the station, present a more accurate picture.

'Chris had been doing hospital radio and he found out that the man who normally helped Timmy the most was going off to university, so he wrote in and asked to replace him,' says Tina.

Evidently, the programme controller, Tony Ingham, had been sufficiently impressed by his letter to invite him in for a chat, so one morning Chris had taken himself off to Piccadilly Gardens. Gazing at the huge colour photographs of its star DJs – Phil Wood, Dave Ward, Mike Sweeney, Suzy Mathis – grinning down from the side of the city-centre building, he must have felt a degree of awe. A caught-in-the-headlamps look was still fixed in place as he moved from reception through to the hospitality area.

Mike Gates, then a freelance broadcasting assistant, was detailed by Ingham to show him around. It was the autumn of 1982, and he smiles at his first memory of Chris.

'There was a circle of seats where the guests used to wait before being interviewed, and my image is of him sitting there, staring through the glass partition, at all the knobs and gadgets in the control room. You know that gormless look he has sometimes? Well he had it then. And he was wearing a sort of Radio One DJ-style jacket: white, shiny, with turquoise stripes on it. He had very thick dark-red hair then, and these National Health specs, and he was like a little schoolboy trying to appear older.'

Had Evans followed Mallett home afterwards? Gates is aware of the legend but cannot confirm it. True or false, he was taken on as one of Timmy's team. He had secured his first, vital toehold on the ladder, working with probably his most influential mentor.

Mallett christened Evans Nobby No-level (as in No O-Levels). Tina Yardley recalls, 'He would go around doing all these ridiculous things. I followed him on to the show later. They had a character called Aunty Boney Knees, who was leaving and they wanted a replacement, so I went along and got taken on, too. The show was very much in the Steve Wright mould, with different characters in the studio.'

Chris and Tina parted soon afterwards partly, it seems, because his life was becoming so hectic.

'I gave up the radio and decided to concentrate on my A-Levels and do a degree and he wanted to get into Piccadilly and do all these hundreds of jobs,' she says. 'We drifted apart'.

The depth of their love may be measured, however, by the

fact that she is one of the very few important figures from his past who have not been forgotten. They still keep in touch by phone and, according to *The People*, Tina 'comforted him' – to coin a well-worn tabloid phrase – after his marriage to Carol McGiffin broke up.

Nonetheless, she acknowledges his fickle side.

'He is very much like that – everybody is his friend for six months. But we have stayed friends because we have something special. It's not just boredom that makes him cut his friends out of his life, although he is very attracted by new ideas and new things. It's just that he gets taken away in a rush of excitement and doesn't have time for anything else. That's what happened with us. He's not one for visiting people on a Sunday afternoon. I never pursued the friendship. He would always come round to see me. When we were eighteen, I remember I was sarcastic about something and I think it quite shocked him because he wanted to remember me as we were when we were going out together. I am still basically the same, but we all change a little.'

Of Chris's feverish ambition, she says, 'He enjoys the struggle to get what he wants, whether it be a new show or programme; money, or stuff like that. I knew I wasn't the same then. He was always working towards something: The Challenge. I think he's at his happiest when he's creating. But when it's happened he's immediately looking for something else.'

While Tina accepts that he now appears spontaneously funny, energetic, driven, she says, 'I saw a different side. We would spend hours and hours sitting together doing nothing. Listening to music – he had very broad-ranging tastes – playing the guitar and things like that. He wasn't loud. We had laughs, but he was never embarrassing, never over the top. That came later.'

It came, in fact, soon after his premature departure from Padgate High. Having passed five GCSEs and two CSEs – a respectable number, but nowhere near the result he might have expected had he stayed at Boteler – he moved into the

Lower Sixth Form. But he regarded school as another means by which to line his pockets. Believing the official tuck-shop to be over-priced, he decided to open an alternative outlet which would undercut it. He bought sweets and biscuits in bulk and sold them at margins which made them cheaper than the school shop but still left him with a decent profit. Definite shades of Martin Evans here. But if the pupils were happy, the teachers were not. Repeated warnings were issued and ignored until finally, rather than toe the line and shut up shop, Chris opted to abandon his A-Level course and leave school altogether.

Today the headmaster of Padgate High School steadfastly refuses to speak about his time there, but in 1995 his French teacher John Higginson told a newspaper, 'He was a real livewire, a very likeable, confident lad. His sense of humour really shone through.'

He was also a prefect and a member of the table-tennis team. However, although his technical drawing teacher also found him plausible enough and noted on an end-of-term report that 'his skills are improving', he added the rider, 'so is his talk-rate'. What was more, Chris was so distracted and tired by his paper-round, and other extra-mural activities, that a third master, Bob Lowe, was forced to 'read him the riot act' because he was not paying sufficient attention to his schoolwork.

Before he set his sights on a job in radio, Chris's early aim was to become a fireman, which he thought would suit his mercurial temperament. The notion that one day he might be rescuing a cat, the next saving someone from potential disaster, appealed to him. The careers officer took one look at his thick-lensed spectacles and shattered that dream. The memory distresses him to this day. In an interview in the July 1997 issue of *Vogue*, Mariella Frostrup describes how the tears trickle down Chris's cheeks and his fists clench as he recalls the incident.

'All I ever wanted to be was a fireman. So when we were sent to the careers officer just before our O-levels I walked in and said, "I won't waste your time, 'cos I'm gonna be a fireman." He said, "Okay, but just one thing . . . what are those things on your nose?" I said, "What?" He said, "Those things, what are they?" I said, "They're glasses." And he said, 'How are you going to be a fireman?"'

His second choice was to emulate Brian Meachin. On a careers form entitled 'If I Were A Newsagent', the sixteen-year-old spelled out his reasons.

'I would have to be able to hold intelligent conversations with people. The prospects are endless if you work hard. You could even open a wholesalers like John Menzies.'

Perhaps his chosen vocation became more deeply imbued than ever he knew. A decade later, when he landed the presenter's job on *The Big Breakfast*, his producer would attribute his popular appeal to the fact he resembled 'a sales assistant in WH Smith's who thought he looked cool'. But now, as he left school and began his first full-time job, the drudgery of marking addresses on the morning newspapers and selling packets of Trebor mints and Benson and Hedges was to provide a rude awakening.

A chain of three newsagents' shops called the Newsheet group – one standing directly opposite Chris's house in Greenwood Crescent, one in Battersby Lane and a third in Woolston – owned by brothers Brian and Tom McLoughlin, was hardly in John Menzies's league. Even so, in the early eighties, petrol stations and corner shops were yet to compete in the same market and they were a highly profitable little enterprise. Brian McLoughlin had been running the Greenwood Crescent shop since Tony Hayes retired in 1980, and knew the Evans family as regular customers. Brian had been a manager at Meachin's, where Chris had had his paper-round, so that when a vacancy arose at Newsheet for a trainee manager, 'the Evans lad' seemed the obvious choice. Chris was taken on at £50 a week – not bad money for a boy who had just turned sixteen – but although the McLoughlin brothers are reluctant to decry him now, perhaps for Minnie's sake, he was hardly the model employee.

For the first few weeks, until he learned the rudiments of making sure the right newspaper went to the right house, doing the stock and cashing up, he was taken under the wing of a more experienced trainee, Stuart Middleton, who was a year or so his senior. It meant that he had to arrive in the shop no later than 5.15 a.m.; early, but not unreasonable, since he need only drag himself out of bed and stagger a few paces across the road to be on time. But Chris was often late, and no wonder. Each evening, without stopping to eat or change his clothes, he would race off from McLoughlin's to Manchester to help out on Timmy Mallett's show, which began at 8 p.m., and would rarely return until the early hours of the following morning. At best he was getting three or four hours' sleep a night. He was habitually late and mistakes caused by chronic tiredness began to creep in.

'I used to ring him from the shop to get him moving, and he was usually still asleep,' says Stuart, now running his own successful greetings card manufacturing business.

'Very rarely did he get in on time, that's why I laughed when I read that he was in trouble at Radio One for not getting out of bed. I could have told them that Chris likes his sleep. Deja-vu there, all right. He didn't get into trouble with Brian and Tom because there were three of us young lads, me, Chris and Peter Smith at Battersby Lane, and we used to cover for each other. But Brian was always on at him to pack the radio in, and I think he came close a few times to getting the sack. To be honest he wasn't good at the job. I was conscientious. I would mop the floor in the morning after I'd done the papers. He never did anything like that. He wasn't as enthusiastic as I was, but I suppose he had a job to keep his eyes open. He just did enough to get by. Plus, he looked pretty strange. He wore these light blue trousers, and his glasses were silver-rimmed then. Some of the young lads used to call him Four Eyes. And, of course, the hair hasn't changed.

'I would say the McLoughlins were frustrated with him because they paid his wages and out of all their employees he was the most difficult to keep tabs on and control. He didn't do things the way they wanted him to. Whereas I used to look up to Brian and try to copy him because I saw him as successful, Chris was his own man, even then. He had to do it his way. There were often mistakes, for example with the papers. He would mark them wrong, and the *Express* would go to the house that should have got the *Mirror*, that sort of thing.'

Unaware of the pre-dawn chaos he was causing, the McLoughlins soon dispatched him to the Woolston branch, where he was to assist and learn from Tom. Standing in a drab grey double-storey block, flanked by a Spa grocery and a betting office, the shop has changed little since Chris first pulled up outside on his newly-acquired blue Yamaha 50cc moped. A Coca-Cola sign hangs in the window. Reddish-brown vinyl, worn through in patches, covers the floor. And, as evening draws in, the rows of magazines and jars of boiled sweets are dimly illuminated by a stark yellow strip-light.

Tom McLoughlin, now sixty-three, is a dour Warring-tonian whose view of a newsagent's life was not quite as rosy as the one depicted on Chris's school careers form. Intelligent conversations? You were lucky if you got a nod and good morning out of some customers. Endless prospects? Endless headaches, more like.

Small wonder, then, that there were times when the boss was totally exasperated by his young employee. Tom's irritation was at its greatest during their paper-marking sessions. At that time of the morning, all he wanted was to get through the monotonous task efficiently and in silence. But, late or not, Chris would bound in off his Yamaha like a new-born lamb and bleat out a greeting McLoughlin came to dread: 'Morning Tom!' he would exclaim, 'How's the world?'

How was the world? How the hell did he think it was at five o'clock in the morning? It wasn't too long before Chris was marking up the papers alone.

And yet McLoughlin cannot disguise his admiration for Chris.

'He knew what he was doing. He was a lad who had it all

upstairs. Well, he's proved that, hasn't he? He was nobody's fool, Chris. He probably liked to make people think that he was, but he wasn't. He was very ambitious, but his sole aim was to have his own newsagent's shop, not learn how to run this one the way I wanted it to be run. He was always going to go to the top and do it his way. He knew where he stood with me because I'm a straight-talking sort of a bloke, but he always thought he knew best.'

To make his point, he gestures towards the computerised till. 'We didn't have one of those in Chris's day, and it's been a Godsend, but if he had been here he would have known better than that bloody thing, too.

'Mind you, him being a mad bugger could be good for business. The highlight of his day was when the kids came in from the local high school, and they loved him. He was like he is on TV now, all arms and legs, telling them what's what. He had read all the pop magazines and he could communicate with them on their wavelength. He would say, "Nah, you don't want to get that mag this week, try this one." He used to entertain them. That was his function, really. He was a bit larger than life with them, and they lapped it up.'

But a parting of the ways was inevitable. Chris narrowly escaped the sack when, left on his own in the shop one morning, a fast-talking travelling salesman persuaded him to buy a job-lot of sports-shoe laces, even though Newsheet had never sold anything remotely like that before.

'You get these fly-by-nights coming round saying, "Buy this and you'll get a free radio" and he bloody fell for it,' says McLoughlin sourly. 'I gave him a rollocking, and I still keep those laces under the counter.'

He says they serve as a reminder of how costly mistakes can be.

Chris may have escaped with his job on that occasion, but there was to be no second chance. To while away the more boring mid-morning and early afternoon hours at Newsheet, he had taken to bringing his radio to work – an early model ghetto-blaster with heavy bass and a booming top volume.

It was bad enough when he had it on softly in the background, studying the style of new DJ interests like Mike Read (who had taken over the Radio One breakfast show from DLT in 1980). But when Tom McLoughlin returned from lunch at two-thirty to find the whole shop trembling to the strains of rock music, he went ballistic.

'I can't remember what he was playing – it was just a lot of noise to me. We had words, to put it mildly, and it was bye-bye Chris, I'm afraid. He didn't like to be told off. I sent him his cards and any money we owed him. The next time I heard him he was on the radio, standing in for Timmy Mallett for the week.

'It's a shame it turned out as it did, really, because he would have made a businessman. He was bright. But when people are just learning a job and they think they know it all but they don't know it all, well, you have to tell them, don't you? It's as simple as that.'

It was an attitude that Chris himself would adopt, though even more rigorously, when his chance came to play the big boss.

Chris's sacking turned out to be a blessing in disguise, by forcing him to focus on what he really wanted. While he was at Newsheet he had been torn between making it as a DJ and owning his own newsagent's shop. Now the only road to take was the one that led to a career in radio, and he took it in the most literal sense. Having been taught to drive by near-neighbour Pat Tranter in his first car, a clapped-out old Mini, he headed east on the M62 to Manchester and asked Tony Ingham to employ him as a freelance, on the same basis as Mike Gates. A deal was struck. He would work shifts as and when required.

Now began his initiation into the unglamorous, often monotonous off-mike side of broadcasting. His tasks were to collect the newscasts from Independent Radio News, arrange interviews, help on the sports programme, get out records from the library, and, when he was lucky, edit the odd tape. He was everyone's dogsbody, and he earned just £2.50 an hour, but the experience he gained was to prove invaluable.

At just seventeen, the learning curve that had started when he was re-christened Nobby No-level had taken a considerable upturn.

CHAPTER SIX

'Nobby! Where's that jingle?'

'Sorry, Timmy. I'm working on it, honest, but I haven't quite got the last line yet.'

'What?! You haven't cracked it yet, you useless little idiot! I told you I needed it in three minutes, not three hours. Sort it out before the next record or you're finished. You'll never make it in radio, Nobby. You're pathetic!'

If any of the hapless producers, cameramen and assorted technicians who have been reduced to quivering wrecks by Chris Evans's legendary temper tantrums want to know where he learned to rule by fear, they should look no further than Timmy Mallett. Although he had started to help out on various other programmes as a freelance broadcasting assistant, Chris continued to play Nobby No-level, the supposedly half-witted fool at King Timmy's crazy court. But while he was frequently humiliated by his boss he was also being given a priceless grounding in the art of producing and presenting exciting, highly-polished shows.

'Timmy worked them bloody hard. He was absolutely cruel to those kids,' says former Piccadilly DJ Tim Grundy. His show followed Mallett's, and he would watch the team operate before the hand-over. 'I mean cruel. He was nasty and would shout at them continuously – he had a lot of the traits Chris Evans developed. He'd go into a record and he was Mr Nice, then he'd close the microphone and become Mr Nasty. He'd never swear, but he'd say, "That was useless. It wasn't funny. You've got three minutes to come up with a funny sketch about marriage. If it isn't the funniest thing I've ever heard you're all fired." And he didn't pay them anything. They'd all come in for nothing.

'I think they'd have a bit of a gripe now and again but, basically, this was exciting radio and Timmy was somebody. He was already on TV, doing the Oxford Road Show and all sorts of things, so they put up with it.'

Grundy, son of the renowned broadcaster Bill Grundy and now a respected television presenter, adds that Mallett, a vicar's son, is also 'a very bright, secretly very caring guy' who donates a large percentage of his earnings to a Down's Syndrome charity because his brother was born with the condition. On the other hand, he is so single-minded that when he goes out socially he never drinks alcohol because that would not fit with his image as a children's favourite

Chris's best friend at Piccadilly, Mike Gates, concurs.

'Timmy was a very hard task-master. His show was all fantasy, unconnected to reality, and he would create these strange jingles and little songs – or rather his helpers, like Chris, would. To him Chris wasn't Chris, even off the air. He was still Nobby, and between records Timmy would shout across the studio, "Hey, Nobby, give me a song for the next link." If you worked on his programme, you just had to do it. So Chris had to make up a song in the time it takes to play a single, and if he didn't do it in time Timmy would get rude and aggressive. Chris didn't dare argue back in those days. No one argued with Timmy. He could get very, very angry. At the same time he was very good fun. He was extremely fast and highly competent technically, and Chris was drinking all this in, learning by the seat of his pants.

'The show was aimed at kids of about fourteen or fifteen, which suited Chris perfectly. Timmy would sometimes be quite obnoxious and disparaging to the teenagers who phoned in, but he could also be very nice and there was always a bit of an undercurrent of Mallett being lecherous on air. It depended what angle he wanted to take. There would be all these competitions and outside broadcasts, too, which is where Chris came into his own. Timmy would say, "If you get down to such and such a street in twenty minutes, Nobby No-level will be there." So lots of kids from the area would flock round him, and he would get them going, whip them up into a frenzy. Chris was always very good with a crowd, and he started to get a little cult following in Manchester around that period, though he was only about seventeen.'

It would be wrong to accuse Evans of copying Timmy Mallett. More accurately, Mallett's constant chivvying and hectoring prised out the jewel of talent that was already in him, then polished and honed it until it became a recognizable gem. Just as importantly, he taught Chris how to make a poor idea into a good one, and a good one great by, in Evans's words, 'putting ten tons of steam behind it'.

Unashamedly eclectic, Evans has culled from dozens of others, from Noel Edmonds and Dave Lee Travis to Desmond Lynam and Frank Bough. Later he would be influenced by New York shock-jock Howard Stern. Though he may have abhorred Stern's gratuitously provocative racist and sexist remarks, his penchant for having his female guests bare their breasts and Stern's obsession with the size of his own 'raisin-like' penis demonstrated just how far it was possible to go on America's airwaves. One day Evans would become a shock-jock, too, though his shocks would be doctored for a UK audience.

Yet if Evans's own fans could be transported back in time and mingle with the assorted gofers, punters and hangers-on who nightly trekked to Piccadilly Gardens in the hope of being heard on Timmy On The Tranny, they would undoubtedly sense that they'd seen and heard all this some-where else. Mallett's studio atmosphere carried distinct over-tones of Evans's Greater London Radio shows, The Greenhouse and Round At Chris's And His Missus, which he hosted with his wife Carol McGiffin. On GLR, too, Chris introduced gimmicky competitions and stunts, like Pregnant

Pause (which could only be played by expectant mothers) and the brilliantly simple traffic jam stress-buster, Honk Your Horn. For Nobby No-Level, substitute Chris's sidekick invention, Colin The Punk. So it's possible to see how the mixture of irreverence, odd characters, stunts and slapstick humour that form the central thread through all of Evans's work have evolved. The phenomenal success of *The Big Breakfast*, *Don't Forget Your Toothbrush*, *TFI Friday* and his controversial Radio One breakfast show can be dated way back to Nobby.

While he was serving his apprenticeship at Piccadilly, Chris was also learning the rudiments of networking, which he perfected into an art-form. Top bands and artistes of the day – including Sade, Cindy Lauper and Toyah – would come in to be interviewed by Timmy, and Chris would often help with arrangements and research. In this way he got to meet Kim Wilde, never dreaming as he swooned over her that he would ever be in a position to go out with her. Another beautiful blonde who caught his eye was Mandy Smith, then making tabloid headlines after the *News Of The World* revealed that from the age of thirteen she had been embroiled in a decidedly adult relationship with Bill Wyman of the *Rolling Stones*. Now about sixteen years old, she also appeared on the station, and, learning fast in more ways than one, Evans made sure he gave her his phone number before she left for London.

'I remember Chris being very excited, saying Mandy had phoned him the other day,' says Gates. 'They were in touch and I'm not sure whether she went to his house in Warrington.'

Less thrilling, but more important in terms of his long-term career, he also forged close ties with people who would become key figures as he continued his relentless attempt on the broadcasting summit – highly talented and ambitious people like Andy Bird, who preceded Chris as Timmy's main helper before becoming a producer. Bird, now co-managing director of Turner Entertainment in London – which screens the Cartoon Network – would later be instrumental in smoothing Chris's path to the capital. For a while afterwards the two men became virtually inseparable, setting up a company together, Big and Good Productions, and devising a short-lived but lucrative show for TV-am called *TV-Mayhem*. Also prominent among Chris's crew around this time was Chris Whatmogh, now a top-rated Radio One producer. His detractors would say that he targeted these cleverer types because he saw them as useful future allies. Tim Grundy, who would later employ Chris as an on-air coffee boy nicknamed White And Two Sugars (that was the way Grundy liked his morning cup of coffee), numbers among them. He described Evans as a 'classic user of people'.

If there appears to be an element of bitterness here, then Grundy would argue that it is wholly justifiable. Despite enjoying a volatile working relationship, they became firm pals, and in time, when the need arose Grundy would put himself to considerable trouble to keep Chris's career on the tracks. His reward, when Chris finally made it to the top, was not only to deny him a return favour, but treat him as if he were some autograph-hunting fan he had never met.

'There are so many of his old friends, people I would have called real friends who, after he found success, just wanted to contact him and say well done, or how's it going, or shall we meet up and have a meal ... but he has cut them all off if they couldn't be of use to him,' says Grundy.

'I'm chair of a charity, The Children's Adventure Farm Trust, and we bought a farm in Cheshire for £368,000 and transformed it into residential care units for terminally ill, underprivileged and poor children. When Chris had become very famous, I thought, well here's a useful thing, he can raise some money for my charity. So I wrote to him. Two very friendly, positive letters ... Chris would have undoubtedly known about the farm because I was very heavily involved in it when he was heavily involved with me. He may even have been to the farm, I don't know. But I got no reply.'

Grundy followed up the letters with a series of phone-calls.

'I remember getting through to reception and saying, "Is Chris Evans there?" I was asked who was calling and said it was Tim Grundy. The girl asked what it was regarding, and

I said that if she just told Chris it was me he would take the call. She came back and said, "No, I'm afraid Mr Evans isn't available." Now, that happened half a dozen times.' He pauses and shakes his head. 'You ask me why I think Timmy Mallett has a warm heart. Because he's helped me several times and helped other people. I don't see Chris helping anybody except himself. I'm extremely sad at the way he's changed.'

This transparently ambitious and ruthless side to Evans became more and more evident as his confidence in his ability grew. Several of the other DJs did not like him, perhaps perceiving him, even at this stage, to be a threat. And he was unpopular among the technicians because, for all his professionalism, he treated their precious equipment with utter disdain. He would leave coffee cups on tape-decks and control panels, where they could be – and sometimes were – disastrously spilled. He had little respect for the tools of his trade and, therefore, it appeared, little respect for those whose job it was to operate them.

'He used to sit in for other DJs when they were on holiday,' says Steve Huckvale, still an engineer at Piccadilly, 'and I remember he devised a competition where, if the contestant got the question wrong, he broke a raw egg over his own head. You are not supposed to have drinks or food near the equipment – that was a golden rule. The engineer was so incensed when he saw what was happening, with yolk running everywhere, that he switched the equipment off and stopped the broadcast.'

Huckvale understood why, but admired Evans's style nonetheless. 'He could have bull-shitted and pretended he was smashing eggs over himself, but he actually brought in boxes and did it. Chris did things properly.'

There were other little mishaps, the majority at least partly caused by what John Clayton, a former senior producer at Piccadilly, euphemistically describes as Evans's 'healthy disregard for authority'.

He says, 'In those days there were all sorts of restrictions and rules in local radio that no longer apply. When you were doing outside broadcasts, which Chris did a lot of, you particularly needed to follow lots of procedures. The engineers were keen that things were carefully thought out, for all sorts of technical and safety reasons. Chris would never follow the rules, and it made you wonder whether he did it to wind them up. They got very cross with him.'

The radio cars always seemed mysteriously to break down when Chris was at the wheel, and when the management replaced them with pristine white state-of-the-art trucks, with the Piccadilly logo painted proudly on the side, he made a mess of one of those, too.

'We thought we'd try to compete with the Radio One roadshow and it was quickly realized that just doing a programme for the stage was poor, so we devised lots of alternative entertainment,' says Clayton. 'Chris got a lot of bookings from the promotional department to staff the stage because he was so good at winding people up and keeping bored crowds entertained for a long time. As I recall, he had a whole lot of barbecues to give away and he was proving how easy they were to use, so he lit one of them. The stage was on the back of the truck – you just pulled the sides down – and it was made of a rubber material. It might have seemed pretty obvious to anyone else that it would catch fire, but not to Chris. The fire extinguisher was needed, and he would have got a major bollocking. He was always getting bollocked, but some people are hard to shout at, aren't they? I don't think these people thought he'd be listening and they probably weren't wrong.'

Such careless behaviour quickly made him a marked man among the station's hierarchy, particularly its new Controller Mike Briscoe, who had switched to radio after many years as a *Daily Mail* journalist and was keen to establish his authority. Like a tetchy schoolmaster aware that his pupils were misbehaving while he was chalking on the board, Briscoe was frequently gunning for Evans. As he was usually to be found at the heart of any mischief, his suspicion was justifiable. He was incredibly accident-prone, too, especially when cars were involved.

On one occasion he was entrusted with the job of driving a group of competition winners to London, where they would be admitted free to a Prince's Trust concert. A mini-bus was duly hired and Chris managed to steer it safely to the top of the narrowly spiralling Piccadilly Plaza car-park. On the way down, however, the van's roof jammed against the car-park ceiling. With horns blaring from the angry queue backed up behind him and the winners growing anxious about the time, Chris hit upon a typically ingenious solution. He let down the tyres and rolled the van down the ramp.

Incidents like these may have infuriated the Controller, but to less elevated colleagues they made Chris a quixotic figure. To Mike Gates, six years older and just down from Oxford, where he had graduated in English, he was also a great companion, the sort of guy you wanted to hang out with, even if he was considerably younger. Others began to regard him with a similar mixture of affection and exasperation. They might not admit it but, like Gates, they were awe-stricken by his audacity; borne aloft on his endless hydrogen cloud of energy. Not only had Chris escaped the Orford bullies, but he found himself playing the role of talismanic leader. Suddenly no one – the bosses apart – wanted to kick sand in his face or make fun of his appearance. He was charismatic, omnipotent even, and it was he who called the shots. When he sat in the pub and told stories everybody listened: who cared whether or not they borrowed a little from fantasy?

One tale concerned a girl from Warrington with whom Chris was apparently besotted. She had gone on holiday to France, he told Gates, and he was desperately keen to impress her. So he had bought her a box of Milk Tray chocolates, then hitch-hiked all the way to France, to the place where she was staying. But instead of presenting them personally he aped the Milk Tray advert then running on television, leaving them in her room and hot-footing it back to Britain. No matter that Evans never told Gates the girl's name, nor that not one of the dozens of sources interviewed for this book could recall the incident or identify her.

'I'm sure it was true,' says Gates, 'He told me about it in

a very matter-of-fact way. The thing about Chris is that the most extraordinary things did turn out to be true. The whole way he was leading his life was amazing. The most extraordinary things used to happen to him.'

Extraordinary indeed. One of his male friends, whose identity must be protected, was given to getting drunk and stripping off every stitch of clothing at parties.

'Chris would be fascinated by this and I didn't know, but before-hand he would warn people that it was going to happen,' said the serial stripper. 'If I didn't do it he would urge me to. He was absolutely fascinated with nakedness, his own or other people's, male or female.'

Mike Gates, who witnessed these ritual stripping sessions is erudite in his attempt to contextualize Chris's reaction to them.

'You know the fairy story, the Emperor's New Clothes? That fits him perfectly, and he is two characters at the same time. On one hand he is the boy who dares to say what he thinks: that the Emperor has no clothes on. On the other hand he's the Emperor, who believes what everyone around him says. And, of course, the metaphor is complete because he is fascinated by nakedness. I have read that he has held management meetings naked and it doesn't surprise me at all. He has got this fascination with it which is not sexual.

'I think it's part of this wanting to get to know what people really are, and get down to the basics. It's something to do with his obsession with having a new start to every day. He does start every day as though he has just been born. Even when we hired a camera for him to make a demo-tape for television, it came through. He had the camera running, and he developed a sort of script and running order. It began with him lying in bed and the alarm clock ringing, and opening his eyes and starting off the day. All very much present tense, very ad hoc and real. "I've woken up, it's a new day and off I go." And I think this thing with nudity is part of the same thing. Here we are. Don't look back, look forward, I've just been born. At the risk of sounding pompous, it's almost Blakeian. On the one hand people talk about him being blasphemous and corrupt, but on the other hand one of his greatest qualities was his innocence. People responded to that.'

Back in the geography class at Boteler Grammar School, it's doubtful that such a philosophical view would be shared by the teacher who ordered Evans to stand up and found himself staring at his penis.

CHAPTER SEVEN

Substituting a safe, relatively well-paid job in retailing for the role of resident clown and teaboy on a local radio station made very good sense to Chris Evans. It certainly did not to his mother. When he broke the news that he had been fired by Tom McLoughlin, her advice was that he should find another job with similarly good prospects as quickly as possible. Either that, or follow his brother David and sister Diane, by gaining better qualifications. Much as he wanted to please the widowed Minnie, Chris was utterly convinced that if he was going to achieve his burning ambition, he simply could not accede to her wishes. Their difference of opinion caused serious friction between mother and son and, for the first time, they began to have rows.

'She used to come in to work and say he was doing her head in,' recalls Pat Daley, who worked with Minnie at Orford Hall. 'She used to despair of him ever making anything of himself.'

Mike Gates, at Piccadilly, saw the arguments from a different side.

'The person he wanted to prove something to more than anyone else was his mother, because his mother is not easily impressed by anything. Certainly not things that he values, like fame and money and celebrity status. I think the thing she values most is behaving in a Christian way and having a good education, which Chris certainly lacks. I think that even now she would view David and Diane as more successful, because they have gone on and got "proper" responsible jobs. I'm sure she loves him and she's very proud of him, but no matter how much he succeeds in his field, I don't think Chris would think he'd won her approval.'

Their relationship reached such a low ebb that around the time of his eighteenth birthday Chris decided he had to get away for a while. The problem, he reflected as he packed up his few possessions into his rusting old orange Mini, was that he didn't actually have anywhere else to stay. His part-time job at this time was collecting the glasses at the Lion, then the most thriving town-centre pub with a strong tradition for attracting big name rock bands. *Deep Purple*, *The Cream*, David Bowie – all had passed through its cobbled courtyard on their way to greater things. He asked around the staff for a temporary place to stay and spent several uncomfortable nights on the floors and couches of anyone willing to put him up. Among them was Sue McNish, a barmaid who was living in a bedsit on Wilderspool Causeway, one of several busy dual-carriageways feeding motorway traffic into central Warrington. In part she was repaying a favour for the night when, pestered in the pub by a persistent old flame, Chris had agreed to join her behind the bar and pose as her boyfriend.

'He wasn't the toughest, but he did it for me,' she laughs. 'He was smashing, was Chris. He was very lively, funny, and everybody liked him. There were always girls around him and I could never work out whether they were girlfriends or just mates.'

Sue, now married, went out socially with Chris several times, and although she insists that they were never more than good friends, they became 'very close for a few months'. Slightly older and certainly more mature than he was then, Chris began to confide his domestic problems in Sue.

'He fell out with his mum over a silly argument. She didn't want him to go into entertainment . . . and I think his mum was concerned,' she says guardedly. 'He asked if he could stay at my place and other people's. I would assume that's why he didn't get on with her just for a time. I think she was just worried about him doing the right thing, as any mum would be.'

Understandably, given his admiration for Minnie and his desire to please her, Chris now began showing signs of his deep-seated melancholy. As he grew older this would degenerate into depression, sometimes manifested as anger. Out in the pub at night, Sue remembers, Chris was the life and soul of the party. Back at Wilderspool Causeway, she glimpsed how he was really feeling.

'He used to sit and chat for half the night and he didn't seem happy. He would mention his dad. He had been dead for around four years, but it obviously still affected him. You could tell he was still upset, and I just felt that he hadn't got over it. It was, "I wish I could turn the clock back . . ." That kind of stuff. On top of that there were the worries about his mum. That's why I was able to talk to him. I wanted to help him.'

His desire to achieve success quickly was also eating away at him.

'I remember once he showed me a letter he had written to Richard Branson – or perhaps it was addressed to whoever was running Radio One. There was page after page; ideas, ideas, lots of ideas about what he would do if he had a job there.'

Mike Gates was among the handful of friends whom Chris trusted sufficiently well to reveal his dark, discontented side.

'Sometimes he would look really depressed. His brow would be furrowed and you could tell. It was pretty obvious: his whole face would look really, really sad. But at the same time, he could have a laugh about it. I think it was just part of his character. Anyone who is as "up" as he can be, and as optimistic, has to come down, otherwise they float away.'

He was unaware of Chris's letter to Branson (or Radio One), but unsurprised that Chris had penned it. 'I always thought his depressions were usually connected with work, at least superficially. Not getting on fast enough. He never seemed to doubt his own ability but perhaps he might have doubted whether it would ever be recognized by other people.'

His doubts must have reached their lowest point when, only a few months after the McLoughlin's fiasco, he was given his marching orders from Piccadilly. The manner of his dismissal was classic Chris Evans, from start to ignominious finish.

His latest girlfriend was another barmaid, a dark, attractive brunette named Dawn, who worked part-time in a pub in the Lancashire village of Astley Bridge, near Bolton. One snowy afternoon the lovebirds decided to go sledging in the steep moorland hills nearby, and, hurtling along at treacherous speed Chris came flying off and fractured his leg. Mike Gates, who lived nearby in Ainsworth, was summoned to ferry him to casualty, where the stricken limb was duly encased in plaster from just below the knee. To anyone else it might have been obvious that driving a car in such a condition was inadvisable, if not dangerous – but not Chris. The next time Timmy Mallett asked him to take the Piccadilly radio car on an outside broadcast, he duly obliged – and inevitably crashed. He was summoned from on high and given his marching orders.

'How he thought he could operate the pedals with his leg and foot in plaster I don't know, but that was Chris,' laughs Gates. 'It must have been the end of his freelance work, and I think he was finished as Nobby No-level, too, because I never saw him for maybe eighteen months after that.'

To less resilient egos it might have been the end of the road. Time to return to reality and apply for one of those sensible, reliable jobs advertised in the *Warrington Guardian* that Minnie had suggested. Chris thought differently. It wasn't very long before he was regarding his departure as another opportunity. A chance to broaden his showbusiness experience. He scanned the papers, all right, but looking down the personal ads it was another type of money-making enterprise that captured his imagination: kissograms. Well, why not? He had already proved himself to be adept at manipulating crowds while doing roadwork for Mallett. All he had to do was think up a better act than the ones already operating and he'd be quids-in. It would be a bit of a laugh as well.

His enforced change of direction came after a chance reunion with his junior 'minder' at St Margaret's, Trevor Palin. The pair had bumped into one another again a few weeks previously, in Orford, while Trevor was on his way home from a guitar lesson, and quickly rekindled their old friendship. By this time Palin was intent on making a career as a singer-songwriter, and Chris had managed to secure him a few unpaid slots on Mallett's show, where he was handed the job of instant jingles writer and dubbed 'Muso'.

'If Timmy told me to write a song about a cigarette machine in a couple of minutes I could usually come up with something,' he says. 'Sometimes we'd stay behind in the studios and record songs, and we'd occasionally stay at Timmy's house in a nice area of South Manchester. But I was never really part of the in-crowd there. Timmy used to treat us like puppets and I didn't like to be ordered around.'

Nevertheless, recognizing that Chris not only had immense talent and self-belief, but possessed the charisma and 'front' to open doors, Trevor, who was far more reserved, was quite prepared to follow his lead. And when Chris suggested that they form a kissogram team – one with a difference – he readily agreed.

'He had done a couple for an agency called Bunnies in Chester,' recalls Trevor, now a photographer for a London advertising agency. 'They had advertised in the paper. He tried one or two on his own, then I remember him saying, "Come with us and play the guitar." But it wasn't worth our while working for anyone else. We only got £15 each, so Chris said we should do it ourselves. We bought a 50cc Yamaha and I'd ride pillion. We made quite a lot of money – about £140 a night – but we would do several appearances some nights and it was knackering.'

They won bookings because their act was the most original in town and word spread fast. Saucy policemen and vicars were old-hat, Chris reasoned, and they couldn't really compete as strip-a-grams because they were usually performed by women. As they were both comically white-skinned, hollow-chested and puny, why not exploit their lack of brawn by posing as the least likely Tarzans Warrington had ever seen? They could liven up twenty-first parties and hen nights by performing in leopardskin loincloths and nothing else. Even better, they could put their songwriting skills to good use by finding out a few embarrassing – and preferably risqué – facts about their unsuspecting victims, and turn them into Timmy-style jingles, accompanied by Trevor's acoustic guitar. Soon, Chris came up with another idea that made the act complete. Before each appointment he popped into the butchers and bought half a pound of plump pork sausages. Then it was on to the chemists for some shaving foam. The cream-smeared sausage was stuffed down his loincloth, female victims were blindfolded and invited to let their hands wander lower and lower . . . The squeals of shock when they reached the slimy pork meat said the rest.

'We would turn up to the function fully-dressed, go to the toilet and strip off. It got to the point where we could even write the songs in the loo beforehand, then reappear half naked,' laughs Trevor. 'Some nights we would do a balloon game, where Chris would have a long balloon tied round his waist and the woman or girl would be guided into position to lick off the cream. It sometimes got out of hand and we got our shorts ripped off, and we'd be literally stood in the nude. We were always pushing it to see how far we could go. It got a bit hairy at times in these working men's clubs. Chris was six foot two but I'm about seven or eight inches shorter, and we must only have weighed about fourteen stones between us. We'd go to these places, and there'd be all these brawny guys eyeing us up as we had fun with their girlfriends or wives.'

One of the early 'victims' was Karen Welch. She was at work in the finance department at North West Water on her twenty-ninth birthday when Tarzan Chris burst into the office.

'He was in a grass skirt, no top, and he had a guitar,' she says. 'He sang a poem, and there was no embarrassment at all. Then he put a sack over my head and he had a sausage down his undies, and he said I had to get a surprise. I just played along with it . . . it was a good laugh.'

This reaction was typical, but had the stunt been pulled on a different type of woman in the more politically correct nineties, who knows what outcry might have erupted?

A more hazardous engagement, Palin recalls, was at the local job centre.

'I was definitely signing on for unemployment benefit at the time, and I am sure Chris was, too, but we were asked to do this booking there for one of the clerks. It was ridiculously risky, but we thought, fuck it, and we did it. It was so funny that we could get away with it. It was a buzz.'

But the ultimate buzz was the night they were invited to an unusual venue: the elegant suburban home of a local doctor. The GP had decided it would be fun to give a dinner party for a few friends, then, when the drinks were flowing, introduce Tarzan and his assistant to his sozzled wife. Far from being intimidated, the wife determined to get full value for her husband's money. Palin still finds it difficult to believe what transpired.

'There were only about six people there, and I'm a bit of a prude, so it was a difficult one to start with. But after we did the act the guy's wife came upstairs to the bedroom where we were changing. She had stripped down to suspenders and a black bra, and I can remember her jumping on the bed and lying there. She was your typical drunk, middle-class wife. She wanted us to spray the cream on her body, so Chris obliged, then we both licked it off. It didn't go further than that. We just licked the cream and had a bloody good laugh about it. Again, it was, how far can you take everything? Can you take a mundane kissogram and enjoy it?' Palin paused, then added, 'Women were attracted to Chris, but at that stage he didn't really realize it. But don't get me wrong: he was definitely interested in them, too.'

Escapades like this are unlikely to have reached Minnie Evans's ears, but she was nonetheless concerned when she learned how her son was earning a living. Warrington on a

Saturday night was like the Wild West. Supposing some violent drunk didn't think he was amusing and thumped him, or worse? She knew from long experience that he wasn't equipped to take care of himself if trouble arose. He had to be protected. The man for the job, she decided, was her near-neighbour Paul Maudsley, brother of Chris's old Woodcraft Folk pal Kenny, who was now a hulking, sixteen-stone body-builder and security guard at town centre clubs. In Orford, rumour has it that Minnie actually offered to pay Paul a small amount to act as Chris's minder, but Maudsley denies the arrangement was ever formalized.

'I used to pass her house quite often, and she found out I worked on the doors of places where Chris was doing the kissograms. One day she approached me and said, "Please keep an eye on my son,"' he says. 'She was obviously worried about him getting hurt.'

Paul eased her fears by promising to watch over Chris – but he felt like reneging on the agreement because of Chris's ungrateful attitude.

'He was very flippant,' he says. 'He would come in and say, "All right, lads, keep an eye on my gear." I thought, who are you to talk to me like that?'

Stung by Chris's ingratitude, Maudsley told him that he would be protected, but only for the price of a round of drinks.

'He was a pitiful excuse for a fella and he played on looking like a wimp,' he says. 'Before he did his act he would come up and ask me about the mood in the place . . . how many lads were in, what they were like. That way he would know how far to go. You get a couple of pissed-up lads and he's got their birds all over him and it could cause a riot.'

Ironically, the only night Chris needed Maudsley's assistance was when he was accosted by a hugely obese woman.

'He was singing a song on his guitar and she was completely bladdered and made a grab for his leotard. Her momentum knocked him off balance and she ended up on top of him. The poor lad was nearly crushed, and I had to pull her off. Quite often the girls would be groping his bollocks while he was trying to sing them his songs, but he wouldn't even blush. I wouldn't mind, but he didn't even look to be well hung! He sometimes got flustered and scared but he had the patter. That arrogance that he's got on TV saw him through.'

As hackneyed and played-out as they may appear today, kissograms were, in their way, as integral to Evans's development as a live show presenter as anything he learned at Piccadilly. They taught him to adapt with alacrity to any given situation, sharpen his repartee and gauge the mood of his audience. Realizing this, and regarding them as relatively easy money, he continued to perform them until 1987, by which time he was twenty and re-established as a fast-rising DJ at Piccadilly. Rather than continue on a freelance basis, however, he got himself on the books of one of the area's thriving agencies, Carter Entertainments. The principals were Neville Carter and his son Geoff, then, and still, a talented DJ on local radio and the club circuit. The Carters provided Chris with lucrative work, either DJ'ing in local pubs or performing Tarzan-o-grams, and looked after his affairs efficiently. He would get £50–£60 for a DJ'ing engagement, from which they took around ten per cent. Their reward for this service was not one, but several sharp kicks in the teeth.

Neville thumbs through the company's old ledgers.

'17 October 1987, he was at Reuben's nightclub, a cheap and nasty night at Warrington General Hospital social club, in an oversized Portakabin, that one. Chris would only get DJ work when we were full apart from this regular booking at the hospital. He used to go there with his mate Ian Daley, who helped him out on a Thursday because he was trying to tap up the nurses. Chris'll not forget the night he turned up there and found he had no speakers because Ian had a gig on himself, and he had told the steward at the club Chris had let him have them. We had to rush down with some spares.

'Then there was the time he nearly got me lynched. I was in hospital at the time and I was due to be let out on the Friday. On about Wednesday one of the staff asked me to fix them up with a kissogram for this staff-nurse who was leaving the day I was going home. Chris said he would come as Tarzan, and of course the word got round the hospital. He was due at 1.45 for a two o'clock gram. By 2.10 he still hadn't arrived and there were dozens of people on the ward. Even doctors had come off duty to watch.

'By 2.20 I was in a state and ringing home for my lift. I had to tell my brother-in-law to take me out the back way because they were so angry that they'd been let down, and they just tied the nurse to the gates and put her in a bath of cold water. Chris had been in the pub next door – he said he thought it was a 3 p.m. appointment. I gave him the biggest bollocking he ever had. But he was a smooth-talking so-and-so and he sat it out.'

Mr Carter kept him on because he was, as he readily concedes, 'bloody good at his job, a loveable rogue'. But, as usual with Chris, he pushed his luck to breaking point. Reluctant to rake over old coals, his former boss refuses to tell the full story behind their parting. But he discloses just enough to make it clear that, neither for the first nor the last time, Chris had pushed the self-destruct button by overstepping the bounds of acceptable behaviour.

'We were really good buddies until he let us down,' says Mr Carter. 'Let's just say we have a set way of doing things and Chris didn't follow it. If there was a record the customer didn't want you to play, you didn't play it. If there was anything they wanted, you tried to get it. If there was anything they didn't want said, you didn't say it. He must have gone against this and the customer complained.'

He adds the familiar refrain: 'Chris couldn't stand being told what to do. We said, "Listen, if you work with us, you work our way or don't work at all."'

It was, he added, 'a forerunner of his argument with Radio One.'

If the Carters felt their trust had been abused, then they would have been appalled had they learned about a far more cynical and calculated betrayal that Evans allegedly plotted while they were still business associates. It happened, according to Ian Daley, when the top-rated Saturday evening television programme *Blind Date*, hosted by Cilla Black, was in its relative infancy. With its irresistible through-the-keyhole formula – hunky young man chooses beautiful woman and whisks her away on exotic and, hopefully, romantic holiday – the programme was a popular newspaper's dream. Fleet Street was briefing reporters to uncover steamy secrets about the antics of the contestants when the cameras weren't rolling. Editors were obsessed with revealing other fascinating facts, too. Were the panel of three potential partners told the questions they would be asked in advance, giving them time to prepare their all-too-clever answers? Was the whole thing rigged to ensure that the best-looking or most effervescent contestants landed the dream trip? In this pre-recession era, chequebook journalism was reaching its frenzied climax and vast sums were being offered for exclusive articles that might be billed along the lines of 'Blind Date: The Full, Shocking Truth'.

Already the consummate tabloid man, Chris Evans would undoubtedly have been aware of this when Geoff Carter was selected to appear on the programme. Handsome, bubbly and naturally funny, he was an inspired choice, even though *Blind Date*'s executives did at first balk when he turned up in multi-coloured jeans, an as yet unfashionable baseball cap and a gimmicky sweat-shirt.

Well used to entertaining audiences with smart one-liners and amusing actions and facial expressions, it was no surprise that he was selected as a 'date', and he and his allotted girl jetted off to Iceland. Soon after he returned he agreed to give an interview about his experiences to Chris Evans, then on Piccadilly Radio, as DJ on the early morning 'graveyard shift'.

Their on-air chat was totally innocuous for two reasons. Firstly, Carter had signed the standard contract undertaking that he would not divulge anything of note about the programme to the media and, secondly, according to Geoff's father, there was little of great excitement to report. Nevertheless, Ian Daley says that Chris was determined to make some capital out of the interview, and was prepared to abuse his position to do so. Unknown to Geoff Carter, Daley claims, Evans kept his tape-recorder running after the interview had finished and cajoled his studio guest into telling him – in the strictest confidence, of course – 'the real Blind Date story'. What juicy nuggets of information Carter imparted cannot be established. But, according to Ian Daley, Evans evidently believed they were worth risking his job for because, he says, his friend then proceeded to try to hawk the tape around national newspapers, aiming to sell to the highest bidder.

'Chris said we could go to the papers and make a bit of money out of it, so we both went round Manchester – the big newspaper buildings,' recalls Daley. 'I went in one and he stayed outside. He came into the *Mirror* building, and we had a big tour round there. We went round three different buildings, but I think it was at *The Mirror* that they actually cleared the interview room and Chris told me what to say: "Don't let them listen to it – we want some money in advance." Daley says that when the newspaper concerned refused to hand over an up-front sum he turned off the tape and stormed out of the meeting. When he returned to Evans, who was waiting outside, and relayed what had happened, he claims his friend's demeanour underwent a rapid transformation. "He just didn't want to do it any more. He made up his mind . . . I put it down to the fact that Geoff was his mate and he was getting a bit of work off him. Once he's made his mind up, it's like he is now with people . . . "We're not, and that's it."'

The Carters never found out how close Geoff had come to being set up. But, looking back on that period, they might wonder why, in the weeks that followed his appearances on the show, a series of chequebook-waving journalists were constantly beating a path to their door.

'For about a month later I was getting phone-calls from different papers,' said Neville Carter, when his son's *Blind Date* adventure was mentioned. 'They were trying to get a slagging-off story about what goes on behind the scenes. All the sleazy stuff.'

One reporter had arrived with a suitcase containing

£10,000 in £20 notes, and later increased his bid to £15,000, he said, but still Geoff had refused to be tempted.

Later, when told about Ian Daley's allegations, Neville Carter spoke on his son's behalf. Geoff had confirmed that he was, indeed, interviewed by Evans about *Blind Date* at the Piccadilly studios, he said. But Chris and Geoff were the only two people present, and it had happened a long time ago.

'Geoff doesn't remember anything about any discussion afterwards, or any tapes.'

He was happy to accept that Chris Evans had done no wrong unless it was proved otherwise, but if he had attempted the deception it would have been 'very, very nasty'.

The story demonstrates an extraordinary lack of judgement on Evans's part. He may well have realized when he allegedly stopped Daley auctioning the tape that if the plot had been hatched and his cover blown, he would have been black-balled by every reputable radio and television station in the country.

CHAPTER EIGHT

Lucrative and amusing as his Tarzan-o-grams were, Chris
soon came to regard them as merely a temporary diversion.
To reach the top in radio and make serious money he knew
he had to gain experience as a grassroots DJ, then gradually
build his reputation. Even in an apparent pop-cultural back-
water like Warrington this was by no means easy. Most of
the busy town-centre venues employed highly experienced
weekend DJs who guarded their territory jealously, especially
when confronted with an aspiring newcomer.

This was particularly true of Ye Olde Lion, the pub where
Chris was occasionally employed as a glass-collector. A ram-
bling seventeenth-century coaching house with several bars
and a huge upstairs ballroom, its late landlord Bill Medland
was justifiably proud to have transformed it into one of the
North's leading live rock'n'roll hot-spots. Even on an unre-
markable evening it would be packed to the rafters by an
incongruous, writhing mass of leather-clad heavy metal fans,
brown-brogued mods, pierced-nose punks, smoothies and
skinheads. When Chris was in his teens, the turntable at the
Lion was the preserve of DJs such as Karl King, Paul Black,
Bob Hayes, the brothers Robert and Brian Foden, and Friar
Tuck – better known to his mates as Kevin Jones from New-
ton-le-Willows – who for some unknown reason spun the
discs wearing a monk's habit. In Warrington these names

were the stuff of Saturday night legend and, before Chris could be the next Dave Lee Travis, he knew he must first breach their ranks. But how?

He badgered Bill Medland for a regular slot, telling him about his work at Piccadilly, but it wasn't forthcoming. To Medland's world-weary eyes, Chris was just an amiable young kid who sometimes collected beer-glasses. No amount of boasting would make him change his mind. It remained that way until the landlord informed Chris that one of the resident DJs was unable to appear, and offered him the opportunity of filling in. Evans needed no second bidding, and hurried away to make plans.

This must be no ordinary gig, he decided, it must be something special. Something that would not only capture the punters' imagination, but impress Bill sufficiently for him to come back with an offer of more permanent work. At the time, Evans and his friend Trevor Palin were operating as the town's first known pop music buskers, strumming Beatles songs while clowning around to fairly profitable effect in the tinted-glass walkway that links a multi-storey car-park to the main shopping precinct. For Chris, whose nasal whine and toothy grin reminded older passers-by of George Formby, this was just another enjoyable pocket-lining exercise, but the more musically talented Palin had serious hopes of becoming a singer-songwriter.

Chris offered to be Palin's manager.

'I think he had ideas about becoming Brian Epstein and DLT combined,' shrugs Trevor. 'He was that ambitious.'

Why not get Palin to play the Lion, Chris mused. A live show would dovetail nicely with his own disco, and the audience would get double the value for their entrance money. Excited by this latest project, Chris set about gaining maximum publicity. He borrowed a camera and summoned Palin to a photo-shoot.

'He did this picture of me sitting on the boot of someone's car, looking all moody and holding my guitar. Then we made some fly-posters from it, on A4 paper. We pinned them up all over town. But there was one little problem – I didn't actually have any songs rehearsed or even a band to play with.'

To Chris this was a minor hiccup. For a start, Palin didn't need a drummer, he said. 'We didn't like drummers. Too big and noisy and too much hassle with equipment.'

All Palin required was a good bass player, and Chris knew one of those. He was an older guy called Kevin – in Palin's words 'a bit of a wino' – whom Evans had seen playing at the Orford community centre. Tracked down by Epstein and his budding McCartney, Kevin duly agreed to join the band, which was christened *The Strings*. They made a hasty debut at the Barley Mow, another humming, centrally-located pub, and it went down pretty well considering Trevor and Kevin had only rehearsed for a few days. Next stop the mighty Lion, gateway to fame and glory.

With the bar staff handing out free drinks while they set up their gear, the gig didn't quite work out as Chris had envisaged.

'We were completely pissed before anyone even got there,' recalls Palin. 'So we got on stage and we couldn't play, and we had this crowd of two hundred people. We burst out laughing, and tried to start again, but the same thing happened. I was playing something and Kevin was playing something else. In the end they had to pull the plug and turn us off.'

It was the kind of ineptitude that would later make Evans explode with anger. Had he been angry then?

'No, it was a big joke, and we got away with it because it was the mad mid-eighties and we were well-liked. People thought this was cool.'

To add insult to injury, when Chris shook off the first flushes of drunkenness he realized that, at 50p a ticket, the returns for the evening would be very small. Ever the master of improvisation, he announced that a bottle of whisky was to be raffled, and cajoled the revellers into buying £60 worth of tickets. When the draw was made, the winner stepped forward to collect his prize and his jaw dropped. The whisky bottle was a miniature.

'No one but Chris could have carried it off,' says Palin, 'but he did because he made it fun.'

Fun it may have been, but Bill Medland was apparently unamused. Chris never did usurp the regular Lion DJs. As for *The Strings*, they had snapped for good.

Chris was rebuffed by other major venues, including the Carlton, then the trendiest nightclub in Warrington. Its boss, Derek McCullough admits he just couldn't take him seriously.

'I think it was me who told him to concentrate on live broadcasts,' he laughs. 'He used to busk outside the front door. He sang Beatles songs slightly out of tune.'

In the opinion of Robert Foden, who later forged a hugely successful disco equipment business with clients like *Frankie Goes To Hollywood* and *Dead Or Alive*, Chris was simply not good enough when he started out.

'He was crap,' he says. 'He would just sit there and put the records on, hardly saying anything. He was sixteen or seventeen at the time. Later, when I heard him on Piccadilly, I was shocked by the difference, but radio DJs and road DJs are two very different things.'

He may have been crap, but Evans was indomitable. He regarded setbacks as battle-scars. The crusade continued. If he couldn't crack the Lion or the Carlton, then he would find some other home for his talents. If it was to be a permanent residence, however, Chris would need his own disco equipment. Ian Daley, his DJ friend, remembers him scraping the cash together to buy his first rig: a tinny set of second-hand FAL speakers and some roadside traffic lights, purloined from off the streets.

'It was dirt cheap and thrown together,' says Daley. 'It would have cost £50, maximum. It was as if all the other DJs were working from new BMWs and he had a rusting old Mini. I used to walk into pubs and ask when was their worst night of the week. They'd say Wednesday or Thursday, and we'd offer to do it for a few beers, and once we got a few people in we'd talk more money.'

According to Daley, that is probably how, late in the summer of 1984, Chris landed his first regular berth, at the

Mersey pub. The Mersey's landlord at the time, Harold Parker, remembers it differently.

'I think I approached him. He started coming in just now and again for a drink, and he was such a talkative man, I said, "How about doing some DJ'ing?"' His shows proved so popular that before long he was appearing at the Mersey on Fridays, Saturdays and Sundays.

'Chris Evans is Chris Evans, isn't he?' says Harold. 'Before he came I would get maybe fifty or sixty people in, but word spread. He was here about six months and pretty soon two hundred would cram in. I knew when he was working for me that he would go far. He was very good at putting money in my till. Youngsters, middle-aged, old folk – there was one seventy-year-old woman called Elsie who was there every night without fail – he appealed to them all.'

Parker is at a loss to explain exactly what that appeal was, but Daley says that Chris innovated his own style.

'Normally DJs in this area were taught to have their decks behind them. But Chris set his up around him, like a radio disc jockey, and treated the drinkers in the bar like a studio audience. A bit like he does on *TFI Friday* now. He didn't want to be the same as anyone else, and helped make the atmosphere.'

Rather than churn out endless Top Twenty hits, heavy rock or Tamla Motown, Chris brought his eclectic taste to bear. He would play everything from *New Order* to Elvis, so that although he came to be regarded as 'alternative', in truth it was impossible to categorize him. Whatever his magic formula, when news of his success filtered through to the Lion and the Carlton, Bill Medland and Derek McCullough must have wondered what they had missed.

After about six months Chris quit the Mersey to take advantage of a new opportunity. It materialized in the form of a gaudy, potted-palms-and-pillars wine bar that aspired to bring a touch of St Lucia to grimy St Helens: The Tropical Fun Club. The club's co-owner, Mike Hollington, was on the look out for a zappy, fresh DJ and Ian Daley was recommended to him. Employed to create a Caribbean calypso party atmosphere, Daley would allow Chris to tag along. Occasionally Evans would be permitted to be master of ceremonies himself, but, as one ex-staff member put it: 'Only when no-one important was in.' According to the source, the bosses did not share Harold Parker's belief in Evans.

'They thought Chris's DJ'ing was useless and said he didn't look the part, either.'

But Hollington – then aiming to be Warrington's answer to Peter Stringfellow – empathized with Chris's determination and decided to give him a chance. A few weeks later circumstances conspired to cement an ill-fated friendship between Hollington and Evans. After a bitter wrangle with his partner, Hollington found himself frozen out of the 'tropics' Fun Club and forced to sign on the dole. Evans was also drifting between jobs and would spend time at Mike's, sometimes sleeping there, and one day his friend came up with a proposition. Hollington's brother worked for the new Docklands development in London and needed a couple of hands to help sort and package a massive mail-shot he had planned. As he and Chris were unoccupied, why not go down to the Smoke and earn some easy money? Evans readily agreed, but was infuriated to learn that he was only being paid £50 to Hollington's £150.

His spirits lifted, however, when he received an invitation to the TV-am studios in London. Timmy Mallett was by now appearing on the breakfast programme, in *Wacaday*, and a phone-call to his old mentor at Piccadilly did the trick.

'To see Chris on that set was incredible,' said a source who was there. 'He was like a little child who's just got his Christmas presents. He was jumping up and down, bombarding Timmy with questions. You could see him watching the presenters Anne Diamond and Nick Owen and drinking it all in.'

Afterwards he told the Hollington brothers, and anyone else within earshot, that he was going to be a television presenter. They scoffed that he was unlikely to succeed against competition from natural TV 'faces' like Philip Schofield, but he wouldn't listen.

Freak or Unique? ☆ 89

'The thing about Chris,' said a friend around him then, 'was that failure simply wasn't an option.'

Many times, after their return from Docklands, Hollington fed and watered the eighteen-year-old Evans, or gave him shelter when he didn't want to stay at home. Chris professed gratitude, despite the Tropical Fun Club debacle. He also had so much faith in Hollington's business acumen that he later urged him to become agent-cum-manager to himself and Tim Grundy, the Piccadilly DJ who also wished to break into TV. Hollington, ten years his senior, turned him down flat.

'He just didn't see how anyone with ginger hair and glasses could make any inroads in a field where looks count for so much,' said a source close to Hollington. 'When Chris became famous he felt a bit like the man who turned down the Beatles.'

Hollington had taken Chris too much at face value and with hindsight it is easy to see why he rejected him. In those days of Thatcherite designer-dressing and culinary sophistication, Evans's self-image was so retrograde he appeared trapped in a time warp. His old friend from Piccadilly, Mike Gates, recalls inviting him for a meal and discovering that he had not yet tasted rice. His diet largely consisted of fry-ups. Bacon off-cuts were his favourite, 'in bread, with tomato sauce, mate, please'. His silver-rimmed glasses seemed to be the first pair the optician had shown him. His clothes bore no resemblance to anything remotely in vogue. In a pre-Grunge era, it wasn't fashionable to look unfashionable. His top-heavy hairstyle was so hideous that Trevor Palin hardly dared to mention it to him. At last, Chris decided it was time to update his image. His pal immediately suggested a new haircut at his own stylist's, Stewart's, in Orford Lane. Chris agreed, says Palin, but still he was reluctant to try anything too outlandish.

'He wouldn't have his hair shaved, he wouldn't take it too far . . . he was conservative but eccentric,' says Palin.

Conservative but eccentric. It was a contradiction that made Chris the most charismatic and interesting guy in town.

His transformation from bullied schoolboy to undisputed peer-group big-shot was almost complete. For a while Trevor Palin was among those content to follow.

'Obviously he wanted to be the leader of the two of us,' says Palin, 'and he was a control freak. But with me he was more encouraging. "Come on, Trev, do something with your talent. Break out of Orford." Chris was so assured. So confident. But, you see, he still needed the company of someone who he knew would be there for him. I was happy to play that role. It was a time for change and progression and he needed to be with someone else with the same outlook. I never looked up to Chris, but I admired him and he was one of the closest friends I've ever had. I've had friends before and since, and it has never been like that.'

Reflecting upon their friendship, Palin now sees that Chris rarely lowered his defences.

'He would go into depressions. He was really moody sometimes. It was just life. It was, "Well, fuck it. What's going on? Why?" We would talk about life. It was more about what could we do to get more out of it. We never went into things in a deep way. It was, "let's live for tomorrow and see as much as we can".'

One evening, whiling away time at Minnie's, a strange thing happened. Chris, he says, fetched a pen-knife and asked him to become his 'blood brother'. They each cut their fingers, held their open wounds together, and swore a pact of eternal allegiance.

'I know it was immature and weird. When I look back on it I find it funny. But we were really close,' says Palin.

This manner of ritual bonding was to become another of Chris's eccentricities. Though fingers were not sliced, he and Ian Daley took similar vows, pledging, says Daley, to stand by one another through good times and bad. Tim Grundy recalls how Chris became 'blood brothers' with the leader of a Manchester rock band. In each case, however, his fraternal vows proved short-lived. Palin, like Daley and who knows how many others, would, when the time came, find himself excluded from Chris's life.

'I have tried to contact him several times. Not because I want anything from him, but just as a mate,' says Daley bitterly. 'I just wanted to say, good on you, well done. He doesn't want to know.'

But at eighteen years old the dependable, yet adventurous Palin was Evans's perfect foil. Bored by Warrington, they began casting their net wider. They would jump into whichever wreck Chris happened to be driving and take off, sometimes for several days. Once, making it as far as London, they loitered outside Stringfellows nightclub. Chris spotted Radio One DJ Bruno Brooks.

'I could only see this short little fat guy and I'm thinking, who's that?' says Trevor. 'Chris knew immediately, and he's all excited, saying, "He's on Radio One. That's what I want to do."'

As usual they were broke, and Palin recalls how they slept huddled on the steps of a bank. Later, when Chris told Michael Gates the story, it became the Bank of England. Evans claimed that they had sneaked inside while it was still open, and spent the night under a boardroom table.

'He said they only woke up the following morning when a meeting started and people's feet appeared next to their faces,' says Gates.

Another case of distorted memory? Palin says they did sleep under a table, but this was on another night and in the YMCA, where they were stirred into life by the hum of a vacuum-cleaner.

During this same London adventure, Chris blagged his way into a DJ'ing job in a Soho club. Heady stuff, but it lasted for a solitary night. The next day, with Palin feeling the onset of 'flu, they decided to head back to Minnie's for a bed and some hot food.

But it was not long before the wanderlust struck again. It was summer and, in Chris's Mini, they headed for the North Wales holiday resort of Rhyl, where they aimed to earn enough money from busking to pay for their booze, board and lodgings. To spice up the trip, Chris also contacted Mallett, suggesting that he should include a 'Nobby No-Level

Reports, Live From Rhyl' slot on Timmy On The Tranny. 'Brrr-i-lliant!' said Timmy, and Chris agreed to phone him each evening.

'On Chris's Radio One show he sent guys down to a phone-box to call him, but we did it first,' says Trevor. 'We would squeeze into the kiosk with a crowd of people who we'd met during the day, busking. We would have them all singing our made-up songs. I can remember the first song we wrote together. We were in Rhyl and it was a lovely summer's morning. We had sneaked into a hotel and had a shower, and we sat on the kerb and wrote a song about Monday mornings and the working man. It wasn't cynical, it was a lament. It asked why should they do that boring job when they could be doing what we were doing? Writing songs about things was our way of communicating in depth with each other.

'Rather than go to the extremes of inventing ideas, we would take very mundane things and use them. We did a fantastic outside broadcast from a fish and chip shop in Manchester. It was called Sammy The Spud and it was all about what the potatoes and fish felt like to be fried and eaten.'

He sings the ditty: '"I looked in the chip-fat and what did I see? I saw Sammy The Spud staring back at me . . ." They were basic ideas, and Chris has simply taken them a step further and made big money out of them. Things that you and I think of every day, he does a show about them.'

In the long, balmy summer of 1984, creating ditties didn't earn Chris much money. Indeed, in Rhyl, he and Trevor lived largely on chip buns. But the young girls on holiday were captivated by the romantic image the two wandering minstrels conjured up, and they were never short of a bed – or at least a floor – for the night.

The intensity of living from hand to mouth and being together virtually round the clock eventually caused friction between Palin and Evans. One morning, when the sun was not shining and takings were low, this escalated into an incident that Trevor still regrets, an incident that illustrates Chris's enormous capacity for selfishness.

'We had no ciggies and it was a shitty day. He slipped off

and spent what money we had left on a chip-bun for himself. I couldn't believe did that. We were like brothers, remember. We were supposed to share everything equally, look after each other. I went berserk and we had a whopping argument in the street. I just hit out, and caught him. I couldn't believe I had hit Chris and we both started crying. He kept saying he didn't know how I could do that to a mate. He wasn't physically violent, you see.

'We had a couple of days where we didn't speak to each other, but we were okay in the end. We came to terms with it.'

Returning to Warrington, the prospect of another long winter of kiss-o-grams and part-time work didn't appeal, so they decided to gain qualifications at college. They had just watched the film *Porkies*, depicting student life as one long round of sex and drunken fun, and thought this was definitely for them.

'So we went to Padgate College and Chris said he was going to study art,' says Trevor. 'I decided to do some O-Levels in photography, English, maths and music. Three weeks after we enrolled I was in a lesson when I looked up and saw this big hippy staring at me through the glass door to the classroom. He was pulling silly faces and trying to attract my attention. Eventually I cottoned on that it was Chris in disguise. He'd gone and bought this long wig and sneaked in to take the mickey. He didn't like college anymore. It wasn't like *Porkies* at all. It was boring. So he did it to get me to leave with him.'

Palin's next move was to apply to join the RAF. But Chris was desperate to cling on to him.

'He drove me to St Helens for an interview and all the way he was telling me how mad I was, and asking me why I was doing it. I told him I didn't want to end up like all the other lads from our estate. He was saying, "but you play the guitar". I didn't get accepted, and Chris said it was the best thing that could have happened.

'My uncle had a business and I started doing some terrible odd jobs on building sites instead. Chris turned up out of the blue again and tried to persuade me to leave the site and go busking. He was completely irresponsible. He couldn't see why anyone would want to do an ordinary job. It was worthless to Chris. That's when we started splitting up.

'I remember one of the last times we met. I went to a club with my girlfriend, Justine, and Chris turned up. He had a long black coat on that I'd never seen him wear before. He seemed 'off'. There was definitely a gap between us which had come from nowhere. I went over and we had a drink together, but it wasn't the same. It was really weird. I've never fathomed it out, but it was probably the time when he had got his own night show at Piccadilly and he was kind of saying, "I'm going to be who I'm going to be." It was quite upsetting, actually. It wasn't pre-planned or pre-determined on his part. It was just that I was going my way and he knew where he was heading.'

A couple of years ago, still trying to fathom Chris and evaluate their friendship, Palin took up his guitar and found himself writing the following song:

'You reach for the stars and you fall into space.
You came from nowhere – now everyone knows your face.
Tell me, do you get lonely when you are alone?
Are you a self-appointed king on a hand-made throne?
Do you ever feel the rain as it runs down your skin?
Did it end when you started, or are you still about to begin?
Do you still trip on sacred ground?
Are you the biggest fool who wears the smallest crown?
Do you ever miss the hand of someone you wanted to love?
Do you take your gifts for granted, given by somebody from above?'

The words sound better when sung, and when you meet Palin you understand that they were not inspired by envy. Watching Chris's TV shows, as Palin infrequently does, he says he recognizes the old buzz of excitement in Chris, but sometimes detects his old mate's sadness, even through a television screen.

'You can see him thinking, "Why the fuck am I doing this?" And now he's achieved his objective, done something he wanted to do as a boy, what will he do now? I think the dreams that he had when he was seventeen or eighteen were pure. Once you get older your priorities become financial. Yes, Chris wanted to make money because we had none. But it was the buzz that he really wanted and I wonder whether it's there any more.'

If Trevor Palin was cast as Chris's loyal straight-man, then his friendship with Ian Daley, from Bewsey, a rough Warrington suburb, fulfilled an altogether different function. Daley, a roving-eyed Jack-the-Lad, was the man to call when Chris felt the urge for some unadulterated debauchery. As mentally agile as Chris in those days, Daley – shortish in stature, chirpy and tousle-haired – also harboured a desire to make it as a DJ. But while Chris's ambition was backed by single-minded application, Daley was all too easily distracted. Particularly when alcohol and women were around. His idea of a great night out was to get 'out of his tree' and 'pull'. The second part of that agenda increasingly appealed to Evans in his late teens.

'The women you used to meet,' sighs Daley, wistfully. 'You could be the ugliest trog in the world but, if you were on stage, women wanted to go to bed with you.'

When they first did discos together he thought Chris 'weird' because he used to have a lot of girls who were simply friends.

'Chris would sit down and have a good chat. I always wanted to try and get into their knickers, but Chris didn't. He was a bit of an agony aunt. And he used to be round at the YMCA playing Trivial Pursuit. He was shit-hot at Trivial Pursuit. Used to do me 'ead in.'

Despite their differences, Chris and Daley became close – even though Daley was a *faux-pas* waiting to happen. Upon first meeting Chris's sister Diane – by now a tall and attractive trainee-teacher – Daley told his mate in the crudest terms that he thought her highly desirable. Chris just shrugged. Ian was Ian and he said that type of thing. And besides, he must be all right if Minnie liked him. She was always ready with tea and biscuits when Ian rolled up, and they developed a rapport.

'I liked Chris's house because it had an easy-going atmosphere – the dog, the piano, the guitar, always a brew on offer.'

The state of Chris's bedroom also made him feel at home. It was, he says, 'A tip. Smelly socks, everything. Him and Minnie used to have some blazing rows about it.'

As for Chris, 'I liked him because he was outgoing and always up to something strange, not your normal run-of-the-mill person.'

Daley was hardly run-of-the-mill either, and, when he was operating with Chris, bizarre things would happen. At seventeen, Daley was living with an attractive teenager, and they had a baby. One night he went out to buy some cannabis (which, he says, never interested Chris) and when he returned to his council house the front door was wide open. He burst in to find Chris, apparently asleep on the couch, with two empty wine bottles beside him.

'I'm thinking, where's my bird? So I goes upstairs . . . and she's fully clothed in the bath, which was full of luke-warm water, cottoning on to be asleep, I think.'

His heart thudding, Daley tried to rouse them, to no avail. Then, understandably, he began making assumptions.

'I think they'd been shagging, heard me coming, she'd run upstairs and jumped in the bath, which she'd run years ago. When I walked in the house she knew what was going to happen. I was very possessive and I'd erupt if someone was in the house, no matter who it was, even my brother.

'I goes mad with my girlfriend, demanding to know what's been going on, went downstairs, Chris gets up, I ended up just picking him up and throwing him out. I felt like hitting him, but I didn't. He swore they'd just ended up getting drunk . . . I'm still not convinced. If they'd both been sat there pissed up, fair enough, but why's she fully clothed in the bath and he's pretending to be asleep? I saw him at the time as being dishevelled – so out he went. I didn't speak to him for a couple of weeks after that.'

Guilty or not guilty, Chris might consider himself fortunate to have escaped Daley's wrath. He later married, but the relationship was so volatile that he was jailed for six months for striking his wife in the face.

'I was seriously provoked – she had already stabbed me,' says Daley, adding, 'I don't think Chris was around then, but he certainly didn't visit me in prison.'

There were other very minor rows, sometimes precipitated by Chris's petty meanness, says Daley. 'He'd never buy you a packet of crisps. In fact, he used to smoke but never had his own fags.'

He admits to having seriously considered using violence against Chris on one other occasion.

'I had to do a wedding disco and he had my little box of records. I had to go round to his house and threaten to break his neck because he wouldn't give them back. He had borrowed them and said they were his. I wouldn't really have killed him, but I was going to give him a good hiding. He threatened to get the police on me. He's a very temperamental type of person, happy-go-lucky when anyone else was there, but he got into bad moods. He'd just change. Comedians are always Jekyll and Hyde and Chris is a bit like that, probably more so now.'

But generally, their time together was fun.

'I remember one particular day when he had an MG, bottle-green it was. We were going to town from his house and this girl he knew knocked and asked for a lift. He said okay, but as there were only two seats he told her she would have to get in the boot. She got in, he shut it and drove off. She was in there for ages while we looked for somewhere to park.'

Daley can't recall Chris having a steady girlfriend, although if he had been serious about anyone he is unlikely to have introduced her to Ian. But he broadened his horizons with a succession of one-night stands – and his appetite for unusual sexual adventure began to develop. Daley vividly recalls one night when he, Evans and another man had teamed up to perform a Tarzan-o-gram and happened to meet a buxom kissogram girl they knew. They all went back to Greenwood Crescent and, with Minnie then working nights, Daley says an orgy ensued.

'We all had a bit of drink, bottles of wine or cider, and me and Chris are playing about on the piano,' says Daley. 'The next thing you know, the other bloke and this girl disappeared. We sneaked upstairs and opened the door, and there he is giving this girl what for. We thought, what're we going to do? We'll join in. So we gets undressed . . . the next thing I was giving her one, then Chris was giving her one. She was loving it. Two of us would go downstairs for a brew and breather and we'd swap over, that's what it was like. That was the first orgy session I ever had. What a laugh.

'Once Chris came out of himself he was a bit of a lad. He wasn't the geek everyone thought he was. When you're busking and DJ'ing, first of all you're dead shy, but you've got to come out of your shell. I think that's what happened to Chris and he went from strength to strength.'

An even less edifying sexual episode occurred when Daley and Evans, accompanied by a postman friend, ventured to Germany on a cheap weekend 'booze-cruise', something of an eighties phenomenon. As Daley recounts the details he finds himself so amused that he ponders re-visiting the scene with his current friends – and it is difficult not to smile along with him. Yet upon reflection there is something vaguely disturbing about Evans's hunger for instant gratification which, by some standards, might be seen to border on depravity.

The larks began soon after they arrived in Chris's car at Harwich and joined other revellers boarding the Hamburg-bound ferry.

'We didn't have a lot of money. There were a load of squaddies, and Chris – quick-thinking that he was – noticed that there were loads of rooms empty.'

According to Daley, Evans managed to spirit away the keys to these vacant cabins and began offering them to the soldiers at £5 each.

'I was gobsmacked with that one because it was brilliant. We made about £75.'

They began spending the money in the boat's nightclub, he says, and Chris and their friend drank themselves sick. When he returned to the cabin the three were sharing, however, his companions were sufficiently recovered to cajole him into participating in a masturbation competition. The tone for the rest of the trip had been set.

In Hamburg they ordered a drink for a bar-room hooker and were ejected for refusing to pay a ridiculously inflated price. Their appetites now whetted, however, they watched a live sex show, then, realizing that the ferry would soon be leaving for Harwich, headed back to the port.

'We were all right pissed by this time, so we're running back to this boat down this dead long, straight street and there's loads of women on every corner. Chris says something to one prostitute – gives her a bit of German – gives her something like £3, and the girl, me and Chris disappear up some stairs. We go into this seedy little room with a sink, Chris lies on the bed . . .'

The woman performed oral sex on Evans, and Daley's condom split, causing him to worry about catching a disease for months afterwards.

They made it to the boat with minutes to spare and laughed all way back across the North Sea. When they reached Warrington, Ian's mum fed them on home-made hot-pot.

CHAPTER NINE

Quite whether Chris's foray into the fleshpots of Hamburg occurred during his relationship with Alison Ward cannot be reliably established. Ian Daley either does not remember or does not wish to remember, and Alison herself is not the type to waste emotional energy torturing herself with events that may or may not have happened in the past.

'I was never jealous of him then and I'm certainly not now,' she says, 'Maybe I thought no one else would be stupid enough to take him on. Looking back, I suppose he might have been unfaithful, but at the time it never entered my head.'

Over the months that we chatted, Alison – who asked for nothing other than that her story be recorded faithfully – proved a refreshingly open, honest and uncomplicated witness. On the surface, she and Chris made an improbable match. None of the adjectives that apply to him – ambitious, brilliant, hyper-active, unpredictable, insecure, malcontent – can be applied to her. Conversely, one would hardly associate Alison's most obvious traits – reliability, steadiness, loyalty, and unfailing cheerfulness – with Chris. He went to grammar school, she went to the nearest comprehensive. Her horizons extended little further than home, friends and family; Chris's were boundless. He is now a star while Alison works part-time at a factory sewing-machine. Indeed, although they were raised barely a few hundred yards apart, even their accents were markedly different. While Chris spoke in slightly mannered, clipped tones that made it difficult to pinpoint where in the North West he hailed from, Alison's voice – borrowing something from Manchester and something from Liverpool – was unmistakably Warringtonian.

Yet according to psychologist Dr Bryan Tully, it is by no means uncommon for a man of Chris's character to become romantically involved with a less dynamic woman.

'Very often, people like this are able to attract beauties and have the women that lots of men are chasing after. But they often end up with another type of woman who may have lower self-esteem. They can then be comfortable without having to be the bright sun all the time . . . and their partner may put up with their dark side.'

This generalization fits, but with two qualifications. Firstly, Alison was attractive and sought after in the circles in which she and Chris moved. Secondly, although she may appear less confident than Chris, whether she holds herself to be less estimable is open to question. What cannot be queried is the fact that he has treated her, and more pertinently their daughter, Jade, with shameful disregard.

Alison, a petite blonde with sparkling eyes and a generous smile, had seen Chris DJ'ing on several occasions before they met, and was singularly unimpressed. Sure, he was funny and kept the night moving, but she had never paused to consider whether or not he was attractive. Alison was then affecting the punk revival look – black leather and chains, cherry-red lips and death-white panstick – and Chris, the technicolour loon, was in a different orbit. But both had started playing squash at courts run by Mike Hollington, the former Tropical Fun Club boss. One of Evans's regular opponents was Clive, the boyfriend of Karen Ward, the eldest of Alison's five siblings. The two men and the two sisters would play on adjacent courts, and Alison soon came to realize there was more to Chris than his looks.

'I didn't fancy him but we used to get on really well,' she says. 'He used to have a really good personality, nothing like the obnoxious person he seems to be now.'

They began going out together in May 1985. Alison had turned eighteen the previous March, and Chris was just nineteen. He made the running, and his tactics were so well-executed they might have been gleaned from a teenagers' magazine.

'We had been to a nightclub and he walked me home because my sister and her boyfriend had left. He brought the conversation round to flowers, and the next day when I was at work a bouquet turned up with no message on it. I wondered who it was from, and I thought it must have been this lad I had been seeing on and off. So I got a friend to ring the florist's and get a description of the person who'd bought them. I only knew one person who was six foot two tall, with ginger hair and glasses.'

Intrigued and flattered – 'no-one had sent me flowers before' – she phoned Chris and invited him out for a thank-you drink.

'He said he didn't know, he'd have to think about it,' she says. 'He said he was afraid it would change things between us. I was gobsmacked. Why else had he sent me flowers?'

But Chris, it seems, was playing games, because when Alison backed off, saying it might be better if they forgot the whole thing, he suddenly came on strong again. Their first date was at the Barley Mow pub in town. Alison can't remember what she was wearing, but how could she forget Chris's appearance? He turned up in blue and white canvas sailor's shoes, beige trousers, and a brilliant orange roll-necked sweatshirt, the colour of which was indistinguishable from his hair.

'He was really quiet,' says Alison, 'I had never known him stuck for words before. Normally he's ten to the dozen, doesn't shut up when he's asleep.'

As she was even quieter, there were many long silences. Still, she says, they felt comfortable with one another, and their first evening together was sealed with a 'great big snog' beside the moonlit lake in Walton Gardens.

Their courtship now under way, there followed an all-too-brief period of storybook idyll. As spring moved into summer, they would zip around Warrington in Chris's bottle-green MG convertible. It may have been battered and rusting, but who cared when music was blaring from the tape-deck and the wind was blowing in your hair? Often, in the evenings, Chris would be DJ'ing, and Alison would join the special crowd sitting close to the turntable.

'They didn't seem to talk a lot,' said one of the group. 'Alison would often just sit their gazing at Chris, almost as if she was in awe of him.'

After the gig they would often stay up half the night at Alison's parents' neat little council-built semi in Gough Avenue. One party was so wild that her parents Maureen and Cliff opted to sleep in their caravan, parked outside.

'Our house was the centre for teenagers in those days,' laughs Alison's mother, Maureen. 'They all used to gather here because they knew they'd get a cup of tea and a bit to eat.'

Round at Chris's, the atmosphere was not quite so cordial. Minnie was fine with Alison. But there was a palpable tension between Chris and his sister, Diane.

'I think, what it is, Chris is so outgoing and sure of himself that she didn't like it. I think, in a way, she was jealous. Or there was jealousy between them. Plus she was going out with this bloke and Chris didn't think much of him. Chris and Diane would just pass each other and not speak.'

Despite his voracious sexual appetite, as described by Daley, Alison says Chris was 'a perfect gentleman' during their first weeks together. Far less modern in outlook than her punky appearance suggested, she found this appealing.

'It was about six months before we slept together,' she says, adding after a brief pause, 'well, maybe three. Anyway, it was quite a long time. That suited me because I had only lost my virginity at seventeen, and only slept with that one boyfriend. Chris said he wanted to get to know me.'

Eventually, however, the opportunities presented when Minnie worked nights proved too tempting, even for gentleman Chris.

'If I slept at his house when his mum was there, Chris used

to be in one room and I was in another, but when the cat's away the mice will play.'

Alison is not the kind of woman who readily gossips about what goes on behind her bedroom door. But during one of our conversations she divulges one or two secrets which may be of more than passing interest to those who hold Evans to be the sexual icon of his generation. From the outset, she says, he was keen to impress upon her how experienced he was.

'He told me he had done it with a couple of his mates' mums. He even told my mother that. He wasn't joking. I can't remember what we were talking about at the time, but certain things stick in your mind. Whether it's true or not, I don't know.'

This boast notwithstanding, their own love-making never reached the dizzy heights.

'I wouldn't say it was three times a night. But, saying that, he was crap anyway,' she says ruefully. 'I mean, I went out with him for two years and I never had a single orgasm and it can't just be me, because it has happened for me since.'

Whether this seriously bothered Chris, Alison is unable to say. But perhaps it was out of some misguided desire to satisfy her that, she claims, his tastes became increasingly bizarre. One night, she recalls with a shudder, they were driving home from Manchester when he stopped the car on a quiet hillside. They got out and started to make love, whereupon he asked her to urinate in his mouth.

'I said, "Oh, no, I don't think so." He just said, "Why? Why?"'

Alison deflected the question back to him. Why on earth did he wish her to perform such a strange act? How could it possibly turn him on?

'I just want you to,' came the lame reply.

Alison again declined and he was left frustrated. But why, indeed? An analyst might find some Freudian link between this desire and his ordeal at the hands of Shaver Browne. Her refusal, she says, did not stop him pestering her for anal intercourse. But again she refused.

'With Chris it was sometimes anything for a quiet life, but I had to draw the line somewhere,' she says.

His reluctance to show her any real tenderness made matters worse. He would only kiss and cuddle her warmly when they were in company, she says, which made her feel as though he were being affectionate for the benefit of onlookers. The other major problem with which she was confronted soon after they started dating was Chris's apparently cyclical decline into despair.

'He would go into deep depressions,' she recalls. 'He was fine with everybody else, but not with me. I worked out that it happened every six weeks. I counted the days. Every six weeks he went down. God knows why. He would say nothing when I asked him what was the matter. Then a couple of days later he would come back and expect me to be the same. But when you questioned him he never, ever talked about it.'

In one of these bleak periods, Chris found himself talking about the final stages of his father's illness.

'He said they brought his dad home from the hospital, and he was upstairs. Minnie used to shoo Chris away from the room,' she says.

But soon the subject was closed, and did not re-open.

You never really had deep conversations with Chris,' she says. 'He never opened up about his family or anything.'

Did Evans ever truly love Alison?

'I think he was infatuated but I can't imagine him being in love with anyone,' said one of their friends at the time. 'Except, of course, with himself.' Chris, he said, 'wasn't a giver. If it was a choice between a night out with Alison and something else that had come up, there was never a contest.'

Small wonder, then, that although they were going out together for more than two years, there were lengthy periods when Alison had no clue where he was. When he was around, he was so hyperactive that her mother, Maureen, says that he would never come in and sit down on the sofa. He would stand on it and bounce down in a seat-drop, as though on a trampoline. Another friend describes how he would constantly chew at his nails and fidget as his mind leapt from idea to idea.

'You didn't just go out and have a pint and a chat with Chris, it was always, "What are we going to do next?"'

Besides working as a DJ and Tarzan-o-gram, during this time Chris was also employed by, among others, Burton's chain of Top Man shops. He was first recruited as part of a team of bubbly 'personalities' who were placed in the group's stores to boost business, and later became a sales assistant. He also worked, very briefly, at Kerfoot Motors, the local Vauxhall dealership.

'He must have been depressed if he was working there,' says Jennine Payton, whose job Chris took over when she was promoted. 'The job was cleaning cars before they went out to the customer. It was about £40 a week, but he only lasted two and a half days. He couldn't hack it. Not being nasty, but it was hard work. It just wasn't him.'

When he wasn't working or popping in for a brew at Maureen Ward's, Chris was busily engaged in his newest money-making enterprise – dealing in bric-a-brac. Like a souped-up Steptoe, he would pore over the small-ads, then race around church halls, schools, council offices – anywhere that he might snap up second-hand items for resale. He got to know the times of car-boot sales and markets as far away as East Lancashire, and whenever he had a spare moment he was up early and on the road. If he wanted company, he would drag friends out of bed. Dave Whittaker, who sometimes accompanied him, was confounded by his drive.

'He was always on the go . . . planning, scheming. Always having a go, doing something. And brilliant fun. It was good to be in his presence because it was an education as well as an experience. You'd go round jumble sales in the middle of the week, picking up all sorts of junk. Electric fires, really naff ones with copper legs, old light fittings from people's houses, glass lamp-shades, heavy, dangerous stuff. Even cardigans, bits of clothing. The first time I did it with him we filled the car with stuff, stayed out all night, had a wash in the morning, then drove straight to Bury market. We had a good laugh and I think we made £7 or £8. But the money wasn't that important really. We threw half the stuff away; it was more pleasure, a chance for Chris to experience that side of life. He wanted to try the business lifestyle, see what it was like being an entrepreneur.'

Alison remembers Chris's market-trader phase with less enthusiasm.

'He did car-boot sales, but he put new gear in the boot, so he wasn't allowed to sell it. You have to have second-hand stuff!'

Whittaker never bullied Chris, but he was among those who had wanted nothing to do with him in his early teens. However, when they became properly acquainted at nineteen, after meeting through their mutual pal Ian Daley, Dave joined Chris's growing band of disciples. He was amazed how this 'big, lanky nerd' had changed.

'He was beaming with confidence . . . but a hell of a nice guy to talk to.'

While his other friends hung around pubs or got stoned on whatever drugs were around, Chris was different. Yes, he enjoyed a few pints of lager, but he wasn't very interested in anything that made him lose control, and you never saw him sprawled out drunk like everyone else. Chris was 'intriguing, interesting'.

Dave lived with his girlfriend in a small terraced house in Brighton Street. They had decorated it themselves in outlandish, post-hippy style, and Chris loved to spend time there. The living room was not unlike the Big Breakfast set, with a yellow-painted gas-fire, bright green carpet and multi-coloured curtains. The shelves were covered with armadillo skins, giant speakers pumped out the heaviest music, and there were surreal ornaments, like a set of ten-pin bowling skittles. Chris told Whittaker it was 'the most comfortable room he had ever sat in', and it was one of the few places he seemed to relax. While he was there, Dave – sensing that Chris was soon destined to leave his friends behind – asked Chris where it was all going to end.

'I told him he should become an actor or a writer. He said, no, he wanted the top slot on Radio One.'

The dream had not changed. As if to emphasize this, when they did venture out from Brighton Street and visit a pub disco, Chris would demonstrate how much better he was than the hapless DJ who was performing. He would ask if he could take the mike for a couple of minutes and end up making him look an idiot. He would have people laughing in seconds and was technically brilliant. Often the DJ was too embarrassed to come back.

Chris and Alison decided to move in together. While they were saving for a place of their own, one of Alison's older sisters, Lynn Lowes, agreed that they could lodge with her and her husband, Andy. It wasn't long before Lynn was regretting her generosity. It wasn't that she and Andy didn't like Chris: it was hard to dislike him for long. It was just that he had such irritating domestic habits.

'If he had a fry-up, fat would be trailed across the kitchen floor,' says Alison. 'He used to loll everywhere, and he would dip every bit of food in his tea.'

They were all delighted when he was taken on as a sales assistant at Top Man, but as he had no decent clothes to wear for work, she says, he would borrow Andy's and try to sneak them back into the wardrobe before he found out. One evening Andy beat him to the wardrobe and he was never again quite as friendly towards Chris.

Even when smartly attired in Andy's ill-fitting shirts, trousers and shoes, Chris still didn't conform to the image required of a Top Man salesman. But clad, once more, in his own outlandishly mismatched outfits, his employment at Top Shop couldn't last.

'I think he was sacked because he didn't go in a couple of times and didn't bother telling them,' says Alison. She was beginning to wonder what he might do next when he bounded in 'over the moon' and announced that he had been re-employed by Piccadilly Radio.

'But this time,' he enthused, locking his bewildered girl-friend in a rare bear-hug, 'it's going to be different'. He was returning not as Timmy Mallett's whipping boy, he explained after trampolining on the sofa several times, but as a disc-jockey in his own right. Encouraged by Alison, he had sent off a demo-tape. It had impressed the station's bosses sufficiently for him to be offered a presenter's post. It was only the dreaded graveyard stint, from two to six in the morning, when the audience consisted of shift-workers and insomniacs, and it was only about £30 a show. But who cared? For the first time he had his own radio programme. A golden chance to vent years of accumulated ideas without playing second fiddle to anyone. The very thought sent his adrenaline rushing and the effect was visible to everyone.

'I hadn't seen Chris since he left Piccadilly the first time round, and when I saw him in the studio again the change was incredible,' says Mike Gates, who was still working at the station. 'He was no longer this cheeky little upstart. He had this aura of power and success around him. It was quite strange.'

In addition to doing his own programme, Chris became what is known in the business as a 'swing-jock' – a locum DJ who fills in for colleagues when they are ill or on holiday. Supercharged with energy as he was, however, even this was not enough for him. When Tim Grundy, who hosted the peak-time breakfast show, asked him to become his sidekick he readily accepted. Now began the most gruelling timetable Chris had yet tackled. After DJ'ing or performing a Tarzan-o-gram in Warrington in the evening, he would drive directly to Manchester, arriving after midnight. Dubbing himself 'The Prince of Darkness', he would then do his own four-hour show. And, when dawn came up, rather than return home to sleep he would fight back his tiredness to appear with Grundy on the breakfast show. After that? Perhaps a little busking or some bric-a-brac selling.

A technician on the station recalls, 'At lunch, we'd all go out for a butty. But one day when I was buying mine, I saw Chris down Market Street straight after his morning slot doing some busking.'

It was not uncommon for him to be on the go for eighteen hours at a stretch.

'You'd think he was on whizz or something, but he wasn't,' says Ian Daley. 'He didn't need it. He was just buzzing on life.'

With that kind of schedule, it was no wonder that he and Alison began to drift apart.

On the breakfast slot, Grundy invented a new persona for Chris: White And Two Sugars.

'We wanted a name and he always used to come in to the studio and say, "Do you want a drink, boss?" And I'd say, "Yeah, coffee – white and two sugars," so that's what it became.'

It was the cue for Chris to take part in the programme. While Grundy (who now drinks his coffee black and unsweetened) played the cool, debonair jock, Evans was cast as the hair-brained little upstart who brought his morning cuppa, but constantly railed against his lowly status.

'His character used to come in, saying, "Mate, mate", in a whinging voice. "How you doin' maa-aate." And we'd work out little routines which he'd come in and do. He'd come in with a supposedly brilliant idea – like going to sell fresh air in cans to the Americans. Or we'd do a gag, the punch-line of which was the title of the next record. But he also did some unpredictable things. Every now and then he'd just slap me round the face in the middle of a link. I mean really slap me. Or just stop a record. In those days they were records, with needles, and he'd just stick his hand on it and fall about laughing as I opened the microphone to try and save the programme.

'This weird style of unpredictability was Chris at his best. He would just do it. No warning whatsoever. More often than not I thought he was really funny, and I'd fall about laughing, particularly the first time he ever slapped me. It was right in the middle of a link, and I thought it was such a bizarre thing to do to a radio presenter while he was live on air. I think he once pushed it too far. He said something that was just too rude or too negative and we had a big row. We came to blows on a couple of occasions.'

One incident happened, Grundy recalls, when Evans rose above his station and deliberately ruined a funny story 'because he was bored'.

'I remember I closed the mike and flew off the handle. I grabbed him and pinned him up against the wall. We pushed each other around a bit. He was fairly volatile.'

They didn't speak to one another for two days, communicating through written messages. The silence was broken by Evans.

'"Life's too short, maa-aate",' he said. 'I think he gave me a hug and we carried on exactly as we were before.'

But their most infamous fight was sparked off by an incident that has now passed into Chris Evans mythology. The Bob Geldof Tape Recording Cock-up. Still basking in the glory heaped upon him for masterminding the Live Aid concerts, 'Saint Bob' had by now grown tired of the spotlight. But after much delicate negotiation, Grundy was granted an audience. To record the interview he and his producer, Mark Ratcliffe – who more than a decade later would succeed Evans on the Radio One breakfast show – jetted out to Gibraltar to meet Geldof. Given the tight budgets in regional radio, this was a rare extravagance, but one that was financially worthwhile. By syndicating the interview, executives had calculated that they would make a handsome £40,000 profit. It all went swimmingly well, Geldof and Grundy got along famously, the great man was more than usually expansive and a special slot was duly assigned for the broadcast.

Grundy decided to leave nothing to chance. It being a weekend, he headed straight from the airport to Piccadilly, and placed the UHER reel-to-reel master-tape – considered more reliable than an ordinary cassette – in a personal locker. Grundy recalls it to have been his own locker but Mike Gates – who was assigned to do the editing – swears the tape was put in his locker.

'Chris didn't have his own locker,' says Gates. 'There was no lock on it, so he could get in and out.'

There is no disputing what happened next. The following

Monday, when Grundy went to fetch the tape, it had vanished. Panic-stricken, he collared White And Two Sugars.

'I asked him if he had seen a tape with "Bob Geldof, Master" written on it, and he said, quite nonchalantly, "Yes, maa-aate." I asked where it was, and he said it was in the machine.'

His anxiety now giving way to nausea, Grundy inquired what it was doing there.

'Well,' replied Evans, casually, 'I was listening to this really funny thing about boxers and I wanted to record it. I didn't have a tape so I borrowed one of yours.'

Evans had recorded over the interview, at the time the most notable of Grundy's career.

'The words "Bob Geldof, Master" were clearly written in red,' recalls Grundy. 'I went bananas.'

Did he think Evans had known what he was doing?

'I think he must have done. He couldn't possible not see the writing. That was Chris. Chris would do things without thinking. He just went looking for a tape, grabbed it, and stuck one in.'

Had Grundy hit him?

'I think so, yeah. I think that was the time when we really did have a real one.'

And had Evans returned his blows?

'I don't think so, no. I think he was a bit disappointed in himself, really, because he realized what he had done and realized how angry I was.'

Chris may have appeared contrite, but Mike Gates's version of events casts doubt on his sincerity. By the time Grundy confronted him, Evans, he says, must have known for at least twenty-four hours what he had done, because he had first told Gates the previous day.

'On the Sunday morning I came in and he was really excited,' says Gates. 'He was always making tapes and he said he'd done a demo about a boxing match. He told me to take a listen. I went in the control room and put the tape in, and it looked familiar. I told him it was the Geldof tape and he just said, "Never mind, listen to the boxing." He laughed.

He wasn't really bothered. He was more interested in me listening to the boxing. He's got such a strong belief in himself that he probably didn't even consider the damage he had done. It wouldn't really bother him.'

Crass thoughtlessness or wanton disregard for a colleague's prized work? No one but Evans himself can say for sure. But more remarkable than his behaviour was the fact that those whom he sabotaged now saved him from the sack. Mike Briscoe, the long-suffering Programme Controller, was ready to fire him. However, Radcliffe – backed by Grundy – successfully pleaded on his behalf.

'Radcliffe claims to have saved Chris's career,' says Grundy. 'Here you have a classic case of a lad behaving outrageously and yet his friends actually rallied round to protect him. Because there is no doubt that I saw genius in him. I think we all saw something a bit special – he was mad, he was unpredictable, but there was a talent there. He was infuriating a lot of the time, but we didn't want to see it all go to waste.'

Did Chris attempt to repay this loyalty? Apparently not.

Interviewed by the broadcaster Henry Matthews for a BBC Radio Five profile on Evans, Mike Briscoe described how Evans's personality changed after his conversion from 'willing prankster' to DJ.

'He became a perfectionist, I suppose you could say, being nice about it. Or being, perhaps, unkind about it, he just became a bit of a bully. He expected all the people on the station to do what he had done, which was, if you like, go and fetch and carry for someone else. And he started getting to be a bit of a tyrant, I have to say.'

Arriving at the station as Evans was completing his overnight slot, Grundy was among those who witnessed this burgeoning arrogance. Evans would harangue the back-room team with only slightly less venom than Timmy Mallett had directed at him.

'I'm sure if you spoke to a doctor or psychiatrist they'd tell you that's what people who have been bullied do. The abused abuse,' says Grundy.

Though they were close friends, Mike Gates was among those who felt the sharp edge of Chris's tongue.

'He wanted some kind of feature for his night programme, so he suggested that I write a sort of Philip Marlowe detective spoof,' recalls Gates. 'I thought of the name, Gambon and Defreitas, and we found some spooky music. The people in it were myself, Chris, and this other bloke, who Chris claimed was a bank-robber, and his girlfriend. We would all read the parts and it went out every couple of nights as a kind of serial. I was doing it for nothing, and it was sometimes very hard to think of a storyline. But Chris, who was a very tough task-master, took it seriously and he used to get really angry if I hadn't written something every day.'

For a while, Gambon and Defreitas became one of Chris's obsessions. Indeed, prompted perhaps by the television radio-detective series, Shoestring, he persuaded Gates to partner him in a private eye agency with the same name. Headed note paper was duly printed and an advert was placed, giving Gates's parents' phone-number as their office.

'We only got one assignment, from a woman who suspected her boyfriend was having an affair,' laughed Gates. 'We set out to tail him but we hadn't really got a clue what we were doing. The ironic thing was that she told us we were far more professional than others she had tried. She called us off because she couldn't afford our fees.'

The detective series brought fan mail, mainly from inmates of Strangeways prison. From the same destination, Evans received a death-threat. One of the criminals believed that by adopting the nickname The Prince of Darkness he was allying himself with the Devil – and pledged to show him what being evil really meant.

'The funny thing was that Chris had no idea who the Prince of Darkness was until then,' says Alison. 'He just liked the sound of the name.'

In any case, regarding all audience participation as positive, he was undeterred. Gates recalls how he amused himself – and his audience – by hooking gullible listeners like hungry fish, then reeling them in slowly to maximize their embarrassment. One listener whose hopes were built up, then crushed, was a less-than-bright man from Manchester.

'Chris was running a competition, and this rather dim-witted chap somehow won it, and Chris said that the prize was a beautiful car. The bloke was obviously thrilled, and Chris made a big thing of it. He said he wanted to present it personally, live on air. When he arrived the poor bloke found his prize was a Matchbox car.'

It was the same trick he had played years earlier at the Lion pub disco, with a miniature whisky bottle, refined and recycled to devastating effect.

'Chris thought it was hilarious. He had a cruel streak,' says Gates.

The streak got the better of him again in the autumn of 1986, after Alison – now living with him at Lynn and Andy's – accidentally fell pregnant.

'I was changing pills and I got caught in between,' she says. 'You know what I'm like. It just went over my head.'

Until then, she and Chris had never discussed their long-term future and settling down to start a family was not on the agenda. When she missed her period he suggested a pregnancy test and insisted on calling for the results himself.

'Have you heard of a phantom pregnancy?' he asked her when he got home, peering over his glasses earnestly. 'Well, you're not having one.'

She still laughs at that typical Evans delivery.

'I can remember coming straight round to show mum the test. I think I was more shocked than anything. He wasn't upset or angry, though – in fact, Chris was fine about it. He certainly never mentioned an abortion, not that I would have considered it anyway. But marriage never came up, to tell you the truth, and deep down I knew we wouldn't stay together. He was too ambitious.'

Too ambitious and too interested in capitalizing on his rising celebrity.

One day, soon after she learned that she was to become a mother, Alison was touched to hear Chris breaking the happy news on Piccadilly Radio. Distinctly less amused was an attractive young girl named Christine, with whom – by Mike Gates's recollection – Evans had been unfaithful around the same time. The fling occurred, says Gates, at one of countless parties to which Evans, a rising young turk on the Northern media circuit, was invited during his second spell at Piccadilly. There, among a group of talented classical musicians, was Christine. Evans's wandering eye fell upon her and they chatted intimately before drifting off together.

When they parted, Gates clearly remembers Chris's words. 'He said to her, after the one-night stand, "Listen to me on the radio in the morning."'

If Christine tuned in expecting a sweet little message, then she got a rude awakening.

'When he was on the radio all he was talking about was Alison, and how his girlfriend was expecting a baby.'

One can only imagine how cheap this made his lover feel. Had Evans, in Gates's opinion, deliberately set out to humiliate her? He ponders the question for a moment.

'He must have realized,' he said. Then, charitable by nature, added, 'but perhaps it was just unconscious.'

Gates indicates that Chris cheated on Alison on other occasions, but he does not believe his friend wished to hurt anyone. 'I think they were all clear what the score was with Chris. They could take him or leave him.'

Among the in-crowd who frequented the clubs and parties of Manchester, this might have been true. Back down the M62, in Warrington, a pregnant Alison remained blissfully ignorant.

CHAPTER TEN

No sooner was Alison's pregnancy confirmed than she and Chris were presented with another, more pressing, problem: finding a new home. Her sister and brother-in-law were moving and, in any case, couldn't be expected to accommodate a baby. Ever supportive, Alison's mother offered to let them stay with her but, while the idea appealed to Alison, Chris was not so keen. Commuting from Warrington to Manchester every night and returning early in the morning didn't make sense, he reasoned. Besides, Mike Gates's parents would soon have a cottage to rent next door to their converted vicarage in the village of Ainsworth, near Bolton. They would only charge £150 a month, and it was much nearer to the Piccadilly studios. He would go and stay at Mike's for a few weeks and Alison could join him when the cottage was vacant. Alison didn't really want to be parted from Chris during the final stages of her pregnancy, but she was too tired to argue. With hindsight, however, she can see that this first separation marked the beginning of a slow decline from which their relationship never recovered.

Distanced from Alison by thirty-odd miles of twisting moorland road and motorway, Chris treated his expectant girlfriend with a confusing mixture of kindness, misguided concern and neglect. Deciding, one day, that she must improve her diet, he arrived at Mrs Ward's via the super-market – not a place he usually frequented.

'He charged in with all this beef, tomatoes and peppers and started cooking some sort of concoction,' says Alison, whose tastes extend to Chinese food but little further. 'He was telling me to eat it, that it was good for me. I managed that meal, I think, but not some of the others. I went right off chicken after he'd cooked me some. He was always trying to cook for me.'

On another day Chris breezed in with what Alison describes as a 'monstrous purple coat' with velvet cuffs and pockets.

'It was disgusting,' she says, 'but I didn't have the heart to tell him I didn't like it. I tried to get out of wearing it by saying it wouldn't fit me, but that didn't work. He said, "You'll never believe it, the girl who sold it to me was preg-nant herself, so I got her to try it on. It's just the right size." I only wore it about three times.'

Rather than receiving meals and gifts, Alison would have drawn greater comfort from some physical affection. But Chris found her swollen belly unattractive, so their love-making grew less frequent as her confinement progressed. His attitude towards her social life also changed. Before her pregnancy he had hated her to go out with friends while he was working; now, because he no longer felt threatened, he encouraged it. Before the pregnancy, he would bowl up to Alison's workplace when her shift finished and whisk her away to the Lake District; now she felt rather like Cinderella, only the Prince of Darkness rarely showed up.

'He seemed to spend every minute of his time in the studio, even when he wasn't on the air,' says Alison. 'He threw him-self into it, and he was always trying something out or making demo tapes. Everything was work, work, work.'

Upon Chris's arrival in Ainsworth, the Gates family felt as though their isolated semi-rural retreat had been hit by a maelstrom. He was a walking disaster.

'He was never nasty or arrogant,' says Susie Gates, 'he was simply full of fun. He was also very affectionate. He would put his arm round me and give me a kiss. It was just that he had so many accidents all the time, and he was so boisterous.'

One early catastrophe happened after he had spent all day at the studio and dashed back for a snack and a couple of hours' sleep, intending to return to do his 2 a.m. show. Before going to bed he put some washing in the machine and soaked his dirty dishes in the sink. But he left the plug in – a fatal mistake, given that the Gates's washing machine emptied into the sink. When he awoke the kitchen was flooded. Racing off to Piccadilly, he left Mike Gates with a bucket, ankle-deep in water. Soon after, the underfelt started to rot and the Gateses were forced to buy new lino. Chris was genuinely apologetic, and the Gateses were too fond of him to throw him out. So the mishaps continued unabated.

Excited by his new countrified image, Chris acquired two fishing rods and some old tackle and persuaded the reluctant Gates into a day's sport at a nearby lodge. They caught nothing, and on their return a disappointed Chris left a bag of unused maggots in the garden shed. A few days later, when Bill Gates opened the door, he found himself amidst a plague of newly-hatched bluebottles.

'The shed had to be fumigated,' says Susie, pinching her nose at the memory. She attributes such mishaps to Chris's 'one-track mind'.

'He was in love with himself and his one preoccupation was to further his career. Nothing was allowed to get in his way. He was like a racing horse with blinkers on. He was never nasty – he just didn't think.'

One evening his thoughtlessness came very close to killing him. While he was concerned about Alison's eating habits, his own were at best unhealthy, at worst unhygienic. Shortly before driving to work in Manchester he was chatting to Gates when, suddenly feeling peckish, he produced some dangerous-looking tuna sandwiches from the fridge. The bread was dry, with curled-up edges, and it was clear that they should be thrown out. Clear to Gates, that is, for he wisely declined to take one. Chris wolfed them down.

That night Chris's job was to field the phone-calls on DJ

Jim Reeve's show, and the Gates family realized something was wrong when Reeve played record upon record, without any listeners' calls.

'Half way through the show Jim apologized,' said Susie. 'He said he couldn't get Chris out of the toilet as he was vomiting and "the other". Around midnight, he said an ambulance had just carted Chris off to hospital. We were sick with worry. We couldn't ring Piccadilly because no-one was answering the phone and we had no idea which hospital they had taken him to. He arrived back home early next morning, looking dreadful, having discharged himself against their advice. They told him he had arrived so dehydrated and poorly that he could have been dead within the hour.'

His misfortune was not only self-induced. He returned to Ainsworth one evening with his hair matted and sticky and his glasses smudged. A concerned Susie asked him what had happened. Well, he said, he had stopped at the lights with the top of his sports-car rolled back when a woman pulled up alongside him. She had just poured herself some tea from a flask and as the lights changed she had hurled it at him, shouting, 'Poser!' Evans swore blind that he had done nothing to provoke the attack.

'Just setting eyes on Chris used to offend people before he was well known,' explains Mike Gates. 'He had this habit of annoying people just by looking at them. Looking at him, you could imagine why he was bullied when he was younger. He also had a way of speaking extremely directly. He would say things that other people wouldn't dare say. I mean, he used to say some horrible things to me, but you got used to it.'

Shorter and stockier than Chris, Gates gave an example.

'Once I had some jeans that didn't fit me very well, and I went to the bar and came back and he just said, "My God! You look terrible from behind." And he would say things about me losing my hair. It was how you took it. If you took it personally you couldn't be friends with him.'

For Chris's sake it was fortunate that Gates did not 'take it personally', for he came to the rescue on countless occasions.

Calamity struck once more for Evans one Sunday, when he and Mike were in the studio preparing for a three-hour special that Chris was to host. Much of the show had been pre-recorded and somehow Chris dropped all the spools. Most of them unwound, and just before the programme began, he and Gates found themselves surrounded by a cat's-cradle of unravelled tape. With only minutes to spare they managed to find the first tape and frantically rewind it. While Chris started the programme, Michael, sweating blood in the background, rewound the others and tried to hand them in the right order to Chris.

They managed it. Just.

Gates again sublimated his own interests when Chris decided, at the eleventh hour, to play in a Piccadilly Radio charity cricket match. They had driven some competition winners to London – or, rather, Gates had driven them while Chris had snoozed in the passenger seat. Chris hadn't previously mentioned the match, but as Manchester neared he awoke and started saying it was important for him to appear.

'He said we should go straight there and that I could sit and watch. But I didn't want to do that because I was absolutely knackered,' says Gates. 'I said I would drop Chris off and then drive home and he said, "Okay, on one condition – you have to lend me your trousers." He was wearing jeans and I just happened to be wearing white trousers.'

Gates reluctantly agreed. Arriving at the cricket ground they headed straight for a disused toilet in order to make the swap.

'We disappeared inside and, to everyone's amusement, we walked out together wearing different trousers. As I am about five foot seven and Chris is six foot two, mine were too tight and his were half way up his shins. I was really pissed off with him.'

The rather expensive trousers were ruined by grass-stains and Chris didn't have the money to buy Gates a new pair.

From such stories one might see Gates as a downtrodden batman, wimpishly pandering to Chris's every need. While he was often prepared to put himself second, this would be a misconception. Older than Evans by some six years and an Oxford University English graduate, Gates is astute and articulate. He now lives in Finland, where he runs a group of successful language schools. He has spent long hours attempting to analyse his relationship with Evans, and he has drawn some interesting conclusions.

'Chris dominated our friendship, but I was prepared to allow that,' he says. 'I found him extremely amusing to be with. Energetic, a strong character. Forget the difference in our academic qualifications. He is also hugely intelligent. After he moved to London he used to keep a journal, which he showed to me. I studied literature and I know good writing when I see it. It was absolutely outstanding.

'There was an interesting article about him in the *Mail On Sunday*, where Andy Bird [who worked with Chris at Piccadilly and later became his business partner] said that you had to remember he was shy. His wife Carol said she couldn't understand what Bird was getting at, but I think in certain situations there was a shyness about him. He would sometimes have an idea to do something, then push me forward to do it instead of him. For example, when we went round Warrington banks and accountants trying to get the detective agency going, he would say, "Go on. You go in." You could call it shyness or it might be bossiness.

'I think, perhaps, he is confused about what his values really are. He couldn't understand why, when we were friends, I seemed to value different things than he did. I mean, at the time I had two very good friends; one was a former school-teacher Roger and one was Chris. And Chris would ask me, "Who's your best friend – him or me?" I think he got the impression that Roger was my best mate and he didn't like that at all. One reason he didn't like it was that he felt uneducated by comparison with Roger. He had only read one book, *My Family and Other Animals*. So, on the one hand he had this admiration for education, but on the other he couldn't quite appreciate why someone might not value achieving fame, or money as much as him.'

The weeks slipped by, and it was late April 1987. The

house that Chris and Alison had hoped to live in was still not vacant, and Alison – by now eight months pregnant – had given up all hope of moving to Ainsworth before their baby was born. But then, suddenly, Chris was on the phone, telling her she must join him immediately. There was no need to wait until the house was ready, he said, he had thought of a brilliant idea. They could camp out in a tent pitched in Susie Gates's garden.

It might have been a warm spring, but of all the insane schemes her boyfriend had ever dreamed up, Alison thought this easily the most crazy.

'Chris,' she said evenly, 'I'm absolutely huge. I'm about to have our baby – there's no way I'm sleeping in a tent.'

It was then, she says, that he shared with her the details of a publicity-grabbing con-trick that journalists still believe to be true.

'He told me not to worry,' says Alison, 'he said it was all for PR. I didn't really have to stay in the tent, but he just wanted me to come along and make it look as though I was. I said that no one would be daft enough to believe that a heavily pregnant woman would be sleeping in a tent.'

The time would come when Alison would not be prepared to bend the truth for the sake of Chris's career. Now, however, she agreed to play along and the scam worked brilliantly, as an article in the 1 May 1987 edition of the *Manchester Evening News* confirms. Headlined 'Good Morning Camper!' and accompanied by a photograph of a grimacing Chris emerging from the tent for his early morning show, the text reads in part:

'When Piccadilly Radio DJ Chris Evans moved to Bolton he did not bargain for such a down-to-earth lifestyle. But that's just what he got. For 'home sweet home' is a tent in a friend's back garden! With the recent warm weather, Chris has even been joined by his girlfriend, twenty-year-old Alison Ward, also from Warrington, who is expecting their first child any day.'

St Margaret's CoE Junior School, class of 1972, with Chris (middle of the second row) perfecting the grin that would help make his fortune.

Boteler Grammar School, 1978. Chris is easily recognizable with the trademark glasses now in place.

The Evans's council home in Greenwood Crescent, Orford, where Chris grew up and where Minnie Evans still lives.

Newsheet, the newsagents where Chris had one of his first tastes of working life.

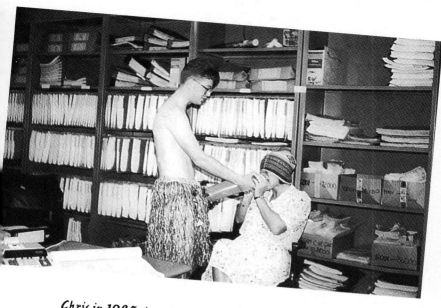

*Chris in 1985, in mid-flight with his
Tarzan-o-gram money-spinner.*

Trevor Palin in 1984, in typical guise, after playing a jingle on the Timmy Mallett Show at Piccadilly Radio.

Chris Evans

PICCADILLY RADIO

Left: An early PR portrait, circa 1985/6.

Below: Like mother, like son. Minnie Evans (second left) dons tinsel and tiara to play a 'Fairy Over Forty' at Orford Hall, the old peoples' home where she worked.

Chris in 1987, brewing tea for his pregnant girlfriend, Alison Ward, outside the tent they purportedly shared in Susie Gates's garden.

Jade Lois Ward, Chris's
daughter by Alison, in an
incubator just hours after
her birth.

Right: As a carrot-topped
toddler, Jade was the mirror-
image of her father.

Maintenance payments
Alison received from
Chris after he left her
and Jade for London.
They bounced.

Alison and Jade: 'I don't think Chris realizes what he's missing,' says Alison.

Chris, in happier times, with his wife Carol McGiffin.

Clocking in: Chris begins work at the Radio One Breakfast Show in April 1995.

Fully recovered and back on top form, with Michael Grade, former Channel 4 Controller, after signing a lucrative new contract in March 1997.

Chris milked the story for all it was worth, deciding to present the following day's radio show from the tent. When the outside broadcast van broke down he rushed back to the studio and simply pretended he was in the countryside.

'I had to let him know when the milkman or postman arrived – he had tapes of their noises in the studio,' Susie Gates says. She also gave him a running commentary on the weather so he could accurately describe the prevailing conditions. It all sounded so authentic that it even fooled the station's chief engineer, who was supposed to authorize all outside broadcasts.

'He woke up and listened to this and went bonkers,' laughs John Clayton, then a senior producer. 'He had carpeted Chris many times for unauthorized behaviour and he drove in frantically, imagining that he would have the chance to take him off the air. Apparently, the sight of his jaw dropping when Chris was sitting there in the studio was something to behold.'

The *Manchester Evening News* also appears to have failed to see through the wheeze, publishing a follow-up story, in which Chris is described as a 'cheery ex-seafood salesman' and a spare-time bric-a-brac trader. Delighted by this unexpected flurry of positive coverage, Piccadilly bosses capitalized by presenting a feature on homelessness.

The great tent myth was still being recycled as late as April 1996, by which time *The Mirror* was billing it as 'exclusive'. The newspaper had dug out an old photograph of Chris with Alison, pregnant and bulging beneath her clothes. Chris had just been given a £500,000 pay rise by Radio One, and the accompanying story contrasted his millionaire lifestyle with the days when he and his pregnant lover were forced to sleep outdoors. Susie Gates is adamant that Chris did camp on her back lawn for two or three weeks, but alone.

'He could survive with very few possessions. He'd be happy with a bench, a nice car and a job he loved,' she told *The Mirror*'s Amanda Ward. 'If it was a cold night he'd come into our house and get me out of bed. I had to sleep on the floor. He was very bossy.'

But Alison has different memories.

'He might have spent the odd night in the tent for a laugh, but not more than that. I never slept in it at all.'

Who cared about the minute details? Not Chris. As far as he was concerned, it was a classic case of not letting the facts interfere with a good story. Encouraged by the ease with which he had manipulated a situation to his advantage, it was not long before he was embarking upon his next scam.

Sick of driving around in shabby old cars, he conspired to get a new one without paying for it. No one in the world deserved a decent car more than the long-suffering White And Two Sugars.

'One day he came on air and said that he wanted a company car,' recalls Tim Grundy. 'I asked him what he was talking about, and he said that I had one as long as Derbyshire, with the company name on it, so why shouldn't he have one, too? I said, "Well, here you are, you've got the whole of the North West listening to you this morning, so just ask any one of those car dealers out there to provide you with a car." Chris said he wanted, of all things, a Skoda, with "Tim Grundy's Coffee Boy" written on the side.'

Within days his wish was granted. A garage boss named Peter Shenk, who knew a public relations opportunity when he saw one, provided Chris with a free top-of-the-range Skoda – the first new car Chris had possessed. The news duly made the Northern editions, but, adds Grundy, 'In true style he blew it up on the M6. He said that someone had left a spanner in the engine.'

As May gave way to June and Alison reached full term, Chris began to betray signs of anxiety about the birth. He asked Alison if she wanted him to be there and she merely said that he could be if he wanted to, knowing that he had a phobia of hospitals.

'I think he told me that it was because he had visited his dad there a couple of times,' says Alison. 'And I knew he would be no use to me, so in the end I told him my sister Karen would come and that he needn't bother. I think he was a bit relieved.'

But his nervousness resurfaced one morning when Alison phoned his radio programme.

'He ran a competition where he described what he was holding in his hand and listeners had to guess what it was. I was sitting with Karen and Clive, and I bet them that it was a prawn-cracker – I was right, of course – but they were doubting me. I settled the argument by calling Chris on his direct line.' She laughs. 'Chris picked up the phone and as soon as he heard my voice he thought I must have had the baby. He was going mad. He kept saying he couldn't believe I would call at a time like that over a prawn-cracker.'

Alison was in labour for three days before the baby was born at Warrington General Hospital, at 11.45 p.m. on Thursday 4 June 1987. Had it been a boy, Chris had chosen the name Wesley. But when the scan revealed that they were having a girl he couldn't come up with anything, so he left Alison to pick. She liked Jade, her mother liked Lois, so Jade Lois Ward she was.

'We left Chris's surname off the birth certificate because we thought we'd be better off financially, with regard to social benefits,' says Alison candidly. 'Looking back I wish we hadn't. If there's a way of changing it, I would like to do it now, for Jade's sake.'

Stepping gingerly into the delivery-room, Chris was alarmed to find that his girlfriend was not cuddling their child, as he had expected. His concern turned to panic when Alison – still intoxicated by gas and air – kept repeating, 'I'm sorry, Chris, I'm really sorry.' Though her memory of those hours is hazy, she may have been apologizing because Jade's delivery had proved so difficult. In fact their baby had been fortunate to survive.

'Jade had what they call a flat birth,' she says. 'Her ribs and stomach didn't go into place as they normally do, so she literally looked flat. Plus the cord was wrapped around her neck twice, and the midwife didn't cut it, she pulled. She wasn't breathing when she was born and they took her straight to intensive care. She was grey and I later found out that she had had two epileptic fits in the first twenty-four hours of her life. She had to go for check-ups every six months until she was two.'

All this was too much for Chris. His head spinning and his heart racing giddily, after just a few moments talking to Alison he staggered out into the corridor and fainted. He had to be helped to his car and driven home.

Alison was not permitted to see Jade until the following day. In the meantime, the nurses gave her a Polaroid picture of her in the incubator, to show what she looked like. She didn't want to go to the intensive care unit alone, so she phoned Chris and asked him to accompany her. Chris returned to the hospital at about 2 p.m. on the Friday and even then, says Alison, he almost had to be carried there. But, having admirably subjugated his fears a little, he was as supportive as any young father could be. He walked into the unit tenderly holding Alison's hand and whispering reassuring words. But when he first glimpsed his little girl – a seven pound eleven ounce mirror image of himself, only with blonde curls rather than red – his emotions overcame him.

'He started crying,' says Alison softly, 'that's the first and only time I've seen him cry. I think he was scared as much as anything, because he had this little baby all wired up, and he didn't know what was going to happen.'

His way of handling his feelings was to bring Alison a huge box of pick'n'mix chocolates, then sit by her bedside guzzling them all.

Jade stayed in intensive care for four days and when mother and daughter emerged from hospital a week later, Alison couldn't stop cuddling her. If she assumed Chris would react the same way, however, she had misjudged him.

'He used to tell everyone about Jade and say how lovely she was,' says Alison wistfully, 'and he bought her toys. But he never made much effort with Jade from the start. He didn't even hold her more than a couple of times, and that was only when I passed her to him while I did something else. I don't think he had any paternal instincts. You know, I just felt that he couldn't cope.'

If Alison's tone is non-recriminatory, then her mother takes a harder view.

'I only saw him nurse his own daughter once,' says Maureen Ward scathingly, 'and even then he stuck his grubby finger in her mouth.'

When they left Warrington General, Alison and Jade stayed at Gough Avenue for a couple of weeks, then, with the Gates's cottage empty at last, she joined Chris in Ainsworth. However, her visions of a wholesome family life in the countryside were illusory. Isolated in a quiet little village miles from anywhere, with a baby and no transport, she had only Susie – whom she didn't know very well – for company. Chris was off working or gallivanting in Manchester. Susie Gates could do nothing to assuage her loneliness.

'She realized he had no time for the baby,' she says. 'I mean, he was nice to her and he was nice to the baby, but he wasn't really interested. He just wanted to be famous. He would make promises – but the minute he turned his back it was forgotten.'

'After only a few weeks Alison didn't want to stay any longer. She was homesick because Chris was working all hours and she had her friends and family in Warrington.'

Susie never heard them argue, she says. In her view: 'They just fell out. One day he loved her, and one day he didn't. He wasn't deliberately nasty, it was just that nobody apart from himself was that important. I mean, look at all the girlfriends he's had since then. One minute he had met a girl and was going to marry her. The next he had forgotten all about her. That's typical.'

Mrs Gates says she only met one woman who seemed to have the measure of Chris: his mother Minnie.

'She had him sussed.'

Alison recalls how, on their few snatched moments together, Chris became increasingly moody and irritable.

'He used to shout at me for no reason that I could see, which he had never done before. He would say he wished I argued back, but I was taught never to shout back because it only makes people more annoyed.'

Back at Piccadilly, his anger manifested itself as depression. 'He had mood swings. He could be quite morose. Most of the time he was a very happy person, bouncy, bright and bushy-tailed. You have to ask yourself whether that was an act. Whether it still is an act. I'd quite often find myself saying to him, "What's the matter, mate, what's going on?", because he'd be sitting there like this,' says Grundy, burying his head in his hands.

'"Come on, Chris, tell me about it."

'"Nothing."

'But the next day he'd be the bouncy Chris he always was.'

Michael Gates believes his angst may have been caused by his perplexingly dichotomous view of himself.

'For a while he had two contrary images of the future in his mind. In one he was going to be this famous person, and in the other he was going to be like the people in Warrington who he grew up with. I remember quite early on, when he was nineteen or twenty, he was talking about him and Alison buying furniture and going down to IKEA and setting up home. And when he moved to Bolton, it was, "Right, let's set up this nice little place together," with Alison as his wife. But I don't think he really believed it. I think Alison believed it, and that he wanted to believe it. But in your heart you knew he wouldn't settle down. Even when he was moving in to the cottage with Alison and Jade there was no sense of reality about it. It was as though he was playing out a charade. You could see this young couple setting up home, but you knew it wasn't happening, really.'

Ill-equipped to handle the responsibilities of fatherhood, at least when Jade was very young Chris tried to play the part. When Alison told him that she was leaving the Gates's cottage and returning to her mother's, he not only offered to join them but went one better. As he was now earning reasonable money at Piccadilly, he told his girlfriend that they could afford a mortgage on a home of their own. Delighted, Alison began scanning the property pages in the *Warrington Guardian*. But her joy was short-lived.

'Whenever I suggested that we should go and look at a place he was always too busy,' she says. 'I wasn't going to nag him, so in the end I went house-hunting on my own. He would stay at my mum's sometimes, but he was flitting between there and Mike Gates's.'

When Chris was at the Wards' home, the accommodating good nature of Cliff and Maureen Ward was tested to breaking point by his slovenliness. Soiled undergarments were strewn around for the house-proud Maureen to pick up and wash; ketchup-crusted plates were left wherever he happened to have been sitting. One minute he was leaping around, whirling his arms and legs like Magnus Pike, as he enthused about his latest five-minute fad. The next minute he was lolling fast asleep on the couch so that no one else in the family could sit down. Waking up with a start, he would promptly switch over the television, oblivious to whether someone was watching another programme. Or if there was nothing worth viewing he would strum a few dubious tunes on his broken-stringed old Eko guitar, which remains in the hall upstairs.

'You had to laugh at him,' says Maureen but, echoing Susie Gates, she adds, 'I just don't think he knows how to look after anyone apart from himself.'

Having previously regarded Chris as generous – if not with his time – Alison was also perturbed by an emergent mean streak. Gone were the days when he fattened her up on best-beef and vegetables. On the few occasions when they shopped together, 'I would be sticking things in the trolley and he would be taking them out just as fast. He asked for the cheapest cuts, and he never gave me any money. He was very, very tight. And by this time he was on a good wage.'

Of all his strange ideas, the craziest was unveiled when Jade was just a few days old. Though still only feeding and sleeping, his daughter, he informed the Ward family in all earnestness, must have a horse. No? Well, all right, a pony would do.

'He said there was no need to worry because he would buy it himself and make sure it was watered and fed,' said Maureen Ward, still confounded by the madness of it all. 'I said, "Fine, Chris, but where are you going to keep it?"'

She wanders over to the window, peels back the curtains and gestures towards a back-garden no more than twenty-feet long.

'He said it could live out there. He was deadly serious.'

After much debate, the Wards convinced him that their tiny lawn was not best suited to become a coral. But Chris, who has always felt a strong affinity with animals, was not to be defeated.

'He was determined that we should have some sort of pet, and a few days later he brought home this great big sheep-dog,' laughs Alison. 'He said he'd got it from a farm. I told him my dad would go absolutely ape and it couldn't stay. He said it had nowhere to go and he wouldn't keep it long, only for a couple of weeks. He said Cliff didn't have to find out. He actually thought he could hide it upstairs in the bedroom but Cliff obviously heard it. Chris said that the dog would never go to the toilet, but it did – always when Chris was out. It saturated the carpet and in the end he took it with him to the studio. I didn't see it again after that. He was potty but in a nice way. You couldn't tell him off.'

Clearly this domestic sit-com could only run for so long. Even Chris was aware of that. When, late in 1987, Alison's sister Karen mentioned that her boyfriend's mother was selling her house at a good price, he decided to make his first major investment. He paid about £25,000 for the two-bedroomed terrace, 285 Lovely Lane, which stands just around the corner from what remains of Bostock Street. In a final attempt to keep their relationship together, if only for Jade's benefit, Alison moved in with him, but her stay lasted just a few weeks.

'He was getting more and more into his job and less and less into me and Jade,' she says. 'I used to think it was a shame that Jade had come along at the wrong time for him, but now I don't think any time would have been right.

'He was away at night so often that I slept with a knife under the bed. He would come in with Ian Daley, eat his tea and go out again. He would ring and say he'd be back in half an hour, then he wouldn't show. It was, "I'm not happy at Piccadilly Radio, I want more." I could see he was angling to move to London and I just didn't want to go. It was obvious what would have happened. He'd have been off with his work set and I would have been on my own in London, even lonelier than I had been at Susie's.'

They parted when Jade was about four months old.

'I was waiting for him, as usual, one night round at Ian and his girlfriend's, and he was in one of his depressions,' recalls Alison. 'About 10 p.m. he came in, and he was fine with everyone else except me. He totally ignored me; walked past me as though I didn't exist. He just said to Ian's girlfriend, "All right? Mind if I get my head down for a bit?"

Then he disappeared upstairs. I thought, that's it, I've had enough. I asked Ian if he would take me back to Lovely Lane to get my things because I was leaving. Ian went upstairs and told Chris, and he just said, "No, she won't", and went back to sleep. I thought, you obnoxious arrogant so-and-so. He had the attitude that I couldn't do without him. I went back to my mum's and it was a couple of days later that he rang. He just said: "I can't believe you did it."'

Incredulous he may have been, but Evans did not try to persuade Alison to return.

'He used to come round now and again,' she says, 'We would take Jade out, and we got on fine, but it was just as friends.'

Soon after, Chris rented the spare room in the house to some girls. Though his relationship with his new lodgers was, by all accounts, platonic, they must have been liberal in outlook. Dave Whittaker recalls:

'Me and Ian would knock for him and he would answer the door totally naked. He would stretch his arms up to the door-frame and dance around, so everyone walking past, and anyone inside, could see. He had obviously just got up, or taken a bath, but the rest of the population would get a towel. With Chris it was, "World! Look at me! I'm mad!"'

During these immediate post-Alison days, Whittaker and Daley appeared to take on a new importance for Chris. Lonely, perhaps, he would urge them to join him on the Piccadilly night show.

'We used to get the red-carpet treatment from the security guards,' laughs Whittaker. 'They used to wave us into the Green Room – I think they thought we were a band.' Once inside Piccadilly Plaza, Evans's 'courtiers' had the run of the place. They would smoke, select records, laze around. Occasionally Evans would introduce them into his performance, or they would phone in from very close by, pretending to be old women and weird characters.

If Whittaker and Daley were not being used on air, then they certainly had their uses elsewhere. To reach the studio it was necessary to walk through a darkened, graffiti-covered shopping complex where drunks and drug-takers often gathered to shelter from the cold.

'One night, this punk in a black leather jacket came up to me and Chris as we were walking through,' says Whittaker, a thick-set, bull-necked man who would appear to be able to handle himself. 'He was muttering something to us about the Vice Squad nicking his bird. He kept repeating it, and then he pulled out a syringe and starting threatening us with it. AIDS was big news at the time. We were shitting ourselves.'

Confronted by the bulky Dave Whittaker, the would-be attacker backed off. Had Evans been alone, he might not have escaped so lightly.

Another evening, Whittaker was at Daley's home when Evans burst in, wild-eyed, limbs whirling, saying his car had broken down and he had to interview Rick Astley in Manchester in twenty-five minutes' time. Astley, also from Warrington, was then the music industry's hottest property.

'He wanted a lift and we were subtly wondering what was in it for us,' says Whittaker. 'He said we could meet Rick, which didn't impress us at all.'

However, as Chris had actually paid for Ian's car – a £50 Talbot Horizon – they felt obliged to rescue him. The three dived into the Talbot and hared off.

'Ian's renowned for not putting oil in cars. We were burning down the M62 and we got about half way when the engine seized. Chris ran down the hard shoulder, phoned the police and told them that he was Chris Evans and he had a vital interview with Astley. Within minutes a police Range Rover arrived and Chris disappeared, leaving us standing on the roadside.

'He didn't need us any more, so he just left us.'

Daley and Whittaker held no grudge. When you hung around with Chris episodes likes this became commonplace. But then, soon afterwards, they began to see less and less of him in Warrington, for his attention lay elsewhere.

As his interest in Alison had waned, over in Manchester he had become desperate to impress another woman: a Piccadilly

Radio news reader named Sara Green. Petite and reed-slim, with short, feathery fair hair and huge, bright eyes, Sara was Alison's polar opposite. Sara spoke elocution English and came from a comfortable background. Sara possessed a university degree and was expected to go far in journalism. Sara, say her former colleagues, was supremely self-confident and 'a little aloof'. In short, Sara was just the sort of bright, highly desirable young career woman that an upwardly mobile radio presenter like Chris Evans should be going out with.

'She was very middle-class, you know, okay ya!' says Alison, who had been introduced to her when Chris took her to Piccadilly. 'Not like us common types. But she was pleasant enough and pretty. Whether he had started going out with her when he was still going with me I don't know. I don't really care, either, to be honest. It's all water under the bridge now.'

Most of the single men on the station secretly fancied Sara, and the problem was, Chris reflected, she seemed to be out of his league. Worse, as he had never attempted to woo a woman of her status and social background, he had no idea how to make the opening move. Day after day, as he passed her in the newsroom or observed her through the glass-sided studio his frustration grew. Eventually he confided his dilemma to Julie Smith, one of his closest friends at Piccadilly, and now a television producer in Scotland.

'He had quietly been pursuing Sara and didn't tell me about it for ages,' she recalls. 'Then he said he needed to ask her out and he didn't know what to say. I don't think he realized how attractive he was then, but he actually had a lot of female admirers. He had charm, humour, and he's quite an invading character: you can't be in a room with him and not know he's there.'

Evans, she adds, had 'a strange taste in women'. Sara was 'intelligent, but seen as difficult. Not that she wasn't very nice, but – how can I put it? I always thought she was quite cold. It was only after she and Chris split up that I realized she was quite a nice person.'

Around the same time, colleagues say, Chris appeared to

be attracted to Julie, too, but she dismisses any possibility of a romance, saying: 'I don't think I'm tough enough to be his girlfriend. I think he loves a challenge in life, and possibly women come into that category.'

Julie Smith is not sure how Chris overcame his shyness to snare Sara, but Tim Grundy remembers precisely how White and Two Sugars drew upon all his innate cunning to become the envy of Piccadilly's red-blooded DJs.

'They were both working night shifts and he needed a bed to sleep in during the day. Sara had a house [in Cheadle Heath, an affluent south Manchester suburb] with a bed that was available during the day. It was a futon, which was a new thing in those days, and Chris somehow found this out. One day he said to her, very casually, "I've never slept on a futon before," and she said, "Well, why don't you try it." At first it was on his own. Then I think it became 'sleeping with' in the platonic sense, and then it developed into a relationship.'

A brilliantly simple ruse. Grundy was not surprised that it worked.

'He had an amazing success rate with women. I think the most astonishing fact is that he's not the most handsome man in the world, but for whatever reason, he can win women over. He was always very good at talking to women. He was always very funny. The little boy lost.'

Towards the end of 1987, if colleagues' memories are accurate, Chris took an extra lodger at Lovely Lane and moved to Cheadle Heath to live with Sara. Neither she nor Chris, nor anyone at all has ever spoken about their affair. Indeed, until now it has remained unreported by the press – odd when one considers that over the past five years the newspapers have explored every facet of Evans's life. By all accounts, however, theirs was a torrid courtship. In Tim Grundy's view this was partly because the relationship was a little one-sided – and for once Chris did not have the upper-hand.

'I think he did love her,' says Grundy.

And was this requited?

'No. I think he was very much smitten and he was annoyed,

or sad, that he didn't quite get the same back as he was putting in.'

He added, 'She was very clever, very astute. In the Selina Scott mould.'

To Mike Gates, Chris's involvement with Sara was 'very much part of his education'.

Gates says: 'He thought, "My God, I've managed to get the newsreader who's got these degrees and, hey, she's a journalist!" It was as though she was the one he was looking up to – but then it changed. He started out being romantic and charming, but then he sometimes cut her off.'

To make matters stickier, Evans had what Gates ironically describes as 'a talent for keeping old relationships going while existing relationships continued'.

Added to which, even when he was besotted with someone – as he clearly was with Sara – Gates says Evans always had an eye out for other opportunities.

'We went to Oxford intending to sleep in the car,' recalls Gates. 'When we got there we walked into a confectioner's and Chris fancied the girl behind the counter. He spent all day talking about her, then plucked up the courage and went back to ask her out. She said she'd like to, but she couldn't because she had no money. Later on he was pestering me to lend him a fiver, and he said he'd throw in a fiver as well. He said: "We'll buy her some flowers and hand them to her with the money for a night out in an envelope." We went back and gave it to her, but she still couldn't come out. But Chris got her number and I think she came to see him later.'

A third opinion of Chris and Sara's relationship is offered by Julie Smith.

'I guessed Chris loved her and she felt the same way,' she says. 'But there were fights. I think that Chris brings that out in people. He can really piss people off. Just by forgetting to do things, for example. If you expected him to call you could be sure he wouldn't. If you asked him to get the milk you could be sure he would forget. She wouldn't be the type to tolerate that. I know they would fight about stupid things like that.'

In the first throes of her fascination for Chris, Sara was evidently prepared to forgive him such selfishness, but over the months their domestic spats became full-blooded rows, and they would part traumatically.

If he was being troubled by his turbulent private life, Chris certainly did not allow this to affect his performances behind the microphone. At Piccadilly Radio his star was in the ascendant and the buzz around the station was that he was heading for great things. Inevitably this made him the prime target of envious colleagues, particularly DJs whose work was inferior, and for whom he sometimes deputised.

'There is an art to sitting in for people,' says the former senior producer John Clayton. 'The convention dictates that, while it's a big opportunity to impress, you don't rock the boat. You don't change the programme. But Chris did. He would always take someone's programme and work only within the broad parameters. He would use them as a shop window show-case and really go for it.

'I remember him sitting in for Dave Ward – one of the station's big-name DJs – one lunch-time. For some reason it was coming live from a place called Bowlers, in Trafford Park: indoor cricket, a health club, that sort of thing. Even more bizarrely, the guest artists in these incongruous surroundings was a really cool Scouse band at the time called *The Icicle Works*. Chris was in his element. He just took control. The club had new rowing machines and he got the band's Mr Super-cool singer, a guy called Ian McNab, to take part in a rowing contest. That was really incredible in itself. The bass player was really gobsmacked, to the point of being offended, that their band leader was doing this. He was wearing a black overcoat and shades, and he was supposed to be all trendy. It was like getting Bob Dylan to go apple-dunking. No one else would have had the front to get the guy to do it, because they would have been afraid that it might backfire and make them look daft, but not Chris. He was prepared to brazen it out, so people would either go along with him or look a complete bunch of tossers themselves.'

Original as he could be, Evans was shameless in culling

from the lesser DJs. On his night show, for example, one of Dave Ward's ideas was to orchestrate a synchronized mass switching-on of bedroom lights across Manchester. On his instruction, thousands of listeners would flick their lamp switches, and, staring from their upper windows, they would see their neighbours doing likewise. In this way, Ward enhanced and unified his following by creating a curious sort of club. When he moved to Greater London Radio, Chris refined and modified this gimmick, urging readers to honk their car horns. But on *Don't Forget Your Toothbrush*, says Tim Grundy, he blatantly recycled the bedroom lights trick.

'In the end he invited Dave down to watch the programme being made, took him out and thanked him,' Grundy recalls.

Bravery, originality, eclecticism and driving ambition. Not a bad set of qualities with which to arm oneself for an assault on the showbusiness summit. Yet there were two more. The first was an uncanny ability to be 'himself' behind a microphone. The second was an obsessive quest for perfection.

'He would always tape his shows and afterwards he would listen to them and back up on things,' says Julie Smith. 'One time he was telling a story on air which was really funny, but by the time he got to the punch-line it had fizzled out and it didn't work. Afterwards I saw him listening to this story on his own, over and over, and he seemed really down. He was saying to me, "Why is that not funny? Why? Why?" I told him it had taken too long to get to the punch-line, and he took a mental note. He was always looking for people to assess his performance.'

Julie is indebted to Chris for helping her to find a foothold in radio. When they first met she was in her A-Level year and helping out as a volunteer on Piccadilly's 'care-line'. He tipped her off about a vacancy in the radio station's library, and she later joined him as part of Grundy's breakfast show team.

'Chris was sort of Tim's PA and I was a smaller PA,' she says. 'I learned a lot from Chris. He was very open with me. He would say, "That's a pile of crap" if he didn't rate something. But I didn't mind that.'

She began sharing a flat with Evans's producer-friend Chris

Whatmogh and another pal, Barry Joseph, and he would give her lifts in 'Snowy' the Skoda, en route to and from Sara's house in Cheadle Heath. Sometimes he would stop off for coffee, or the group would go out on the town, and for a while Julie became one of his very few confidantes.

'Half the people thought he was funny and half thought he was an arrogant wee shit,' she says. Julie came in the former category. 'Chris is the only person who has ever said to me that they were going to be rich and famous, and done it. He said it to me one day and I just laughed at him. He was confident, yes, but not arrogant. One thing about him is that he would never profess to be good at something he's not good at. So he would never claim to be great at, say, football. But if he was genuinely good at something he would be very up-front and say: "Here, I'm good at that, let me have a go."'

Julie describes Chris as 'a guy's guy' – though, back then, he was 'not a big drinker'. Laddish misfortune appeared to follow him around, however. 'I remember when his car broke down and we had to tow it back to Warrington in Sara's Nova. You know you're supposed to keep the tow-rope tight? Well, when we got there, after we'd safely got all the way from Manchester, the rope slackened then jerked tight, and it pulled his bumper right off.'

Looking back on those days with fondness, she says: 'He owes me a fortune in crisps and petrol, but he was always kind to me. I don't think he means to piss people off like he does. I think he likes to think he can cope on his own. I mean, he can need people, but he doesn't want to appear to need people too much. They can contribute to his life – that's okay. But he doesn't want to seem to need anybody. I don't know enough about his childhood to know why this is. Chris told me his father was dead, but only because I asked. He didn't volunteer the information. He thought a lot about his mum. She was the most important thing in his life. I just knew that, from the way he met her and talked about her. There were flowers on Mother's Day, he went shopping for her, phoned her. I thought he was quite unusually considerate to his mum compared with the average twenty-year-old.'

Although his opinion of Evans has been tarnished by experience, Tim Grundy also clearly enjoyed working with him and saw admirable qualities.

'I still have happy, nice memories about Chris. We really did have a laugh. We were having extreme highs and you can't have those without extreme lows.'

One of the extreme highs for which Grundy is indebted to Chris came when White And Two Sugars stitched up Mick Middles, a *Manchester Evening News* rock journalist. According to Grundy, Middles began gunning for Piccadilly Radio during a difficult period for the station.

'Some of the attacks were quite personal and I think some must have been aimed at me. Anyway, I decided he was a bit of a shit and I would teach him a lesson. Chris was only too happy to help. He and I went into a corner and wrote a complete pack of lies. We decided Chris would pose as a member of a fictitious group trying to get an article in the *Evening News*, and we'd see just how much Mick Middles knew about rock music.

'Chris phoned Middles and said he was a friend of "Barry from *Simply Red*", and that he'd been performing at a gig on Tuesday night at the Ritz. Everyone knows that there's no Barry in *Simply Red* and that Tuesday night at the Ritz was wrestling night. But Chris was brilliant. He said he had performed at such and such, and there was no such and such. He said the gig got rave reviews and had Mick heard of them? Did he enjoy their music? Chris ran through this script and this poor bloody journalist absolutely lampooned himself because he said, "Oh, yeah – I've seen you. I know who you are", and all this business.

'It was recorded, but as he hadn't been told it was being taped we couldn't run it. So we took a transcript and read it on air, with Chris playing himself and me playing Middles. Ten minutes before we did it, which was 8.20 a.m. – peak listening time – we said if anyone knew Mick Middles to tell him to turn the radio on. And we completely screwed this guy into the ground.'

By putting one over Piccadilly's arch-rivals at the *Evening*

News Chris may have endeared himself to the radio station's management. If so, he wasn't perceived to be a good company man for long. The honeymoon ended at Mike Gates's leaving party. Gates departed abruptly over bitter differences with the station boss Mike Briscoe. He planned to use his out-of-court dismissal settlement to start afresh in Finland, but before he left the country Chris hosted and arranged a special 'do'. Evans not only insisted on acting as DJ but, remembering how his old friend loved jamming on the electric guitar, he hired one for him to play on his big night.

'It was marvellous, a real example of his generosity,' says Gates.

Evans, however, was evidently just as interested in making fun of Piccadilly's enforced 'generosity' towards the sacked Gates. Mike Briscoe had been invited, and with the festivities in full swing, Evans asked for silence.

'He said he'd just like to congratulate me for screwing some money out of the company, or words to that effect,' says Gates. Evans's reward for showing such public loyalty to a pal – or disloyalty to the company, depending on one's viewpoint – was to be hauled into Briscoe's office the following day and informed that his salary would be halved.

'He wasn't bothered at all,' says Gates, marvelling at his old friend's devil-may-care attitude. 'He just said, sort of, "Fine", and carried on.'

On the surface, it was a supremely self-sacrificial gesture, but it was one, perhaps, that he could well afford to make. Unknown to Gates, Briscoe and the Manchester crowd, Chris had already consigned Piccadilly Radio to the past.

CHAPTER TWELVE

Whizzkids generate their own mythology. Unlike other beings, they rarely achieve anything by getting lucky, or having a well-placed contact, or happening to be in the right place at just the right time. Whizzkids create their own luck and they don't need anyone's help. If they appear perfectly positioned to capitalize on a big break, then it's their own finely-tuned antennae that have positioned them there.

But does it really work like that?

For every Branson or Barrymore there are others of equal talent who never emerge from the shadows, for no reason other than that is what destiny dictates. How, then, did the fates conspire to assist Chris Evans?

Accepted wisdom holds that Evans's rise to the top happened in three easy stages, roughly as follows: 1) Misunderstood Genius cracks hilarious-but-risqué joke on air, gets threatened with sack and is so supremely confident of ultimate success that he tells boss to stuff job. 2) Misunderstood Genius is spirited away from The Sticks, materializes in London and gets discovered. 3) Misunderstood Genius's brilliance bursts forth, whereupon he achieves the wealth and fame he so clearly deserves.

As with all the best myths, there are elements of truth here. The strongest revolves around the on-air joke that cost Evans his job at Piccadilly. More than nine years have elapsed since he uttered the notorious words, so, unsurprisingly, the story has changed considerably in the telling. But Julie Smith was alongside Chris when the seminal incident occurred.

Evans was doing a 'swing-jock' shift because the action happened in the afternoon.

'Chris had been talking about a newspaper article in which a wealthy woman had left a fortune to a cat,' says Julie. 'He said he thought it was outrageous that she hadn't left it to a children's charity or something. Then there was another story on the radio news about cats being fed caviar. At this point Chris said he liked cats, too ... lightly grilled with garlic butter.

'Four cat-lovers phoned to complain and Mike Briscoe, the Programme Controller, called Chris during a break in the show for the 5 p.m. news. He said that if Chris continued to make jokes like that he wouldn't be able to use him any more. Chris was annoyed about being told what he could and couldn't say, but he was more angry that Briscoe hadn't waited until he had come off the air to make his point. He thought the interruption was unprofessional because it could have really ruined the show.

'I was in the record library, and he phoned me and asked me to get him *Aztec Camera*'s "How Men Are". They were one of his favourite bands and he said he wanted that to be the last song he ever played on the station.'

Julie knew better than to try and talk Chris round herself. She could tell from his tone that he was deadly serious about his intentions and so she dashed round to the newsroom to see the one person who, she thought, might just be able to persuade him to see sense: Sara Green. But the urbane newsreader – who had presumably just read the cat story on the news slot – waved her hand dismissively and declined to intervene.

'She just said, "Oh, he'll sort it out", and left it at that,' Julie says.

The next thing she knew, a misty-eyed Chris was heading towards Briscoe's adjacent office, mumbling: "If Mike Briscoe wants to see me, I'm going to see him."

'There was some heated conversation in the background,'

she says. 'He was arguing with Mike and he must have said, "Forget it", and he walked out. I remember having to get my bag, and I said, "Where are you going?" He said, "I'm leaving and I'm never coming back". He was really pissed off. He just walked out into the street."

Mike Briscoe's version of the saga varies slightly from Julie's. He recalls that Chris cracked his joke after a news item about a serious act of cruelty against a cat.

'Immediately after the news bulletin, with no jingles, no records or anything else, Chris Evans said, "Oh, I think that's terrible about the cat. I like cats. I like them lightly grilled on both sides." The phones at the station lit up with outraged animal-lovers complaining.'

Straight after the show, Briscoe says he summoned Evans for an explanation.

'I was expecting Chris to say, "Yes, fair enough, okay, I won't do it again." But for some reason he decided not to do that and he said that he would do what he liked on the programme; that I was being very silly and pompous about it all. And I said he couldn't do what he liked, and his response was, "Well, if I can't do what I like you can stuff your job, mate." With that he walked out of the office and I never saw him again.'

Despite the discrepancies, the story suggests that stage one of the accepted wisdom is substantially accurate. Yet just how spontaneous was Evans's show of defiance? Superficially he seemed to genuinely regret losing his position, for soon afterwards he met Julie Smith's sister and advised her: 'If you ever think of jacking your job in, think again. The excitement lasts five minutes.' Yet according to friends he had been desperate to hit London for quite some while and, when he stormed out of Briscoe's office, his removal plans may already have been well advanced.

Tim Grundy is adamant that 'he did not have a job to go to'. But, interestingly, he recalls, 'He came out of the meeting with Briscoe and said, "I've just told him he can stick his job. I'm going to London. I'm going to find my fame and fortune."'

Evans's own perspective on his departure, as related to Loyd Grossman in *The Sunday Times Magazine*, January 1994, runs as follows: 'I walked out thinking the world was my oyster and that I was really good. I got paid every third week. Left on a Wednesday and was due to get paid on a Thursday, but because I'd broken my contract they didn't pay me at all. And then the garage rang up and asked for my car back. So literally, within twenty-four hours of walking out on one of the biggest radio stations in Britain I had no money and no car. I was a twenty-year-old [he was actually twenty-one] totally unemployable, arrogant little shit. I'd blown it in a big way.'

Grundy's reaction to the incident is a measure of the esteem in which he then held Chris.

'I think I must have gone to Briscoe and said, "Don't let him go, he's good." Briscoe said, "He's not that good. He's just told me he's the best jock on the station. What do you think about that?" Well, that was an insult to me because I was the breakfast-show DJ. I said, "Well, okay, a little over the top, but he's a good jock."'

Briscoe – who was later succeeded by Grundy as Programme Controller – was not to be swayed and, as Evans wouldn't eat humble pie, the turbulent relationship between Piccadilly Radio and Chris Evans was over.

Why, then, did Chris feel sufficiently brave to walk out on the job of his dreams? Interviewing him for the July 1997 issue of *Vogue*, broadcaster and journalist Mariella Frostrup posed this same question to her friend.

'I just don't have any fear,' he told her. 'Danny Baker says my emotions are fireproof and when you lose your dad they just are.'

Until this point in their conversation, Evans's comments about his childhood had been 'startlingly brief'. His blockage temporarily removed, however, it was as if he is picking up the thread of interviews given years earlier.

'When someone you love dies you think, fuckin' hell, don't want any of that; better get on with it; didn't realize it could happen,' he told Frostrup. 'And so you run and run and run, looking backwards to make sure you're getting further away, and then, if you're not careful, you've run so fast that you realize that you're running away from his death, but towards your own.'

If this loss-induced lack of fear had spurred him to jump off Piccadilly Radio, then at least he had a reliable safety net: his loyal and talented friend Andy Bird. Former Piccadilly producer 'Big Bird' had just landed a producer's slot with a Richard Branson-backed company called Radio Radio, then newly formed to pioneer an innovative concept in British broadcasting. As the Prince of Darkness knew only too well, most regional stations had pitifully low night-time/early morning ratings. Advertising revenue was minimal in the small hours and they could ill afford to pay in-house DJs to cover the shift. By offering a syndicated service fronted by big-name presenters like Jonathan Ross, Ruby Wax, Bob 'Bomber' Harris and the veteran Johnnie Walker, Radio Radio aimed to bridge the gap. When Evans heard about it from Andy he instantly began to see the possibilities. Impressing influential names like Ross and Wax might save him years of fruitless toil. If he worked with one of them he could hot-wire his way straight to the top.

Ian Daley offers another indication that Chris had staked out his future even before the Briscoe debacle. Daley continued to provide Evans with occasional through-the-night company at Piccadilly until shortly before his departure for London. Towards the end, he says, 'Chris kept saying he didn't want to do the show any more – he had made up his mind'.

Daley, who was still struggling to make a few quid in Warrington's pubs, found this hard to believe. 'I told him he was fucking barmy, that he should at least be leaving if someone had offered you a better job with a different radio station.' Evans hadn't accepted the advice. 'He must have thought he had something to go to. He never let on to me, but he wasn't stupid, and he wouldn't have quit Piccadilly if he wasn't pretty sure how it would all work out.'

To support his theory, Daley relates a forgotten incident which, because much of Piccadilly's archive material was lost during its move to new offices, can not be dated. One night, he says, Evans announced to his small cult of prisoners and shift-workers that he was hosting his very last show.

'He said he was going to have a party to celebrate and he invited everyone to come down to Piccadilly and join in. He said anybody who turned up in their nightdress or pyjamas, carrying a bottle of champagne or decent wine, would be allowed in. He probably could have got battered . . . there was only one security guard on, and he was probably risking his job as well,' says Daley. 'Before you knew it, there were maybe twenty-five people outside, some really nice women in nice short-cut nighties. This one guy had a crate of champagne, so he lets him in and we all sat round the studio getting pissed. Well, Chris didn't get pissed because he was driving – he's like that, Chris.'

The man with the champagne, he says, owned caravans near Manchester Airport, and after the show the party continued there. 'I buggered off to this girl's flat and Chris pissed off home. I didn't see him for a day and a half after that. I was stuck in Manchester because I didn't have a car. Eventually I got through to him on the phone and he came to pick me up.'

Evans set foot inside the Piccadilly studios one last time before he hit the southbound motorway. A few days after storming out on Briscoe he returned to take Julie Smith to lunch. Tactful for once, he suggested they meet outside. But shortly before the rendezvous Julie collapsed with a searing pain in her lower abdomen. An ambulance was called and, as she lay waiting, she glanced up at the closed-circuit TV monitor and spotted Chris in reception.

'I told them I wanted him to be with me and they brought him through. There was all this muttering, "But, er, he's just been sacked", but Chris didn't care. He comforted me and went with me in the ambulance to hospital, and the next day he came back and held my hand while they took a blood sample. He may be ambitious and know what he wants, but the way he behaved that day shows what a good, considerate person he is.'

Shortly before heading for London's bright lights, Chris also extended a philanthropic hand towards Daley. Or rather, that's how it seemed at the time. Having failed to persuade his friend to join him in London, he gave him a parting gift – his old Dacia.

'He said he was going to better and brighter things and asked if I was coming,' says Daley. 'I said I couldn't because I couldn't leave my kid, and all that. He just said, "Well, I'm going, so there's the keys to my car – you can have them because I won't be needing them any more."'

Daley was deeply touched by this gesture. Until he went to the rear of 285 Lovely Lane to take possession of his new vehicle. Never in the best condition, it had been completely wrecked by local children. The wheels had gone, the seats were ripped to shreds, the windows smashed. In short, it was valueless.

Fond as he had been of his fawny-brown Dacia, Chris is unlikely to have given it a second thought. Old cars, old friends, old jobs, old memories were all sent for scrap. In any cast, the tasteful headquarters of Radio Radio was not the sort of place to arrive in a shoddy Eastern Bloc car. Situated on the first floor of an elegant building in Rathbone Place, just off Oxford Street in the heart of west-end London, its occupants were in the vanguard of late-eighties chic. When Chris turned up there for his interview in early 1988, a month after the company had been formed, even he appeared a little subdued.

'He was a very polite young man,' recalls Liverpudlian Rob Jones, a one-time Radio Luxembourg DJ who became Radio Radio's managing director. 'He was obviously bright and sparky, but he didn't put his feet on the table and say, "Give me a job!" Andy Bird told me he had just been fired by Mike Briscoe but I wasn't worried. It all sounded fairly innocuous. Besides, I knew Briscoe because he was subscribing to our service – a BBC type of man. Andy said Chris was a real talent and that we could get him cheap, and I really liked him.'

Chris may have come cheap by Radio Radio standards, but the salary on offer, around £18,000, was about double the pittance he had been paid at Piccadilly. Jones invited him to help produce Jonathan Ross and, although Chris badly wanted to continue presenting, he knew he would have to bide his time. This was an opportunity not to be spurned. Mere mortal DJs are not afforded the luxury of a producer. They are simply handed a play-list and a set of instructions by the controller, and left to fend for themselves. Ross, then already acclaimed for his Friday night Channel 4 chat-show *The Last Resort*, came into an altogether different category.

'He was a very big catch and very much the thrust of how we were going to market the service,' says Jones. 'Chris was out of work, so he wanted to start as soon as possible, and he did a brilliant job. He came up with some great ideas. A normal DJ might say, for example, "Right, let's have the request spot", but Chris would invent a catchy name for it, like the Hot Pants Spot. He'd say, "If you're out of breath at the moment call us now . . ." It doesn't sound much, but there was a double-entendre. It would be, "Why are you out of breath?" And he would be putting these words into Jonathan's mouth.'

Although Ross is a more measured and sophisticated act than Chris now aspires to be, he was generally enthused by his assistant's zany ideas. But once, when Evans went over the top, Ross refused to play along.

'"No, Chris!" he snapped. "That's way too Mallett!"'

Evans was not yet sufficiently well-established to bare his teeth publicly, but inside he was seething. With one crisply-delivered put-down Ross had not only belittled his latest wheeze; he had, by implication, accused him of imitating Timmy. Insults always hurt far more when they carry a grain of truth. The wounded Evans stormed off to find Rob Jones and began to browbeat his boss.

'"Jonathan's only saying no because he can't pull it off," he said petulantly. "I can pull it off. Come on! What do you think, Rob?"'

Jones tried to appease him, but he continued: '"Put me on! I can make it work!"'

Jones was sympathetic but unmoved. 'I saw Chris's frustrations. He thought he could be a better presenter than Ross straightaway, and he was nagging to be given his chance the whole time. My claim to fame is that I said he would never make a presenter. He was very Manchester at the time, much more so than he is now, and as we were a national service putting on a blatantly regional guy would have brought complaints from the subscribers. And in places like Newcastle and Birmingham they'd be going, "Who is he?" The people we had were already nationally known names. I said, "You're a much better producer than you would be a presenter. He was excellent. As a person I don't like him all that much, but professionally he's almost a genius. He takes a very simple idea and make it much bigger and more exciting. And yet he's reinventing the same set of ideas the whole time.'

His route to the national airwaves temporarily impeded, Chris set about removing the interference. According to Grundy, who was kept updated on his former coffee boy's progress, on arriving in London he temporarily moved in with 'Big Bird'.

'Andy took him under his wing and they started planning his future. They were never apart.'

Evans's first smart move, says Grundy, was to 'target' Jonathan Ross in the most transparent fashion.

'Chris was determined to achieve success and he saw Ross as his meal ticket and went for it big style. He didn't ever admit that he was shamelessly getting close to him, but it was pretty easy to spot because he never stopped talking about the man. He was totally besotted by him.'

Ross was by then sailing in uncharted waters of television presentation technique and when Chris moved into TV he would set a similar course.

'Jonathan was ad-libbing and didn't use an ear-piece or an auto-cue,' says Grundy. 'Chris doesn't use an ear-piece or an auto-cue, either. Chris has "idiot-boards" everywhere [placards held up, in full view of the camera, with instructions on]. Jonathan does exactly the same. There was hero-worship going on there.'

This 'cuddling up to Jonathan' was, by some accounts, carried out to faintly ludicrous proportions. Evans began frequenting the same haunts as Ross. Perhaps unconsciously, he affected some of Ross's phrases and mannerisms. Much later, the two men found themselves members of the same exclusive North London health club, the Lingfield – although an employee recalls that Evans joined first. In the early eighties, Ross lived in north London's Chalk Farm before moving to the more affluent Southend Green, on the fringes of Hampstead. Was it purely coincidence that when Chris began searching for lodgings he staked out his territory within striking distance of that area? Not at all, in the opinion of Grundy, who says he 'moved within a hundred yards of where Jonathan Ross lived'.

In the opinion of another anonymous source close to Evans around that period: 'When Chris is impressed by someone he is totally taken over by them and takes on their persona. I remember once, when he was reading a book about Einstein, the author said that Einstein drank black coffee. Up to that point Chris usually drank tea. But from then on he started drinking black coffee.'

From a professional standpoint, Ross was the most important contact Chris made at Radio Radio. But on a personal level, by far his most notable new acquaintance was the station's deceptively austere-looking traffic manager, Carol Deirdre McGiffin. Although Carol wore glasses and concealed her impressive figure beneath dark, rollneck sweaters and sober skirts, after work at the pub she could behave outlandishly. Rob Jones recalls how his first encounter with her caused him totally unjustified marital strife. Although there was never any hint of romance between them, she decided to get him into trouble by daubing lipstick marks below the waistband of his light-coloured trousers.

'Stupidly I got home really late that night and hid the trousers from my missus 'cos I was a bit pissed. I thought,

"God, how will I explain that?" She found them and I got a call at work the next day . . .'

The other thing that happened to Carol after a drink or two was that her exhibitionist streak emerged. Without any warning, the outwardly demure businessman's daughter from Kent would matter-of-factly push up her jumper and bra and expose her not inconsiderable breasts to stunned onlookers. She reserved her most talked-about performance for a Christmas party attended by Richard Branson. Then working for the Music Box television station, part-owned by Virgin, she stripped down to her knickers, leaped onto a table, and persuaded Branson to dance with her.

'A couple of drinks in her and she'd strip in the office,' said a source who worked with Carol at Radio Radio. 'I've met other girls who do this. The reaction of guys is fairly spectacular. She has the confidence to do it because she knows she looks okay. It wasn't an everyday experience, but if there was a good drinking session going on, Carol would flash her tits.'

Chris's own preoccupation with nakedness had first surfaced in his days at Boteler Grammar School. To suggest that Chris and Carol somehow recognized one another as kindred spirits could be stretching the bounds of fantasy. Nonetheless, from the day they first noticed one another at Radio Radio there was a tangible spark between them.

'It was an open-plan office and we were having a programme meeting – an ideas exchange,' says Rob Jones. 'There would have been the Programme Controller, Chris Vesey [now at Classic-FM], Andy Bird, the Head of Music, Phil Ward-Large, John Revell [then a producer and later to become an integral part of Chris's life], my PA Alison, myself and Chris.

'Carol was in the corner earwigging the meeting, but not part of it. She hadn't much to do: it was her job to schedule any adverts that came in but at that time there weren't very many.'

Evans, he says, was behaving in his usual manner – loud and highly amusing – and Carol, who had never encountered anyone so uninhibitedly funny before, was 'creased up'. Though Carol, then twenty-eight, was six years older than Chris, when Rob Jones glanced across at her desk he foresaw the future. Her eyes were twinkling, and he smiles when he says, 'Knowing her, I thought, "Look out, look out." She's a brilliant personality – infectious. She was sitting there sparking off him like fuck. He was quite cool with her to begin with because I think you are if you know you've sparked someone's interest. You stay cool, above it . . . keep firing and firing, with no eye contact.'

Carol herself is less effusive, but she, too, acknowledges the significance of that encounter.

'Actually it wasn't the first time we had seen each other,' she says. 'We sort of met briefly when Chris came down from Manchester the previous year to do some work for Music Box. But, yes, he was very funny and he did get me laughing. We became friends from then on.'

The bond was cemented over after-work drinks with colleagues at the Bricklayer's Arms, which became Radio Radio's office pub. Colleagues grew increasingly accustomed to seeing them giggling together, oblivious to the rest of the assembled company.

During their chats, Carol may have told Chris all about the drama that had dominated her life earlier that year – if he hadn't already read about it in the papers, that is. An article in the now-defunct *Today* newspaper had insinuated that she had been 'comforting' Anne Diamond's husband Mike Hollingsworth, for whom Carol worked as a personal assistant, when their marriage hit the rocks. Both Hollingsworth and Carol vehemently denied that their relationship was anything more than professional. *Today* later paid an out of court damages settlement. Carol's share is estimated to have been £20,000 to £30,000.

Such intrigue may have enhanced Carol's allure, but it was her blunt, feisty character that really impressed Chris.

'I know definitely what he saw in her – and certainly later on – was an honesty,' says Jones. 'I mean, she couldn't give a fuck. You couldn't meet anyone less sycophantic than

Carol. She wouldn't care. She would say to God Almighty, "Listen, I think you got part of the Creation wrong." And I think Chris respected that and thought he would get an honest answer out of her. She would say what she really thought.'

In the back end of 1988, however, Chris did not appear to be looking for another girlfriend. He was still apparently enraptured with Sara Green and she with him. In order to stay together, as soon as the opportunity presented itself, she quit Piccadilly to join him in London. She was snapped up by Greater London Radio, the BBC's new station for the capital, and the couple found a one-bedroomed flat off Camden Road. Although the rent was about £120 a week – extortionate by Manchester standards – by pooling resources they were comfortably off. Both worked long hours, and spare time was spent exploring their new patch. Chris loved Camden because, like his own brain, it never seemed to switch off. On Saturday mornings he would drag Sara up at the crack of dawn and urge her to join him bargain-hunting at London's most happening market. The enormous variety of ethnic cafes, restaurants and delicatessens stirred his hitherto latent interest in food. If they were eating in, Chris would surprise Sara by arriving back at the flat with some exotic new vegetable to cook.

'Hey look!,' he would exclaim, like an over-excited schoolboy, 'We've got to try this!'

Sara didn't like to burst his bubble by telling him that she already had.

Evenings were often spent on the sofa, with Chris eager to check out the plethora of independent radio outfits now jostling for attention in London. But there was so much to tempt him out: unusual movies, stand-up comedy bars, pubs filled with intriguing faces. Sometimes, too, Chris and Sara would venture beyond their price-range. Striding hand in hand up Haverstock Hill and entering the serenity of Belsize Park and Hampstead, they were reminded of the material rewards that conquering their respective fields could bring.

Orford must have seemed like a distant mirage. Chris maintained regular telephone contact with his mother but his visits were becoming increasingly rare. When he did return he could barely bring himself to see his friends for a few minutes, and then it appeared to them that he was only out to impress. Ian Daley recalls how Chris came round to his house and began strumming the guitar.

'He knew all these fancy new chords. He must have been hanging about with musicians.'

Chris called on Dave Whittaker twice.

'The first time he wanted me to help him buy a second-hand Spitfire but I couldn't go, so he left,' he says. 'Then a couple of months later he turned up with his car-boot full of promo-records that hadn't been released. Things like Elvis Costello's 'Spike', *The Marquee* album, and one by Sam Brown. He said I could have them all. He had obviously got them free but it was a nice gesture.'

After months without contact, Evans also phoned Mike Hollington to suggested a game of squash. But when he arrived at his old mate's house and found Hollington momentarily preoccupied with builders he shot off without saying goodbye.

And what of his daughter, Jade? When she was about six months old, Alison decided to have her christened. On one of their regular visits to 'Nana's' in Greenwood Crescent, she asked Minnie for Chris's phone number and called him to inquire whether he would be attending.

'He said he couldn't because he hadn't got the time,' says Alison. 'I just said, "Fine", and left it.'

The service, at the Church of the Transfiguration in Birchwood, near Warrington, went ahead without him, but at least Minnie and his sister Diane were there to represent the Evans family.

'I would have liked him to come,' says Alison. 'His daughter was being christened and it wasn't as if we weren't on speaking terms. But I think his mum was more upset than me. She thought he should have made the effort.'

Susie Gates says that around this time Chris and Alison turned up in Ainsworth, pretending they had got back together.

'I said, "How lovely", and gave them both a hug. Then they burst out laughing and it wasn't true.' But eventually, she says, the conversation took on a more serious tone. 'Alison said that she wouldn't let Chris see Jade because he promised her everything and then she never saw him. Alison could see where it would go if he only saw Jade now and again. She thought it was better if he didn't see her at all.'

Alison says Chris saw Jade for the last time when she was eight or nine months old.

'He came up and took us out to Chester for a day. I felt that I had to go with him when he took Jade out because I was afraid he would lose her! We went round the shops, had some tea, had a laugh, but he never came again. He used to phone now and then, and he always asked how Jade was, but it was all done out of duty.'

Chris returned to his former landlady's house just once more, to introduce her to his latest friend, the television journalist Fiona Foster, then a rising star in London and now with CNN in Atlanta. There was no mention of Alison or Jade, and Susie Gates thought that Chris's life had altered beyond all recognition. But for one incident.

'He and this girl left the car in the car-park,' says Susie, 'and just when they were returning to it, it blew up. Chris had parked it above a manhole cover and the gas underground had exploded. I couldn't help thinking that with Chris, some things will never change.'

CHAPTER THIRTEEN

In October 1988, just a few months after Radio Radio rescued Chris's career, he was moving onwards – if not immediately upwards – again. Before he departed, however, one more stroke of good fortune befell him. In the not-too-distant future it would radically alter his status, from well-paid hired-gun to independent programme-maker and multi-millionaire.

Chris's break came when Radio Radio's managing director Rob Jones announced that the fledgling service needed a promotional quiz or competition. Something offbeat and, if possible, original, that would seduce listeners into staying tuned late into the night. Jones convened a brainstorming session, and as suggestions were kicked around, he says, someone mentioned a novel concept that they'd heard on an American radio station. Contestants turned up at the studios with packed suitcases, and the winner immediately jetted off on a free holiday. The idea, though it was enthusiastically received, did not materialize on Radio Radio, largely through lack of sponsorship. But Evans must have stored it away in his memory bank, marked Do Not Delete. Three years later he resurrected it as the Channel 4 quiz show *Don't Forget Your Toothbrush*, the rights for which were subsequently sold in more than twenty countries.

'In the meeting were John Revell, Andy Bird, Chris Evans,

myself, my PA, Carol McGiffin and Chris Vesey,' says Jones. 'I have a feeling that it was me that raised the suitcase idea, but I wouldn't swear to it.'

Evans evidently holds a different memory, because shortly after receiving the first royalties for *Toothbrush* it was not Jones but Revell who found himself a substantial beneficiary.

'I heard that for some reason, one Friday afternoon, Chris walked into Virgin – where Revell was by then joint programme controller – and slapped a cheque for £150,000 on his desk. It was buttons compared to what he was getting for *Toothbrush* but that was his pay-off to John. I think he was wise because a few others of us might have said, "Hang on. If there's any rights going, all of us sat down and ripped that idea off." I could have claimed it – and I've thought about it to this day . . .'

Jones is just as irked by the manner of Chris's parting from Radio Radio.

Having just been appointed to launch the BBC's Greater London Radio, on 1458-AM, its ambitious young bosses Matthew Bannister and Trevor Dann were scouting for fresh, affordable young talent. Jones knew several of his staff had been head-hunted, and, believing Evans to be among them, he confronted him with the rumour.

'I may even have given him a pay-rise that day,' he says. 'I may have said to him, "I really value you, here's £21,000 or £22,000". I wanted to keep him, definitely.'

Evans's response, he says, was emphatic.

'He looked me in the eye and said, "No. Swear to God, I'm not leaving." It was a bare-faced lie'.

At 5 p.m. that day, just hours after attending a potentially sensitive future ideas meeting, Chris was on his way to GLR. Evans, Jones says, didn't even have the decency to tell him personally that he had changed his mind. He left that to Bird.

If Piccadilly Radio was Chris's kindergarten and Radio Radio his reform school, then GLR was his finishing academy. The work he produced there, he opined to Bryan Appleyard of *The Sunday Times Magazine* in June 1997, was 'probably the best thing I've ever done ... legendary'. Moreover, as it was broadcast in London rather than Manchester, it would bring him to the notice of influential ears.

For the moment, however, he didn't reach any ears at all. When the station began transmission, Evans's job was to produce another precocious young talent, Emma Freud – the cultivated daughter of Clement Freud and great grand-daughter of Sigmund – whose weekday show was broadcast from 10 a.m. until twelve noon. Confronted with Chris Evans from Orford, Emma must have thought Bannister was pulling some sort of joke. But any amusement soon evaporated. With Evans, it became clear, her superior social pedigree and her growing reputation as a media ingénue counted for nothing. He had been grafting in radio studios for six years and he knew his way around as well as most and far better than a callow newcomer like her. He also wanted her job. When she made the slightest mistake he would pick up on it and if she really screwed up he mocked her, or bawled her out. He may have been the underling and she the star-apparent, but it was Emma who was forced to sharpen up her act; Emma who wilted and, at least once, wept in the face of Chris's demands. Today she is magnanimous enough to recognize that his brusqueness and originality brought the best out of her.

'One of Chris's scams was to get Emma to work behind reception at GLR on Secretary of the Year Day,' recalls Miles Mendoza, still a producer and researcher at the station. 'He then phoned in, posing as a difficult listener and tested her out. He really had her going, and it made for great radio.'

Bannister evidently admired his style, for in the spring of 1989 he acceded to Chris's constant nagging and put him where he most wanted to be: behind the microphone. He was given a Saturday afternoon berth in place of the veteran Andy Peebles, who did a sports show.

'It wasn't particularly popular at first because people were expecting 'Smashie and Nicey' presentation with sports results, and there was Chris taking the piss out of football,' says Mendoza. 'About three or four months after that Dave

Pearce left for Kiss-FM, which created a gap on weekday evenings, so Chris moved to that. At the same time he landed a Saturday morning show.'

The two slots demonstrated Evans's versatility, for they could scarcely have been more different. He titled his Monday to Thursday show 'Interference' and aimed it at a far younger audience than GLR's intended chief target group, aged twenty-five to forty-five. But while the music was un-ashamedly mainstream pop – Jason Donovan, Kylie Minogue, *Bros*, Betty Boo – the presentation was light-years ahead of everything in town. Borrowing heavily from Mallett, and responding to the soaring national interest in environmental issues, Evans set his show in an imaginary greenhouse. To make it as lifelike as possible, he bought three or four dozen huge green plants, and each evening he and his volunteers would ferry them from his office to the studio. The only light came from an angle-poised desk lamp, and the central heating was switched to maximum temperature. When Chris exploded onto the airwaves, exclaiming, 'Hi! I'm Chris Evans and you're listening to Interference, live from the greenhouse,' sweat would already be cascading down his back.

The greenhouse was inhabited by two archetypal Austra-lian girls, dubbed Skippy and Charlene. And, since real green-houses have insects, in best Timmy tradition, Chris invented two: Filey Flea and Fergie Flea. In a throw-back to Nobby No-Level, Fergie was played by a young ad salesman named Andy Davies, who had regularly phoned in to Emma Freud's show, and was keen to break into radio.

'We used speeded-up voices and fought all the time, as radio fleas do,' laughs Davies, who now edits Jack Docherty's Channel 5 chat-show. 'A lot of Chris's best ideas were spawned at GLR, and it was great fun.'

In time, Andy Davies was to become the latest in a long line of loyal best friends: a line that stretched back through Ian Daley and Dave Whittaker to Trevor Palin, Mike Gates, all the way to Johnny Hoyles and Glynn Povey. When Chris and Sara split up it was Davies with whom he would share a flat. And later, when Evans moved in with Carol McGiffin, it was Andy who would offer him shelter whenever they rowed.

But before Davies, Chris found another stop-gap companion in Vince Rogers, then a twenty-eight-year-old news reporter at the station. Rogers was amusing, discreet and utterly reliable – the sort Chris called on when the central heating broke down at home. Although they were often together, however, their friendship remained predictably superficial.

'I remember him telling me that he sent his mother money, but he didn't talk about his family background,' says Rogers, who now covers whimsical stories for GLR. 'He never reminisced; it just wasn't his style to talk about family or childhood background.'

Running, running, always running.

So what had Vince and Chris talked about?

'Work, usually. He had the Saturday afternoon programme, and I would help out. We were always working out what to do next. Like once, when the FA Cup Final was on at Wembley, the joke was that I couldn't get in. He had me there, holding my mike to the stadium wall so you could hear the crowd.'

As Chris's star rose, so Rogers found it more wearying to be around him.

'At first we were quite chummy, but then he got a bit much for me. He's one of these people who's a presenter permanently, not just when he's on TV or the radio. He's kind of 'on' all the time, which is great when you employ him as a presenter, because all you have to do is stick him in front of the cameras and away you go. But some of us are more shy and introvert, and can't handle it that well. He always wanted to be the centre of attention in restaurants. I preferred being quieter. He would start being loud and very, very extrovert.'

The denouement almost inevitably involved a car.

'I was living at Shepherd's Bush and he needed to get home late one night and couldn't afford a taxi,' says Rogers. 'I happened to have two old bangers and told him to take the

Mini. It was red and C-registered, a 1966 model. He borrowed it and I never saw it again. He lost it.'

Lost it? Spanners in the engine and gas-main explosions were conceivable, but surely even Chris was incapable of losing a car?

'It was a Friday night and the next day he went somewhere up Wembley way – this is what he told me. And something happened like the car got clamped; so he paid to have the clamp removed and went back and found that someone had nicked the wheels. And it was eventually just towed away by the council. He always just seemed to get into trouble. He was incredibly accident prone. He never paid me for the car and I was a bit angry at the time. Mind you, he paid the fine, which was good of him.'

Rogers began to find less stressful ways of passing the weekend, but there were always others eager to fill the breach.

'Usually, when people have ginger hair, you think, "Yuck! Ginger hair",' says Carol McGiffin. 'But Chris charms people in the most amazing way and they become addicted to him. And once addicted, they can't let go. Chris doesn't do this deliberately. It's just that he has this quality which makes people want to be around him. People want to be in his gang because he appears to be having the best time ever.'

Among those who joined his gang at GLR was Holly Samos, later to be one of Chris's girlfriends and to achieve quasi-celebrity status as 'Holly Hotlips', one of Chris's back-up team on the Radio One breakfast show. Holly, who helped out on Interference, shared a flat with another of the charmed circle, a researcher on Interference named Claire Houghton. Claire, known at the time as Lady Huge – not because she was obese but because 'huge' was a show buzz-word – was co-opted on to the *Toothbrush* production team. Her previous flatmate was best friends with Julie Smith from Piccadilly. And then there was Duncan Gray – the first researcher to brave the giant plants and talking fleas in Chris's sweltering greenhouse – who became a leading producer and popped up, toast-like, on *The Big Breakfast*. And so the wheels rolled on. In Chris's intrigue-filled kingdom all the courtiers are interconnected, however tenuously. Perhaps they were once colleagues; perhaps they were lovers; perhaps they can only be linked by rumour or gossip. Instinctively, Evans knew how to manipulate this network to his best advantage; how to push the right buttons and pull the right strings. It was an intoxicating departure from his brutalized childhood. Who would dare to punch him to the pavement and urinate on him now?

His sphere of influence was strengthened significantly with the success of his GLR Saturday morning programme, which he called Round At Chris's. Regarded by many fans as his finest broadcasting achievement, at the outset its ratings were so low that they barely touched the bottom of the scale. By the time he left, however, in April 1993, it was among the three most popular programmes on the station and had seen off practically all the opposition throughout London. Its success came gradually and was largely down to word-of-mouth.

'For the first year or so Chris was putting most of his energy into Interference,' says Miles Mendoza, 'but when Round At Chris's took off it became a cult thing. Anyone who lived in the capital and was under thirty was likely to be collared by their mates and told that they had to listen to this weirdo on GLR because he was totally original and utterly mad.'

Round At Chris's can be viewed as the control freak's ultimate dream. Aiming to recreate the sort of post-party atmosphere that might have been found in, say, Dave Whittaker's Brighton Street sitting room, Evans invited listeners to drop in to the studio and act as raucous accessories. Soon a hard-core of about two dozen were spending every Saturday morning round at Chris's, in reality a spartan ground-floor studio on the Marylebone Road. Then, when the audience grew to fifty or so, an overflow room had to be used, where latecomers watched the show on a screen. Surveying them all from behind his desk, the twenty-three-year-old Evans – chubby-cheeked and partial to bright yellow sweaters – was in his element. An outcast misfit in Orford, now *he* could decree who was 'in'.

He would play 'lookalikes' with them: 'spotting' Dustin Hoffman or Jennifer Saunders in amongst the faces. His manner was sufficiently cordial to seduce them into believing that they were privileged members of his club. But, at the same time, they were never permitted to attain the degree of familiarity to which they may have aspired.

One of the group, Colin the Punk, became a lackey in Chris's old Piccadilly image, and was named – what else? – White And Two Sugars. Only Carol McGiffin, not yet his lover but given the esteemed role of reading the show's 'What's On?' listings, and Andy Davies, by now Chris's rookie producer, were genuine friends. Chris apparently found this social dynamic so agreeable, even intoxicating, that he has replicated it ever since. Fast forward to the mid-nineties, substitute Carol for current girlfriend Suzi Aplin and Andy for current producer Will Macdonald, and the GLR studio becomes the exclusive bar on the set of *TFI Friday* in the Riverside Studios, Hammersmith.

'He presents the show from that bar – and who controls the bar?' says one former close friend. 'I'm sure a psychologist would say he's created this inner sanctum, which only he can let people into. And all the hoi-polloi are left downstairs, watching the band. He has this pathological need to surround himself with an audience all the time. He has to be the centre, the focus of all attention.'

Among Chris's Saturday morning set was Nicky Putt, who commuted fifteen miles from Carshalton, Surrey, for more than a year, but was always in her studio seat well before 10 a.m. No matter that she came from Carshalton, one day Chris christened her Nicky The Knicker Seller from Sutton and that was her name from then on.

'It was just a great laugh – better than vegetating in bed at the weekend,' she says. 'You felt a sort of belonging. Chris would say anything on the air to get a laugh in those days. He just didn't care. But he was very loyal to his audience. When a TV crew came to film him one day they wanted their own selected audience, and he was very scathing, very pissed off. I mean, what other DJ would let anyone in there, off the street? After the show he would talk to us and we would go off to the pub over the road.'

For a long time 'the pub' meant the Prince Regent, known to the gang as the Cheese Dish. But one lunch-time, the landlord took objection to Colin the Punk's mohican hair and refused to serve him.

'Chris just said, "Right, we're all going, then,"' recalls Vince Rogers. 'And, to a man, twenty-five people followed him out of the door. That's how influential he was.'

Chris never went back and thereafter they all drank at the Rising Sun.

One of the few durable friendships Chris formed at GLR was with Danny Baker, who hosted the weekend breakfast show. In the late eighties the outspoken East Londoner was still struggling to operate a studio tape-desk. One morning, Evans was on hand to witness his early fumblings and offered to help.

'Here you are, maa-aate,' he said, sauntering over to Baker, 'let me give you a hand with that.'

Swallowing his pride, Baker allowed this cocky young northerner to show him the ropes. He was obviously impressed, for while Evans continued to present Interference, he was soon invited to take on an extra job as Baker's producer. Today Baker is not only among Evans's few genuinely close confidantes, but co-writes scripts for TFI Friday.

'Danny Baker is one of the few people who can intimidate Chris,' says Maria Costello, who first met Evans while working at the Lingfield Health Club and became his PA for six months during 1996. 'He is very forthright and uses subtle put-downs that keep Chris in check. Quite often Chris feels obliged to do things that Danny says.'

Away from the studios, Chris's life was changing equally rapidly. Within a few months of Sara's arrival in London it became clear that the relationship would not last. Vince Rogers's diary places them together for Christmas 1988, but by the time they celebrated Chris's twenty-third birthday, on 1 April 1989, there is no mention of her. Nor did she accompany Vince, Chris, Fiona Foster and her boyfriend on holiday to Norfolk six days later. By June they were temporarily reconciled, socializing together at a Greenpeace concert. But there are no further mentions of Sara in Vince's diary, which, by 6 January 1990, notes: 'Lunch with Chris and Carol.'

By Miles Mendoza's recollection, Sara remained at GLR until later that year. Her next known job was in Norwich, where she presented the regional news magazine programme for BBC East. Chris has never spoken about the parting, but Carol McGiffin makes it plain that the split between Chris and Sara was particularly messy and unhappy, not least, Carol admits, because she and Chris began their affair before he and Sara were formally finished.

'Sara is the only person with a worse story to tell than mine,' she begins, then stops herself from elaborating. 'I know that she hates me, but she has got no reason to. I think she reckons I forced him to marry me, that I planned it, but that is just not true. Chris sort of implied that I had just organized the wedding and he couldn't get out of it. In fact he asked me three times before I said yes. But, yes, he was still seeing Sara at the same time as me. So you can understand her point of view. And who's to say he didn't marry me because he wanted to piss her off?'

Evans was unusually slow in revealing his affections for Carol, but Julie Smith gained the distinct impression that Carol had her sights fixed on him when they were still on Radio Radio.

'I went to cover the Reading Festival for Piccadilly and on the Saturday night Chris was working and invited me over,' she says. 'He was in with Jonathan Ross, and I was introduced to Carol. Chris had never mentioned her but I got the feeling that she was a wee bit over-protective. She was like, "What does she want?" Me and Carol went out for a beer and she wasn't very friendly. It was, "How do you know Chris? What are you doing in London?" It was very uncomfortable. I met her again at something else later, when Chris wasn't there, and she just said, "Oh, I remember you", in a very patronising way. Chris used to say I was gorgeous, and nice things like that, and I think Carol was quite jealous of anyone.'

Nonetheless, the friendship remained platonic until well after Chris replaced the Canadian DJ Adam Bate as Carol's lodger in Belsize Park, in mid-1989.

'We'd go to bars and cinemas and have a really good time,' she told Matthew Wright of the *Daily Mirror*, 'though it was a long time after he moved in before we got serious.'

Even in the early days she might have seen the writing on the wall, because they soon began to row.

'He was really tight with money. We constantly argued about how he wouldn't buy any deodorant or toothpaste.'

By now, though, Chris was under her skin. They kissed for the first time on an expenses-paid jolly in France, and she told Wright: 'The first snog was fantastic. We'd been taken on a freebie to Dunkirk and ended up having this mad snog for hours on a place above the beach.'

Their ardour was dampened on the return ferry. In a repeat of the Hamburg jaunt, Chris was horribly seasick.

Carol meticulously chronicled the development of their affair in a diary written on her personal computer. She was then a woman approaching thirty, but the language she uses is more like that of a teenager experiencing a crush for the first time.

'I'm going mad. I can't get him off my mind,' one entry reads. 'What the fuck is going on? I lay in bed for three hours thinking of him then went to the gym for three hours and thought more . . .'

Seven years after the relationship began, Carol now lives alone in a tastefully-furnished basement flat off Haverstock Hill, in the heart of their old stamping ground. It is with a mixture of wistfulness and embarrassment that she reads the extracts aloud. After a while, she breaks off.

'I knew that I wanted to go out with him but it was like I didn't think I should, because deep down I knew that in the end he would piss me off,' she says.

Then she returns to the diary. Their early courtship, it reveals, was conducted against the incongruous backdrop of the 1990 World Cup in Italy, when England reached the semi-final and lost on penalties to Germany. An ardent soccer fan, Carol's attentions were divided, but Chris emerged the winner. She describes how they made love for the first time almost as an act of celebration. England had just defeated Cameroon; a match they had watched amid much drinking and patriotic revelry in Belsize Park Mews. As the jubilant in-crowd toasted a thrilling 3–2 quarter-final victory, Chris played Tamla Motown records and led the conga around the mews. As the evening wore on, he and Carol became increasingly amorous and eventually, unable to contain themselves, sloped off. The experience was, she says, more amusing than earth-moving.

'It was just really, really funny,' she giggles, refusing to explain. When the gossip spread, as surely it would, Carol knew that Holly Samos – then Chris's girlfriend – would not have been laughing. If Carol was concerned then her diary does not reflect the fact. She records the football score, and adds, almost as an afterthought: 'Wonder what Claire [Houghton] thought of me sleeping with Chris. Isn't she good friends with Holly?'

Faced with a battle for Chris's affection, Carol's tactic was to allow him a very long rope.

'Holly is about nine years younger than me and, at that time, she was only around twenty years old,' she says. 'I told Chris, "Look, if you need to go out with a young girl and get it out of your system then do it." So he did it, but pretty soon he dumped her entirely.'

A few weeks after choosing Carol over Holly, Chris told her he loved her. Rather, he insinuated that he loved her, just like Hugh Grant in the film *Four Weddings and A Funeral*, because somehow he just couldn't bring himself to utter the magic word. It happened one night when Chris was about to drive away from Carol's flat. As she waved him off he wound down the window, popped his head out, and said simply: 'I do, you know.'

'You don't?' responded Carol bashfully.

'Yes I do.'

'You don't?'

'Do.'

The cryptic exchange continued without 'love' ever once being mentioned.

Up in Preston, where he was now working after leaving Radio Radio, Adam Bate was surprised and disappointed to learn about the romance.

'Him and Carol was a complete shock to me,' he said, 'I mean, I can see the attraction: both are fast, funny, surrealistic people, and McGiff is unusual: very tomboyish and feminine at the same time. But I'm not a big fan of Chris Evans. I think he's out for number one. He'll screw who he can and get what he wants to get. He'll look at you and smile, but he'll stab you if he can. He was pissed off with me. Basically, my radio jocking was based on my deep Canadian accent. He didn't have that and every chance he got he threw a shot at me. There was nothing between me and McGiff, but he must have been jealous.'

Evans threw his cheapest shot after Bate returned to London to visit Carol and found himself invited to be a guest on Round At Chris's.

'I did a little bit on air and then he came on, straight after, and took the piss out of my voice. I had thought I was among friends. He's sharp, bright and fast, but I don't think he's a very nice human being.'

Bate says Evans was surrounded by 'an entourage of five, six, seven people – the kind who laugh at him and stroke his ego.' The talk was all about how he had sounded on the radio, how a particular gag had gone down. 'I would say he was painfully insecure,' he concluded.

If Carol recognized these foibles, they were not about to deter her. In the early months of their courtship she was ecstatic. 'Life doesn't get much better than this,' she recorded in her diary after accompanying Chris to Andy Davies's college reunion ball. Chris introduced her to his mentor, Timmy Mallett, took her to Warrington to meet Minnie and his brother David, though not his sister Diane, with whom he no longer remained in contact.

The other person they never visited, as far as is known, was Chris's uncle, Billy Evans – a tragic and unknown figure in the Chris Evans Story. Billy, now in his seventies, is the bachelor brother of Martin and Harry Evans. Billy cannot care for himself, has always found learning difficult, suffers a speech impediment and, for many years, has resided in sheltered accommodation. First he lived at Orford Hall, where Minnie Evans and Pat Daley worked as nurses. After its closure in 1993 he moved to Houghton Hall, just opposite 319 Greenwood Crescent. According to Pat Daley, who was Billy's key-worker at Houghton Hall, he often talks about his famous nephew and listens to him on the radio: Pat used to tune in for him. But, she says, when she was Billy's care assistant she never once saw Chris visit his uncle after he became well known.

If he had, she says, 'there would have been a fuss and I would have heard about it, whether I had been there or not.'

Chris and Carol viewed the world through an upturned beer-glass, usually filled at the Haverstock Arms, a cosy pub half way up Haverstock Hill. Attracted by its plain-speaking Irish landlord Andrew Carey – now the barman on *TFI Friday* – and its compelling gallery of faded actors and sixties pop stars, they made it their local and became permanent fixtures. Memories of those days may have been blurred by booze and time, but Carol preserves them in dozens of photograph albums. Click! Danny Baker and the crew lurch towards the lens outside the Havvie on a sunny afternoon. Click! Chris and Carol sit side by side on a sofa engulfed by Christmas streamers, glasses in hand.

When the pub closed they would wander up to Primrose Hill to play Frisbee, picnic and swig more wine. They laughed loud and often, though their jokes were straight from the school playground. One jape, recorded gleefully in Carol's diary, was typically lewd and lavatorial. They were all at a party, drunk to the eyeballs as ever, when one of the guests – a stranger – asked to be shown to the toilet. There happened to be two, only one of which flushed. Carol deliberately directed her to the broken loo. To the woman's eternal embarrassment, Andy Davies and Chris then went to inspect it and reported back to the party-goers in gory detail.

Hilarious? Chris thought so. He was so impressed by Carol's raunchy sense of humour that before long her radio show role was aggrandised. Round At Chris's became Round At Chris's – And His Missus. As their signature tune, 'Happy Days', faded, he and Carol would hit the ground running with a music hall-style 'I say, I say' routine. If the jokes sounded hackneyed or unpolished that was the effect Chris wanted.

'They were usually written in the pub on a Friday night,' says Nicky Putt. 'Chris said he hated rehearsing and wanted to do things on the spur of the moment. He liked them to be spontaneous.'

Music punctuated a chaotic melange of sketches, gags, wisecracks, follies, contests and scams.

'Each week Chris sat down with his team and they came up with twenty ideas, ten of which would be Chris's,' says Mendoza. 'Fifteen were chucked out, five went on air and, of those, two were usually brilliant. Those that weren't he ditched. Some of the best ones he took to Radio One.'

One of Mendoza's favourites was Pregnant Pause. Chris discovered early on that, perhaps because of its heavy-rock bias, GLR's audience largely consisted of men. To redress the balance he devised a competition for pregnant women only. All the questions were maternity-related, a 'pregnant pause' was left before the next record, and when an entrant was full-term an Overdue Alarm sounded. Although the prizes were not huge – dummies, baby powder – within weeks the phone-lines were jammed.

'It sounds simple, but in the seven years since not a single competition has come close to getting as many calls as that one did,' says Mendoza. 'No one would have said to Chris, "We need more women", but from the outset he had a better populist instinct than anyone on the station.'

Another long-runner was The Kids Are All Right – But Only If They Are Completely Wrong. Children under ten won a bottle of Wild Turkey bourbon if they could answer three questions incorrectly. Pure Timmy Mallett. Not quite so Mallet was London's Loudest Humming Thing, in which vibrators – real or imitation – were hummed down the phone. In Marks Out Of One, people called to say how much they fancied someone, and gave them marks . . . out of one. Anyone who phoned during Laugh In The Bath had to be soaking in the tub, and answer questions under water. Then there was Tickle Your Trout, reserved for people listening while in bed together.

'What do we shout?' Chris would ask the couple.

'Tickle your trout!' they rejoined.

Why? Well, why not?

Motorists were encouraged to wind down their windows and yell 'Billy!' at passers-by. But perhaps strangest of all was Comedy College, which worked so brilliantly because it introduced visual humour to radio. Chris played a schoolboy named Smithers, whose lamented refrain was: 'It's no good, I'm just not funny, Sir.' As he spoke he would disappear under his desk and reappear with, say, a dustbin on his head. The studio audience howled with laughter, but the listeners were left wondering why.

By alternative pop radio standards, Chris's guests were slightly cheesy. Jimmy Tarbuck, Bruce Forsyth; vintage comedians who might have been considered by some to be past their sell-by date. Chris didn't care. He unashamedly regarded them as heroes. Not that they might have known from the way he treated them. Instead of being invited to plug their latest pantomime or answer banal questions, the star guests were invited to play Person or Personality?, a quiz designed to test whether they were still in touch with reality. Questions were along the lines of "How much is a loaf of bread?" Later, when the show moved to Sundays, he would interview a vicar, and the feature's name changed to Parson or Personality?

'He wasn't interested in contemporary icons of pop culture at all,' says Mendoza. 'He was just interested in entertainers of whatever field. You'd be more likely to hear Cliff Richard than Shaun Ryder. But he was into music – new music formed an important part of the show.'

Round at Chris's *pièce de résistance*, however, would have been impossible without Carol. In an extended pre-written sketch, read out in children's storybook-style, she and Chris played John and Jennifer Rumpy-Pumpy. Every adventure climaxed – literally – with the words, 'I know, let's have rumpy-pumpy!' Whereupon Chris and Carol would flood the airwaves with the oohs and aahs of their cataclysmic simultaneous orgasm.

London had never experienced anything like this, but if Bannister and his deputy Dann feared a backlash, they certainly weren't complaining. By the middle of 1991, Round at Chris's And His Missus was such compulsive listening that the entire industry was talking about the loony northerner.

Then one day, John and Jennifer Rumpy-Pumpy came up with what turned out to be a very silly idea indeed.

'We know,' they thought to themselves. 'Why don't we do the decent thing? Why don't we get married?'

CHAPTER FOURTEEN

'Then Evans came in and the fucker was really ugly,
a ginger-headed bastard with these great goofy
glasses. He was as unlikely a television presenter as
you could wish to see. Even though we were going
for an unconventional look, he had a great face for
radio.'

DON ATYEO, Managing Director of The Power Station,
British Satellite Broadcasting, April 1990 – April 1991

Before we find out whether Mr and Mrs Rumpy-Pumpy lived
happily ever after, let's turn on the television.

The date is 29 April 1989, the time 7 a.m., and we are
among the few hundred thousand Britons foolish enough to
have invested in an oblong-shaped TV aerial predictably
dubbed a 'squarial'. Foolish because within a year Rupert
Murdoch's Sky, with its dish-shaped receivers, will have won
its power struggle with British Satellite Broadcasting and the
squarial will be obsolete. Today sees the launch of the nation's
first non-terrestrial television station, and from the five new
channels we have selected The Power Station. Cornflake-filled
spoons hover between bowl and mouth as we are confronted
by a multi-coloured madman who makes Kenny Everett seem
as charismatic as a newsreader on the Pathe Gazette. Firing
off gags like an AK-47, here is Chris Evans in his latest incar-
nation as inaugural breakfast-time host on the rock video

show *Power Up*. So perfectly natural does he appear, so comfortable with the medium, that no one would guess he's an untried beginner.

Watching Evans on the monitors at BSB's gleaming new headquarters in the Marco Polo building, on the south side of Chelsea Bridge, Nick Powell and Steve Woolley can afford to congratulate themselves. As co-chairmen of Palace Pictures, winners of the £1 million a year Power Station franchise, the shrewdness and bravery of their first major appointment is plain to behold. What they cannot foresee is the one split second of recklessness which will very soon threaten to pull the plug on the Power Station altogether.

Chris's ambition to present his own TV show had smouldered since Timmy Mallett invited him and Mike Hollington to witness the making of *Wacaday*. But even he must have been surprised at how quickly the opportunity arose. It came because Woolley, and Don Atyeo, who had quit the editorship of *Time Out* to run The Power Station, were both addicted to Round At Chris's.

'We wanted fresh new people who had not worked in terrestrial TV, and we had taken on Suggs and Boy George,' says Atyeo. 'At the time, I loved listening to Chris Evans on GLR, and also Chris Morris. They weren't conventional DJs like the old farts from Radio One. They were very anarchic, very presenter-led, very outrageous, a different sort of humour. GLR was a good little station then and it gave these guys their head. Anything could happen, and it was very funny.'

Powell was alerted to the two Chrises' potential and both were approached. Atyeo – a bluff Australian now heading Murdoch's music channel in Asia – will never forget the interviews, conducted in a small, airless office in Wardour Mews, Soho.

'Chris Morris came in first and he was very shy and nervous, almost reticent . . . so we dropped it.'

He was followed by Evans. When Atyeo, who had never met him before, ran his eye over the 'ugly, ginger-headed bastard' he didn't know whether to laugh or cry. He pressed on, however, and within a few minutes Chris had won him over. By the end of the session Atyeo had made up his mind to break with the televisual convention that requires presenters with bland good looks, and recommend him for the job. His executive producer Lindsay Shapero remained unconvinced.

'Lindsay didn't like his sense of humour,' he says. 'She thought he was kind of juvenile and laddish – and all the things that he is. Remember, this was before the start of magazines like *Loaded* and the lad culture, and he stood out like a dog's balls to women of a certain feminist bent. He got up her nose a lot and she was always on his case. She never liked him and she would have loved to have canned him. Lindsay and Chris fought for ever more.'

Any lingering doubt in Atyeo's mind disappeared over the next few days. Evans had pre-booked a holiday in Cyprus and he was terrified that while he was away the post would be offered to someone else. So much so that on arriving in the eastern Mediterranean he began bombarding Atyeo with postcards re-stating his credentials.

'They would stop in mid-sentence and start again on the next card,' laughs Atyeo. 'He was taking the piss, but he obviously wanted the job and he got it.'

When he returned, Chris was offered a salary of around £25,000 and asked to start working on pilots. He left the staff of GLR to become freelance and quit Interference, taking Claire Houghton with him as *Power Up*'s researcher. But, hedging his bets, he continued Round At Chris's. It meant a gruelling schedule almost identical to the one that would prove so disastrous when Chris tried it a second time, fronting both *TFI Friday* and Radio One's breakfast show.

The working environment didn't foster a sense of well-being. The Power Station was shot in a converted Spaghetti House processing factory in Parson's Green, West London, which staff dubbed The Abattoir because, says Atyeo, 'it stunk of dead meat and garlic'. Discarded Coke cans and cigarette butts littered the entrance, and the drab, characterless studio was totally surrounded by a sound-absorbing curtain, the colour of which changed according to the back-drop required. Welcome to the glamorous world of television.

Power Up was recorded one day in advance, but because tapes were edited in the Marco Polo building, an hour away in bad traffic, and there was a need to safeguard against technical hitches, the pace was as frenzied as on a live show. The crew would begin rolling in at 7 a.m., shooting would start at eight and finish around 10.30 or eleven, and the programme went out between nine and 11 a.m. next day.

Ideas meetings were held and suggestions made, but from day one it became clear that this was to be Chris's solo creation.

'He did things I have never seen before or since,' says Atyeo. 'He invented these three characters, Me One, Me Two and Me Half, and they were different alter-egos, or facets of himself. Me One was a much brasher version of Chris Evans, if you can think of anything as disgusting: full-on, up, bright, breezy, Super Chris. Me Two was nerdy. Me Half was shot with only half his head showing: a junior Chris Evans when he was six years old or something. He would come in at 5 a.m., really early, and have conversations with them, but he would record only their responses. Then he would put these recorded responses away and fifteen minutes into the show one of the monitors would come alive, and it would be Me One saying, "Chris, Chris, what are you doing over there?", or whatever. And he would talk to Me One and remember precisely what that part of the conversation was going to be, even though it had happened hours before. It was just extraordinary. He never missed a beat. Everyone would wait for him to fuck up and forget what he was meant to say but he never did.

'One Christmas he came in and did one where he had all three characters on three different monitors. Imagine how difficult that is, but the fucker could remember it every time. That was pure television from someone who had no television experience.

'Totally original. I was really quite in awe of him. I was coming from magazines to television and I was nervous as hell . . . but he just bowled in there and from day one just took it on, and didn't give a shit and made it work as well as his radio programmes. He was very, very good. He was a nightmare to work with, and a real tyrant. Very demanding. A total dictator. He was used to being a one-man band in radio and he came into TV where you have a bunch of fragile egos – producers who wanted to run the show, writers who wanted it their way. TV is not usually about letting presenters run the thing. Ninety-nine per cent of the time they are talking heads. Puppets of the producer, showroom dummies. Evans was none of that. He was running it and if anyone got in his way they got bulldozed.'

Dictators may be feared but they win few friends. Especially twenty-three-year-old dictators yet to perfect the subtle art of persuasion. Moreover, Chris was demanding far more of his camera crew, soundmen, runners and carpenters than ever their job descriptions envisaged.

'He invented, as his set, a cartoon house with blue sky and electric clouds and a sun, and he would just drag them into the action,' says Atyeo. 'One guy became Man In The Kagool and would wear a Kagool buttoned over the top of his head. Some characters would remain for months and others would disappear after just one link.

'One day in January I drove into the car-park and it was pissing with snow. And there was Chris Evans sitting stark-naked at a desk with all these characters in jock-straps. He'd said, "Let's go and do it out in the snow as if it was the middle of summer." Cameramen were sitting there shivering their balls off and filming this maniac as if it was totally normal, which is brilliant.'

Brilliant to watch and brilliant fun for those crew members who shared Chris's zest and humour. For the rest who simply wanted to make sound recordings or record footage and get off home, it was an ordeal. And they weren't being paid any extra for acting as foils and stooges. Chris differentiated between the enthusiasts and the killjoys by referring to them as the A and the B Crews. When the B Crew were on, the tension was heightened by Chris's habit of tearing up sketches or links just as they were due to be shot and substituting them with something else ricocheting around his synapses.

'He was very frustrating to work with for producers because he was constantly fucking them up by changing things,' says Don Atyeo. 'They would be up in the gallery tearing their hair out. It doesn't lead to well-ordered TV. But Chris was a genius. He would just invent these things in three minutes. It was anything that came into his head. He had producers in agony. He's such a demanding fucker and an egotistical son of a bitch.

'He's not a nasty guy. He may have become that but he was just very single-minded about what he wanted to do, and it was always right. He had a hand in everything, the playlist, the style, the links. *The Big Breakfast* was very much an extension of what he developed at The Power Station. Very few people saw it, because no one bought a 'squarial' – maybe 200,000 at most – but those who did, say he was a genius. If someone tried to tell him he couldn't do this or that he would make sure he could do it. From day one he made the transition from radio to TV, which is extraordinary. If you didn't like his sense of humour, like Lindsay Shapero, then he was irritating and loutish, but that was just her. Everyone certainly respected him for what he did.'

Some six weeks into *Power Up*, Atyeo decided a cool head was required to conduct the orchestrated chaos. The task fell to Jules Fuller, now also a senior Murdoch TV executive based in India. Evans was not hostile towards the bright young newcomer. Rather, he responded in the manner of an adolescent who seeks to test the resolve of an authority figure to see where his breaking-point lies.

'He was always getting his dick out in the studio, off camera' sighs Fuller. 'I'm not sure why. Because he can, I suppose. I would walk into the studio and his dick would be sticking out of a hole in the curtains surrounding the studio walls. He popped it away and we carried on the show.'

Boteler Grammar revisited. In time, Evans's ubiquitous penis would re-emerge with dire consequences.

For now, Fuller was unruffled. He won Evans round by

performing hand-shadow tricks on the wall: rabbits, space-rockets, bikes. Chris loved all that. Plus, he says, 'It was easier for me to do stuff opposite him because I could take the flak and he would listen to me – now and again.'

His unflappable professionalism can be measured by the fact that Evans later invited him to work on *Don't Forget Your Toothbrush* and remains his friend.

'He's a difficult bugger to get on with professionally,' concedes Fuller. 'When we were working together he always seemed to be on a complete self-destruct. We would work on something and he would come in and re-write it at 7.30 a.m. "Let's dump it in the bin and start again." It was deeply frustrating, but the end result was always better. He would go off at a complete tangent. "Oh, fuck it, let's do something else." The classic phrase was: "It's funny, it'll work, don't worry", and nine times out of ten he was right. You never clash with someone when you see that what they're doing is good.

'But he was always incredibly demanding of people's time. And that legendary short fuse that he's got . . . he would rant at me or Don and that was fine. We could take it. It's never justified, but sometimes he got better results. But I would say to him, "Don't shout at the guys who are writing the scripts for you or some little PA." Sometimes he would understand that, others he wouldn't.'

On one occasion, when Chris's bullying went too far, even Fuller's coolness deserted him.

'He was bawling out the runner in the studio in front of everybody because he hadn't done something. And actually the runner had no idea what he was talking about. Chris had communicated something to someone else who hadn't told the runner.'

Incensed by this iniquity and unable to make Chris see sense, Fuller exploded.

'I just said, "Outside, now!" and we were nose to nose screaming at each other. To this day I was convinced he was going to thump me and I was going to thump him. And every time I tell him, he looks at me and says, "Do you really think we'd come to blows over a fucking television programme? Don't be so ridiculous." But at the time he was shaking, I was shaking. And then as soon as everybody had let off steam it had gone.'

Chris's temper was at its very worst when one of his sketches – meticulously mapped out in a hard-backed exercise book – was spoiled because someone had forgotten to bring in the right prop or fumbled their lines.

'Cueing videos would be a nightmare,' says Fuller. 'He would often talk over the intro of the song because that's what he did on radio. But there he was in control of the buttons. He could cue the record himself and time it right. When someone else is cueing there can be one or two awful seconds where nothing happens. And when you are working at his sort of pace the timing has to be good. If not he was all over the place.'

More ranting and raving. Fuller gauged from Chris's appearance and temperament that he must himself have been victimized as a boy, and he says: 'I may have thrown that at him once. "Were you bullied at school?" And he'd scream at me even louder.' Had he touched a sensitive nerve? 'I think we had a good enough relationship to say anything to each other.'

During at least one such argument, Chris turned on Fuller and hurled the insult he still uses, both as an unspoken threat and a weapon: 'You don't fucking care about the show any more.' He then refused to speak to his producer for three days – his standard 'sent to Coventry' period.

'After that we sat down and I said it was ridiculous, because I cared more than anyone else,' says Fuller. 'It would be dead easy to turn round and say, "This guy's a fucking arsehole", but I genuinely don't think he is. If the guy was an arsehole and he wasn't very talented that might be different. I genuinely think he's running faster than most people. That's why he goes into this massive self-destruct mode.'

Fuller did not admire Chris's tendency to fall back on smutty jokes when the ideas temporarily dried up.

'I was saying, "Chris, you don't have to be rude to be

funny." When there was a lack of a joke he would be as risqué as possible. That was his way out, and I know that he's gone back to that, and now he's got a name that's fine. But at the time we were doing BSB it was a new kids' show. You try and win your audience over before you slag them off.'

One day, when the inspiration was not flowing, Fuller suggested that Chris flick back through his exercise book.

'"No chance," he said. "The day I go back to a gag I'll stop."'

Atyeo also disapproved of his penchant for vulgarity: 'He was always pushing it a little too far and we got quite a few warnings about smuttiness.'

His bosses sometimes wondered whether he resorted to lewdness to outdo the other presenters, for although they were all part of an exciting new venture Evans was not one to extend the hand of friendship. He was particularly wary of the larger-than-life Australian Jono Coleman, who presented the *Swing Shift* from 8–10 p.m. and who now forms one half of Virgin's Russ and Jono breakfast team.

'Here were two funny guys coming from radio with different sensibilities,' says Atyeo. 'They would eye each other up like a couple of dogs on heat: make snide comments. There wasn't a lot of love lost between those two, I can tell you.'

Jono denies any animosity. 'He was a lot humbler in those days,' he says, 'he was a really nice guy to work with. Our careers have run parallel but he's made a lot more money than I have. Why? He's got red hair.'

The presenter Chris treated most dismissively was Sonia Saul, an attractive and talented newcomer, for it was her misfortune to encroach on his patch. Atyeo asked her to co-present *Power Up* with Chris to 'pretty the show up'.

'Chris Evans was an ugly bastard and we thought he might be a turn-off and it would be nice to have someone who was good-looking and cool to balance him,' he says. 'Also, she had done some TV or acting so we thought we would put them together and Chris Evans could fuck up and she could carry on with the show. It was going to be equal shares.

'But from day one he eclipsed her and it really pissed her off because she could see the audience disappearing into Chris's pocket. She got more and more marginalized. He threw her out, steam-rollered her because he was so on top of it, and she got less and less links. We tried to separate them by putting her back to reading the news, which is where she started, but even that failed. He didn't think that fitted because he thought she was too straight. We changed her round and she did other stuff. He used to come to me and grumble about her and she would come to me in tears about him. He wouldn't swear at her ... he was never a prick to people in public. He was just a lot better than most people; a model TV guy. I always liked him. He did cause us problems, old Chris. He was an odd guy. He was pushing it all the time and you had to watch him because he always tried to slide in stuff.'

Was Chris attempting to 'slide in stuff' the day he almost shut down The Power Station by exposing himself? Fuller and Atyeo have their suspicions, but Nick Powell disagrees, and the question will never be resolved. The facts cannot be disputed, however. During the long, hot summer of 1990, Evans had taken to presenting the show in a pair of baggy but very high-cut knitted shorts, beneath which he never wore underwear. He had invented something Atyeo calls a conveyor-belt game. 'It was a piss-take of *The Generation Game*. People walked underneath the camera with objects and he pretended that they were on a conveyor belt, and you had to guess what they were. He used to leap around the studio while this was happening, in these shorts, doing these high karate kicks.'

One warm morning, mid Bruce Lee impression, Evans's flailing penis escaped from the leg of his shorts. It was visible for such a short time that it completely escaped the attention of the editors, but not, alas, that of watchdogs at the Independent Broadcasting Authority (soon to become the Independent Television Commission). The earlier polite reminders about smuttiness had clearly been ignored. Now it was time to get serious.

When the IBA's outraged complaint was formally lodged with Bob Hunter, one of the principal management executives at BSB, he phoned Nick Powell and summoned him to a crisis meeting. Powell, then co-chair of a company with an annual turnover of £30 million, protested that he was too busy to trek from Soho to Battersea.

'No, you don't understand,' came the sombre reply. 'This is extremely important.'

'I got there and he stuck this tape on and I couldn't see anything wrong,' says Powell. 'He put it on slow-motion and I still couldn't see anything.'

It was only when Hunter used the stop-frame that Powell realized what the furore was about.

'Sure enough there was Chris Evans's dick appearing from his shorts,' says Atyeo, who was also shown the frozen frame.

Powell continues: 'I said I couldn't believe Hunter had brought us all the way for this. I was sure that the IBA had better things to do, and I would make Chris wear bicycle shorts in future. Just at the time BSB were concerned about their relationship with the IBA and they didn't want any problems. While it was ridiculous that they should concern themselves with something the public couldn't see, I wanted to be supportive of them. I also wanted to be supportive of Chris and I didn't want him to go off and do other things. I phoned Don and told him there was a problem and he should speak to Chris. I don't think he did it on purpose. He was just wearing athletic pants. It was more a case for laughter than for concern.' Evans, he added, never caused him problems. 'To this day he's always been friendly and amiable. A perfect gentleman.'

Atyeo paints the incident in a more sombre light. Hunter, he says, refused to accept that Chris had exposed himself by accident.

'Hunter said we were off the air. We had lost the contract. This was a major issue at BSB and I was petrified. I had blown Nick Powell's investment and my head was on the block.' He returned to The Abattoir and made mincemeat of Evans. 'I'm sure he did it on purpose even though he denied it. He was so shifty. He was pushy for the hell of it. He liked to jazz it up. He was utterly reckless. He almost closed down the station. It shook him up for sure, because I'm quite a mild-mannered guy but I was totally pissed off. He was quite cowed by it. I shouted at him.'

Atyeo also butchered Fuller. 'Don said, "You'd better come here", and grabbed me by the head and pulled me downstairs and went fucking ballistic. Every show had to be watched before it went on air after that,' he says.

Had Chris done it purposely?

'Well, the debate rages. He always says he absolutely didn't, thought he was off camera. I'm still convinced to this day that he knew exactly what he was doing. When The Power Station was closing down I went back over some old rushes to pull together a 'Best Of The Power Station' compilation and I found two other sequences where he had been kneeling down in front of a prize or something and his dick was hanging out. I found one where there was a big stack of Coke cans – a year's supply we were giving away – and there, sure enough, he was crouched down on his knees beside the cans and his dick was poking through the bottom of his shorts again. He was always wearing very short shorts and no pants. But the last time I saw him, a year and a half ago, I brought it up, and he looked at me as if I was an alien from outer space and said, "Do you really think I'd ever really do something like that?" At the time, yes, I absolutely did think he'd do something like that.'

A few days before the crisis erupted, Tim Grundy had arrived on the scene. Like some paramedic called to rescue a drowning man, the Piccadilly DJ had hastened to London to try to stop Chris blowing his biggest career break. It was Andy Bird, Grundy remembers, who urged him to counsel Evans.

'He rang me up and said, "He's being rude to everyone, he's wild, out of control, he needs levelling out."'

Happy to help – and seeing a chance to check out his former coffee boy's high-flying new circle – Grundy arranged to stay for a week in Belsize Park. His timing was impeccable.

When Grundy went to The Power Station, he says, 'Chris was in the boss's office. Very nearly got sacked.' Evans appeared concerned.

'He came out in the car-park and we had a long chat. He was quite upset because he claimed it was entirely innocent. But that's Chris – he did daft things. He would do things at Piccadilly like flash in the windows. Just like a schoolboy; giggly stuff really. Chris would do almost anything, never mind take his clothes off. That's what he thrives on. "You don't think so? Well, watch this!" That's him.'

As they chatted, and he observed Chris at work, he saw that his friend had changed considerably in their two years apart, and not for the better. Endearing shades of the old Evans were still there, but he was now driving around in a black Saab daubed with the autographs of famous people like Cliff Richard. And, one afternoon, spotting a beautiful girl boarding a bus he gave chase, flashing his headlights to attract her attention. Also, when Tim, Chris, Carol McGiffin and Bird went to a restaurant which caused embarrassment by declining to accept either a credit card or cheque, Evans took revenge by walking off with the window sign.

He betrayed insecurity when discussing his relationship with Carol. 'For some reason he got it in his head that I didn't like her, because every time I spoke to him after that it was, "You know Carol . . . you don't like her, do you?" I said I did, because she was a very nice person. She wasn't the warmest person with me, but likeable and intelligent. But he continued to ask me what I thought of her right up until she left him.'

The reason Bird had summoned him became apparent each morning at The Abattoir.

Grundy was pleased when Evans suggested he should appear on the show. 'I was The Man With The Fish. I walked on with a big dead salmon and all the soundmen would shout "Oh, no! It's The Man With The Fish!" I'd reel off some ridiculous information and Chris would ask, "Is that fish dead?" And I would give some surreal answer, like, "No, it's learning Spanish."'

But he was appalled at the arrogant disdain Chris showed for the staff: 'I guess there is a cruel streak in the way he treats people,' he says. 'He was just nasty to everybody, totally superior to lesser mortals like soundmen, cameramen, secretaries.

'He'd shout at them a lot in the way that Timmy used to shout at the kids. "Get over here! Get it right!" Just pressure, pressure. "Come on! Do your fucking job!" And that's the last thing you need in a television studio. You're a team. If the cameraman decides to point the camera somewhere else you haven't got a programme. Just because you're the presenter doesn't mean you're better than everybody. He was playing the big I Am. Bursting through the doors: "Here! Look at me!" And I guess he's ten times worse than that now from what I can see.'

Grundy could understand how fame and adulation were affecting him.

'There was lots of money being thrown around. I remember the producers giving Chris £600 cash as we left the studio and saying, "Go and buy some new clothes." I think he got that amount every other week and he just shoved the cash in his trousers. He was also surrounded by people who were basically sycophants. When that happens you can start believing your own publicity and the myths about yourself. You have to be a very strong person and rise above it, and say, "Actually, why don't you all piss off", and get some real people around you, which is what he should have done.'

To bring him to his senses, Grundy varied his tactics.

'I have been quoted as saying, "You're behaving like a cunt", but I don't know if I really did say that. It wouldn't be at all unlike me at that stage of my life. But I tried to be subtle, too. We went out and had a good chat and we got along very well. Just by being there I was reminding him about how he used to be and what we used to get up to. And I would certainly have talked about the importance of being a team member in television and not being superior. I remember telling him to be very careful because television people move so quickly. If you're rude to a secretary one day, eighteen

Freak or Unique? ☆ 189

months later she's an executive producer. We just lived together for a week and everywhere he went, I went.'

In the short term, he says, his mission was accomplished.

'He certainly changed and became a nicer person. I checked. I phoned back sometime later and asked somebody. He got a lot nicer. It was confirmed to me that he was back down to earth and that he had apologized to everyone. He said he wasn't going to be like this ever again.'

The transformation lasted, says Grundy, until Chris achieved celebrity status on *The Big Breakfast*.

'At first Paula Yates said he was too nice. But it started to change maybe three or four months into the programme, and he went back to being the little monster he was before.'

Jules Fuller, in whom Chris occasionally confided after his furies subsided, says there was 'a time bomb ticking in his head'. But while he could barely tolerate the pressure of working at both GLR and BSB he refused to ease up.

'I think it went to his head,' he says. 'I remember a time when he was going slightly out of control. I would think, "Oh, fucking hell, this is lunacy. I can't deal with it today", because I knew he would be shouting and screaming.'

Evans, he says, 'went by rotation from being one of the wisest people I had met to one of the most insecure, to one of the people who had life sussed out more than anyone could have. He was a real conundrum.' When he gently probed for the cause of his angst it became apparent that its source was his 'difficult childhood'.

'Chris says he was let down in childhood. He's never really opened out to me on this stuff but you can gather from the nights we sat and had a few drinks that he's never really satisfied. I think he really hated his father for dying on him. He blamed his father for leaving him. I reached that conclusion. He told me his dad had died and his death really affected him. His dad was the strength for him. Chris hated the fact that he had been abandoned by him so early. He already felt different from other kids. This was just another thing that set him apart. He's clawed his way up to what he is. Made himself. And he feels maybe he's also been let down in the past by people who haven't got the same thirst that he's got. You get the feeling from talking to him that he doesn't really want to go back on his early life so he doesn't like anyone else to. I think he had a couple of girlfriends that he got quite badly hurt by, too, and I think he would like to quietly forget his home town, and that whole thing.'

The merger between BSB and Murdoch's Sky took place in November 1990, and the following April The Power Station vanished along with the 'squarials'. At the chaotic closing-down party, Jono Coleman recalls how everyone swapped jobs. He was a cameraman and Chris, ironically, became a lowly floor-manager. Scenery was trashed, souvenirs stolen, and the staff wept into their champagne over the demise of once-promising careers. As he joined in the wrecking spree, however, Evans felt no self-pity. Plans for his TV resurrection were already being jotted down in his hard-backed exercise book.

CHAPTER FIFTEEN

Alison Ward had just moved from her parents' house to a small council flat in Morgan House, Orford, when one September evening in 1991 the phone rang. Chris's voice didn't surprise her. While in London, he had been calling intermittently to pass on his news and ask after her and Jade, now aged two. But his opening line struck like a sledge-hammer.

'I only rang to let you know I'm getting married,' are the words Alison recalls him saying.

'Pardon?' she managed to reply.

'I said I'm getting wed.'

'Okay, right. Who to?' asked Alison, not jealous, she says, simply incredulous that any woman could be so foolish as to commit herself to Chris.

'Oh, her name's Carol,' replied Chris, who hadn't mentioned having a girlfriend before. 'She's a producer.'

'Oh yeah, what's she like?'

His voiced lowered conspiratorially. 'Well,' he whispered, 'she's nothing much to look at. But apart from that she's all right . . .'

Charming, thought Alison. What a way to describe the woman who was going to share the rest of your life. But just then Carol McGiffin must have walked into the room, because Chris's tone suddenly became chirpy again, and he said: 'Oh, hang on, she's here now,' and he put her on the line.

'She just said "Hello, Alison", and she sounded quite nice. I said, "How can you be so stupid? Do you really know what you're doing, marrying Chris?" I meant it. I wasn't being rotten, I just knew he wouldn't be a good husband. He wasn't any way ready. Carol just sort of laughed and said, "Right, well, nice to talk to you, I'll hand you back to Chris."

'What have you said to her?' he asked anxiously.

'I told her she must be mad.'

'You shouldn't be saying that. Aren't you going to congratulate me?'

'All right, congratulations . . . I think.'

With hindsight, Carol might wish she had taken Alison's advice, for although there would be periods of ecstatic happiness, the coming years would bring her much pain and heartache.

The warning signs had been there long before her first and only conversation with Alison. After a stressful day down at BSB in Parson's Green, the anger Chris had aimed at Jules Fuller and the *Power Up* team would be re-directed towards her. As much as she loved him and wanted to comfort him, Carol was too feisty to allow herself to become an emotional punchbag. Neighbours in Belsize Park grew accustomed to their shouting matches and the sound of shattering china.

'He never physically attacked me,' says Carol, 'but he had a temper like you wouldn't imagine. He would throw stuff at me and I would chuck it back. I remember once when we broke just about everything we could get our hands on, and when it was over we sort of stood there, exhausted.'

Chris found Carol's frankness and feistiness refreshing to begin with. But once their friendship evolved into a love affair he sometimes found it intolerable. Carol would say, 'You're doing that wrong . . . you shouldn't feel like that.' She and Chris would argue over every individual item. Chris was particularly sensitive to any slight criticism of his performances or career moves and there would be a lot of professional arguments. They also rowed over the most trivial issues.

One Saturday morning on Round At Chris's, when both still had flats of their own, Chris read out Carol's home address in Glenmore Road, Belsize Park, on the air.

'I was peeved,' she says, 'so I retaliated by reading his. He was furious and afterwards flew into a screaming temper.'

He was also almost pathologically – and unjustifiably – jealous, she says. And it is interesting to note that the green-eyed monster surfaced most aggressively when Carol was in contact with old friends.

'I have known my best friend, Helen, since we were ten years old and Chris hated that,' she says. 'He couldn't understand it, because he hasn't got any friends left from those days. I only had to be on the phone to her for him to fly into a mood. It was, "What do you want to speak to her for? Get off the phone!"'

When he lost control he was oblivious to who might be listening.

'He used to invite people back after the show and one morning this couple couldn't get in because Chris and Carol were having this massive argument,' says Nicky Putt from the GLR crowd. 'Chris and Carol were hurling things across the room but the couple were so flattered to be invited that they wouldn't go away. They kept knocking and saying, "Chris, Carol? Is that you in there?" They never did get in.'

Chris was unashamed. The following week he singled out the would-be interlopers in the audience and related the incident to listeners in minute detail.

But Carol had more to be concerned about than his raging temper. The hypochondria that would haunt him as his fame increased had already begun to surface.

'If he got the slightest thing wrong with him, even a headache, he thought he was dying,' she says. 'He always thought he was dying. Really dying. I was forever running to the chemist for some medicine or pills.'

It is clearly a fear linked to his father's premature death, but, Carol says, the subject was never raised. 'He only ever spoke to me about his father twice. He just hates talking about his early life.'

Had he done so back then he would have received Carol's sympathy. Not now, though.

'He's not the only person whose father died when he was a teenager,' says Carol, whose own parents split up when she was very young. 'He just has this nasty side and he needs to find an excuse for it.'

Equally disturbing was his tendency to disregard the feelings of others. Never did this trait manifest itself so crudely as over Christmas 1990, when he and Carol arranged to meet up with his old friend Mike Gates. The two men had kept in touch by phone since Gates emigrated to Finland back in October 1987, and had seriously considered forming a car importing business.

'Cars over twenty-five years old aren't taxable in Finland, Chris had this idea of buying classic British models over there and then selling them back home,' says Gates. Their previously attempted rendezvous had, however, failed miserably through a familiar lack of planning. 'Chris was then with Sara Green and they thought they'd visit me but he didn't bother to phone until he reached Stockholm,' laughs Gates. 'When they did, they found out that I was away for the weekend. Everything was spur of the moment.'

This time, keen to acquaint Evans with his new bride, Kirsi, Gates left nothing to chance. As he and his wife were staying with his parents in Ainsworth, they agreed to visit the Britannia Hotel, in central Manchester, where Chris felt flush enough to book himself and Carol into a suite. Slender and fresh-faced, Kirsi is a typically reserved and correctly-mannered Finnish woman. Susie Gates describes her as 'very very modest, very shy, and absolutely soft-hearted'. Nonetheless, she was intrigued at the prospect of dining with this exciting young English showman of whom Michael had so often spoken, and on the drive from Ainsworth she mentally rehearsed some polite opening lines of conversation. Her illusion was rudely shattered even before the introductory drinks had been poured.

'Well! Fancy that! You two going off to the altar and everything,' said Evans breezily, running his eye over the couple. 'This is amazing. I thought you told me you didn't like her, Mike?'

Kirsi's face froze and Gates glared at Evans in disbelief. Such an appallingly insensitive remark would wound anyone's wife, but particularly a foreign guest patently unused to this crass, yobbish style of humour. Not that Chris appeared to be joking. He didn't wink or smile despite cynically betraying the confidence Gates had placed in him a few months earlier.

'Kirsi and I had gone through some bad patch, or whatever,' he says, 'and I might have told him about it, probably did at one stage. But actually to say that was breaking the convention of how you behave with people. He would break those social conventions. They mean nothing to him. I wasn't particularly offended myself because I know him, but people who don't know him could be terribly offended. It's difficult to discuss him in a normal context because he's not normal – and I don't mean that in a negative way. He is exceptional and exceptional people have eccentricities about their behaviour that you can't judge by normal standards. The positive things about him outweigh the negative ones – if you know him well. Kirsi didn't, and she didn't think it was funny at all.'

Oblivious to her discomfort, his behaviour, if anything, grew worse. 'He broke wind openly in front of Kirsi,' says Gates. 'Just farted and wafted it around the room and laughed, and said, "Oooh, it's a really stinky one!" sort of thing. And this is a grown man.'

By now Kirsi was sickened but they somehow made it to the restaurant. As they dined it became clear to Gates that this must be their last supper.

'Kirsi was appalled by his behaviour,' says Susie Gates, who was given a full account later. 'He was bragging and name-dropping about all the famous people he had met. He was still very impressed by those things in those days.'

Whenever Mike reminisced about their old, rabble-rousing days at Piccadilly, a fork was raised to silence him.

'When you meet someone after a long while it's natural to

remember how things were,' says Gates. 'But he got really irritated. He said, "Why are you always talking about the past?" It threw me a bit. I was saying, "Do you remember when . . ." and he couldn't cope with that. It annoyed him.

'The thing about Chris is that he lacks insight into himself. He has the ability to be extraordinarily creative but not the ability to analyse. And because he is the way he is, he doesn't like the past, only the present and the future. So that's where he lives his life. He would think analysing is a past-oriented activity. You can see that by the way his journal was written. It's all in the present tense. Every morning is a new day and he winds his engine up and off he goes. Everything's throwaway: there's a fast turn-around of possessions, people, the lot. He carries it all with him like some sort of avalanche and then it floats away and he collects something or someone else. It's all pretty chaotic.

'His view of life is almost existentialist: you try to do as many things as possible, and you are doing things the whole time. And his success as a human being is measured not by the relationships he makes and keeps, but by the energy he can create. But I don't think he's happy doing it. That's the irony. I mean, this thing with his mother and her sense of values being different from his. Probably deep down he must wonder, "Is she right?" Oscar Wilde said that ambitious people usually achieve their ambition, and that is their punishment. I think that applies to Chris. He might be trying to find some stability and happiness through all he does, but it probably won't work even if he gets to the next stage, and the next after that. He should be commended for what he's achieved, but he probably won't really be happy until he's lost it all. Maybe that's why he self-destructs all the time.'

It is a fascinating appraisal, but Kirsi Gates has no desire to join her husband in pondering the complexities of Chris Evans's tortured psyche. Over in Helsinki his name is taboo in their home, and if Mike wishes so much as to discuss him on the phone then he must speak from his mobile phone or his office.

If Carol disapproved of her boyfriend's behaviour she kept

her feelings well hidden. Mike Gates believes she may have been too smitten to care.

'Carol was obviously very much in love with Chris and pro everything he did,' he says. 'Anyway, she's quite a livewire herself, a bundle of laughs, and she would have gone along with something like that.'

Sifting through the many interviews she has given, or sold, to national newspapers, this seems a fair assessment.

'When I first saw him I remember thinking, "Ginger hair!" But it didn't matter. It was as if he was swathed in charisma,' she gushed to Jane Warren of the *Daily Express*. She didn't 'normally go for men who are as dangerous as Chris – and I don't intend to again', but she was unable to resist.

She told *The Sunday Mirror*: 'Chris has a distinct childlike quality. It's a major part of his appeal.'

Expanding this theme, she told *The Daily Mirror*: 'He was much more fun in those days. We had the perfect relationship until we started getting serious.' She added: 'He can be extremely volatile. He's someone who finds life quite difficult and lives every day as if it might be his last. The closer we got the more we argued. Chris could argue with Mother Theresa. We had a row one time about buying deodorant or something equally serious. He went and slept in another room.' The following morning she awoke to see him leaving with his pot-plants. 'I can't take any more,' he told her, but within days he was back.

In fact, she confided earnestly to Deborah Ross in the *Daily Mail*'s *Weekend* magazine, the attraction almost proved fatal: 'If we'd stayed together I'm pretty sure we'd have finished up killing each other.'

Amid all the thousands of words Carol has spoken about their relationship, however, there is one shockingly sordid episode she has, until now, never disclosed. She relates it while attempting to illustrate the depths of his insecurity, and how low it could make him stoop. The story is revelatory in other ways, too. It exposes Evans, in the years when superstardom was fast approaching, as a man desperately wrestling to control his personal relationships. A man, moreover, who was prepared to use heartless, Machiavellian tactics to do so.

Carol had just landed a dream job with the Disney Channel and decided to celebrate by taking a sunshine break in Jamaica with her best friend Helen.

'When I said I was going away with a mate, Chris just flipped,' she says. 'He was like, "Why did *you* get that job? What are you going away for?" Then he devised this cunning little scheme. The weekend before I went away, he said he was going away, too. He made up a pathetic lie that he knew I wouldn't believe, that he was taking some band gear up to Manchester for a friend. I knew he wasn't. He was up to something.

'Anyway, he didn't go to Manchester, of course he didn't. He came back just before I was due to fly out to the Caribbean and he had obviously been to Norwich to see Sara. I knew he was double-dealing before we were married and realized that he had gone off with Sara to piss me off because he didn't trust me to go away on my own. But what he did then was shocking. Fucking awful. Disgusting.'

Evans, she says, beckoned her over to him, saying: 'Aren't you going to give me a kiss?' As she did so it became evident that he had arrived, unwashed, from a very recent love-making session with Sara, for the sickening scent of their passion was redolent about him.

'Bastard!' hisses Carol. 'I said to him that he smelled of something, and he just said, "Oh! I don't, do I?" He had been two-timing me with Sara and . . . that is how he wanted to get his revenge on me.'

Evans, she says, then confessed – as if it were necessary – that he had been with his old flame.

'I just said, "Yes, I thought so" and walked out of the flat. He followed me and told me to stop. Then he was begging me not to go away, and I was saying that I didn't want him here.'

The obvious question is, how could she have married a man capable of inflicting such calculated cruelty and humiliation upon her?

'I know people will ask that,' she says. 'But you have to

feel sympathy for anyone who feels so deeply insecure that they would do something like that. You have to understand that Chris is a very sad, fucked-up human being. Not happy at all. That is why he is so manipulative.'

She pauses. While telling the story she had been sprawled out on her sofa, diagonally opposite the cartoon of Chris and her at GLR that still hangs on her living-room wall. But now she sits up and straightens.

'And it's all down to his looks,' she says, her voice a mixture of anger and pity. 'It has everything to do with his looks. How would you feel if, because of the way you looked, you got sand kicked in your face every day when you were little? I felt sorry for him and I wanted to protect him. He was so obviously insecure.'

Even among their mutual friends, the issue of who proposed to whom remains a matter for debate. Carol is adamant that it was Chris, and that it happened after another argument.

'I went to his place one Sunday morning to tell him, "I never want to see you again." We ended up having a bit of a row and stuff, and then he said, "Let's get married",' she told *The Mirror*. 'I suppose he thought everything would be all right if we got married and I believed it. I really couldn't imagine living without him. I suppose that's why I went round. I wanted to make him do something to keep me. I seriously believed that getting married would cure all the ills, and ten days later we did.'

It was such an impetuous decision that they might have married immediately, but Chris was going on holiday to Malta with Andy Davies and Claire Houghton, so they had to wait until he returned. In the meantime Carol booked an appointment at Camden Register Office and Chris milked the unfolding drama for all it was worth. The manner in which he broke the news varied from doom-laden to theatrical, depending upon the audience and stage.

In Malta he appeared deeply gloomy.

'We were playing pool in a bar one night on holiday and just as he was about to take his shot, he said, "I've got something to tell you",' recalls Davies. 'The way he said it, I honestly thought he was going to say he had a terrible disease. It was the way he looked: all concerned. But he just said, "I'm marrying Carol when we get back. Okay, whose shot is it?" Then he carried on playing.'

When the shock wore off, Davies agreed to be best man.

By the time they came home, Chris's angst had lifted and he was ready to celebrate. He threw a party for about forty friends and colleagues at a Camden club and Jules Fuller recalls how Carol phoned him in high spirits, beckoning him to join the fun.

'I got down there and there was lots of laughing and joking and Chris was in a particularly funny mood. I kept asking him what was happening, because I'd heard there was a big new thing, and he just said, "Don't worry about it." An hour and a half later he got on stage and said, "Right, Ladies and Gentlemen! Bit of a shock for you . . ." And he was looking straight at me . . . "Me and Carol are getting married." There was stunned silence across the room. He got off stage and he said to me, "I was watching you all the time. Your jaw nearly hit the floor." He cracked up with laughter at my face.'

It is not clear when Chris let Minnie in on the secret. Nor have her feelings about the union ever been recorded. Her daughter Diane's marriage to Paul McAlinden having failed, perhaps she was apprehensive, but Carol is confident that she approved, for she says they have always got along well and she still maintains contact.

Alison Ward says she heard differently: 'His mum told my mum that she never liked Carol. She just said, "You know what southerners are like."'

Whatever the truth, neither Mrs Evans nor any member of either family was invited to the register office on 17 September 1991. Chris and Carol apart, just five close friends were there: Davies, Claire Houghton, television presenter Gary Monaghan who would soon join Chris on *TV-Mayhem*, pop band manager Martin Patton and Carol's pal Helen, who, with Davies, acted as a witness. Low-key would be one way to describe the event; farcical another. Vows were exchanged at

3.30 p.m. before Deputy Superintendent Registrar Mrs Susan Bloom, in the Regency furnished marriage rooms at the new town hall.

'The entire wedding took perhaps fifteen or twenty minutes,' says Mrs Bloom. 'He wasn't really famous then and I didn't know who he was until afterwards, when he came to the fore. He certainly wasn't wacky. I'd say he was subdued.'

Things slid rapidly downhill thereafter. Someone shot a video, but Carol says she later taped over it. The solitary wedding photograph was left undeveloped for so long that it did not come out. From the town hall they went to some forgotten bar, where so much champagne was drunk that the marriage certificate was lost. Moreover, as Chris had just taken a break he could not go on a honeymoon, so their wedding night was spent amid the romantic splendour of the Holiday Inn, a stone's throw from their respective flats, in Swiss Cottage.

It would be easy to say that the wedding day set the tone for the rest of the marriage. Easy, but not altogether fair. Determined not to repeat the mistakes made by her parents, Carol tried hard to make it work and, at times, so did Chris. They moved into his untidy, CD-strewn flat, The Studio at number 76, Parkhill Road, NW3, and she set about turning it into a refuge from his stressful career.

'I tried to create an environment where he could relax,' she told the *Daily Express*. 'You can't tell him directly what to do but I wanted the warmth of our home to rub off on him.'

So seriously did she regard her new role that she soon gave up her job.

'With hindsight, I don't think it was healthy,' she says, 'but it was what I wanted to do. To begin with Chris was grateful but he began to get annoyed that I was relying on him for life.'

At least one person was delighted at her decision, however: Alison Ward. Until Chris married Carol, she says, the cheques he sent towards Jade's upkeep – then £150 a month – invariably arrived late. Two also bounced, and one, dated 1

June 1990, she keeps for posterity because Chris signed it twice, once on the front and once on the back. A daft message scrawled on the reverse reads, 'Cheers Ali, here's a spare signature in case the other one rubs off in the post.'

'After they got married things were a lot better,' says Alison. 'Carol started looking after his affairs and I got the cheques on time every month. She seemed to be looking after his business. Maybe that's what it was, really, more of a business arrangement.'

Carol would disagree, but there is no doubt that in the days immediately following the wedding there was much business to attend to. Earlier in the summer, Evans had heard on the grapevine that TV-am – about to face a tough franchise battle – wanted to beef up its Saturday morning children's output. Out came the hard-backed exercise book. Taking brushstrokes from *Power Up* plus all his old favourites – *Tiswas*, *Swapshop*, *Wacaday* – and adding licks of originality, he and Andy Bird devised a series punningly called *TV-Mayhem*. Claire Houghton was also drafted in to the team. The concept was tabled with TV-am's charismatic boss Bruce Gyngell, and a deal struck.

It was no ordinary deal. Foreseeing that their comparatively expensive programme might be axed if TV-am lost its franchise, Tim Grundy says Evans and Bird hired the best possible contractual lawyer.

'Normally when you do a TV contract you might pay the brief between five hundred and a grand, but they paid this guy five grand up front,' says Grundy.

Bruce Gyngell recalls agreeing to buy seventeen shows, sufficient to cover the autumn quarter, with an option for renewal. However, the key clause stipulated that should *TV-Mayhem* be scrapped mid-series, Evans and Bird's company, Big And Good, would be paid up in full. And, of course, this is precisely what happened. On Tuesday 19 October 1991 it was announced that TV-am would be replaced, on expiry of its licence, by GM-TV. And so, just seven weeks after a baseball-hatted Evans and Gary Monaghan had kicked off the series, the plug was pulled.

Grundy was then presenting *People Today* for the BBC in Manchester, and it was in his office there that Evans phoned him to break the news.

'Andy and Chris had to keep their faces straight when Gyngell called them in and told them,' he says. 'They said, "Well, that's terrible. We're really sad about it." Then they went out of the building and punched the air. They sent their solicitor in the next day and he came out with the cheque.'

Grundy asked Evans what he would do next.

'I'm retired. Retired, maa-aate. RE-TIRED!' came the euphoric reply. 'I'm going to collect classic cars and play golf.'

When Chris had calmed down Grundy reminded him that he was only twenty-three years old.

'He did, indeed, buy a few classic cars,' Grundy adds. In fairness, it ought to be recorded that he also ensured that everyone who had worked on the project was fairly compensated, too.'

So, just how high was the *TV-Mayhem* pay-off and why did TV-am agree to it? By some estimates it could have topped £250,000, but Bruce Gyngell says he 'doubts' that it reached that figure.

'£250,000 would have indicated that he had a £10,000-per-show contract or something . . . If he got £2,000 a programme I'd be surprised.'

It wasn't a case of the show being sub-standard, says Gyngell. It was just that cartoons were cheaper, and profits had to be maximized for the shareholders in the months that remained before the company closed. There was also an element of pique: 'OK, they've stuffed us, now what can the ITC [Independent Television Commission] do . . . they can't say, if we don't run more children's programmes they'll take away our licence. They've already done that.

'We probably didn't spend enough money on the programme but . . . I thought it was exciting and it would have got a lot better if we had spent more time on it. It was a bit of a cross between *Tiswas* and *TFI Friday*. Chris sat at a desk and people kept walking across, and there were funny shots using funny voices, and he used the crew. I think *TFI* is a more sophisticated version of what that show was. Not *Big Breakfast*. That was much more frenetic.'

Had Gyngell encountered difficulties in dealing with Chris?

'I'm sure he was easier to deal with in those days. He wasn't as big as he subsequently became . . . wasn't a prima donna at all. I mean, he called me Mr Gyngell. He was quite polite. But he could well have said to me something like, "How much do you get in your job? I wouldn't mind taking it over", because that's Chris Evans. I don't know him now . . . all I know is, seeing him on air, he's an extraordinary spontaneous talent. A lot of people like that are difficult to handle, but that's part of life.'

Was Evans, in his view, a genius?

'Well, it's not a word I'd actually use, but I think he's a man who totally understands his medium and its range. A child of television. And I think he's much better on television than he is on radio. He almost works as though the television isn't there.'

Many would argue the opposite, and certainly Carol enjoyed his radio shows more, for there she was in the thick of the action. While Evans had been cutting his teeth in television, Round At Chris's had taken on a momentum of its own, and by Christmas 1991 it was cooking, as rare video footage shot by Nicky Putt's boyfriend shows. The film, portraying John and Jennifer Rumpy-Pumpy at their vintage best, is revealing in several ways. As the countdown to airtime begins, Chris purges himself of the urge to swear by bellowing, 'Bastard, fuck, fuck, bastard.' Then, during their 'I say, I say' joke, Chris calls Carol Wifey-Strifey and she addresses him as Gorgeous Hunk Of A Husband. Meanwhile, Andy Davies, nursing a hangover, is the butt of Chris's anecdotal humour.

'Andy bought a Lancia Beta Coupe . . . saved £2,000 for the car . . . got them down to £1,600 . . . the second day the manifold started going. He took it to a garage . . . got it back three weeks later' . . . and so on. Davies grimaces good-naturedly. Later Evans jokingly warns him to hold the correct cue card 'or I'll fire you'.

Evans interviews Bernard Matthews and asks – as only he could – 'When did you first start off with turkeys? What first attracted you to them?' But at one point, when he introduces his mother into a monologue, the humour and bathos become inseparable, leaving the studio audience nervous and uncertain how they should react.

'My mum phoned me up and asked what I'm doing for Christmas,' he begins, simply enough. 'She said we're having a sit-down meal.' Pause. 'Is there any other way to eat a meal, other than sitting down?' He proceeds to relate how his mother has worked hard all her life, but hasn't much money. His dad died a few years ago, he says, and all she has left is her dancing classes. Her dancing partner was a woman named June and last Friday, at a Christmas party, 'June just felt dizzy and dropped down dead.'

'All she's got in her life is dancing and on Friday her dancing partner for the last three years dropped down dead,' Evans repeats for emphasis. 'There's no punch-line. I just thought it was cheaper than a therapist so I told you lot about it. The rest of the show is for my mum.'

Since the age of thirteen, Chris had been running away. Running from the pain of prematurely losing his father and from the guilt he had suffered since failing to attend his funeral. Running to achieve as much as he could before he, too, was stricken by some terrible illness. Running to impress his mother, though there was never any need.

By early 1992, however, Chris was beginning to realize that he could not escape his demons by running, no matter how fast or how far. Before the year's end he would feel compelled to turn and confront them.

On the surface, there could not have been a less likely period in his life for the watershed to rise, for all his efforts were beginning to bear fruit. Although *TV-Mayhem* had been short-lived, he was so clearly a future star that it was only a matter of time before his next big break in television. Thanks to his pay-off he was richer than he had ever been, and he had a wife with whom to share his success. On top of all this, early in 1992 he had been contacted by a man he regarded as a broadcasting legend, the veteran BBC Radio One Controller Johnny Beerling. His then wife, he said, greatly enjoyed Round At Chris's, and as Philip Schofield was leaving the station, an opportunity had arisen. How would Chris like to bring his brand of humour to Schofield's vacant Sunday afternoon slot?

Freak or Unique? ☆ 207

Evans didn't need asking twice. Joining Radio One would bring him within striking distance of hosting the Breakfast Show, the dream he had clung to since boyhood. Perhaps he wouldn't retire and collect classic cars after all.

The show, running from 2.30 to 4 p.m., commenced in March 1992. As his audience would be replete with roast beef and Yorkshire pudding, he titled it Too Much Gravy. The prospect of working from the Egton House studios once occupied by DLT, Noel Edmunds, Steve Wright, Mike Read and so many more heroes was exhilarating, if nerve-wracking. Yet soon after he began the weekly trek to Langham Place he was beset by a crashing sense of anti-climax and dis-appointment. From his days as Nobby No-Level he had striven, tooth and claw, to reach this building and now that he had done so it all felt wrong. His GLR show was infinitely better, he told friends. He could be himself over at the Maryle-bone Road studio. Here, amid the clubby atmosphere of the mainstream BBC, he felt stifled, misplaced. But it wasn't just that, there was something else which he couldn't even put his finger on.

He confided his frustration in Johnnie Walker, the seventies glamour boy of Radio One, with whom he had stayed friendly since their days at Radio Radio.

'I met him in the corridor and he said, "Johnnie, I'm so upset. All I ever wanted was to work at Radio One, it was the realization of my lifetime's ambition. And now I'm here it's completely crap",' recalls Walker.

In his confusion, Evans searched for a reason and homed in on the most obvious and vulnerable target: his callow producer Lucy Armitage. Then still a trainee, her only pre-vious experience had been as a researcher at sedate, harmoni-ous Radio Two, where she worked with Gloria Hunniford, Anne Robinson, John Dunn and Derek Jameson. The contrast between her and John Rumpy-Pumpy, aka The Prince of Darkness, could scarcely have been greater.

'They made the mistake of giving Chris a rookie who was shitting herself at producing him,' says Walker frankly. 'And the word from the bosses was that she had to control this guy. All his ideas were being diluted and squashed, and he had far more experience than her. He said he was being wrongly produced. They needed to put a producer with him who would let him have his head. He told me he was going to have to leave, and he left not long afterwards. I admired him for that. A lot of other DJs would have kow-towed.'

Walker was well-placed to empathize. An old rebel himself, his transition from the pirate station Radio Caroline to the BBC, in 1969, went smoothly at first. But towards the end of his seven years there he was constantly squabbling with executives who wanted to stop him playing album tracks by the likes of Lou Reed and Steely Dan, and switch to middle-of-the-road pop.

'These rows are nothing new,' says Walker. 'Kenny Everett was another example. He was always trying to get away with things and they were always trying to stop him. But with Kenny they realized he was outrageous and backed off.'

Highly as he rated Evans, the uncompromising Beerling had no intention of allowing a newcomer the same leeway.

'I wanted to change the producer but I couldn't make that change – I was overruled by Johnny,' says Paul Robinson, then Beerling's number two. 'He felt he wasn't getting this from Steve Wright, Simon Bates, so why this guy? That was the attitude. I can see his point to some extent. Johnny was a completely different animal from Matthew Bannister [who would become Evans's next boss at Radio One]. I worked for them both. Matthew knew Chris from GLR and . . . tolerated a huge amount.'

Beerling's view has mellowed a little with time. But he concedes: 'It was difficult with Chris because he had been more or less his own man, and very successfully, at GLR. And I think it didn't sit comfortably, working with another producer. He didn't like the discipline and strictness of conforming. It wasn't a particularly happy relationship with Lucy Armitage. I know, because I got both sides of it. With hindsight it probably wasn't a sensible allocation of a producer to a presenter. Perhaps it would have been better to have someone more experienced. But what we weren't trying to do, necessarily, was simply take the GLR show, which was very metropolitan, and put it on nationally. It wasn't a great moment in the station's history.'

It wasn't a great moment in Lucy's career, either, Robinson says: 'There were fireworks between her and Chris all the time. She's a bright woman, and good, but there were shouting and screaming matches, and there was one point when she was going to walk out.'

Today, working in the more temperate environment of the World Service, Lucy attempts to play down their differences. But although she was then twenty-four and Chris almost twenty-six, she makes their working relationship sound like that of a newly-qualified teacher vainly trying to control the most difficult boy in the class.

'I see lots of Chris now because we live in the same area. We have a very good relationship,' she begins. 'At the time we were both very strong-minded and we'd both just started at Radio One and we wanted to make our mark. You can imagine I met my match, bloody hell! When he walked through the door my life changed – quite radically.

'We didn't clash . . . I think you'll find that lots of people say Chris can be fantastic to work with unless you fall out. Paul often thought we'd fallen out when we were just having very constructive arguments. I think the show was really good and Chris would say the same.

'But because I was new I was always doing what I was told. Johnny Beerling would ask me to make sure he played his trails or that he didn't turn up late for his interviews. And because I was naïve I would say [she adopts a stern voice]: "Chris, please can you play your trails", or "Please can you turn up more than two minutes before we go on air." At GLR he used to bounce through the door two minutes before they went on air, which was fine. But at Radio One they wanted him in half an hour before or they'd start off emergency procedures. It was just because the BBC obviously has very strict rulings to make sure it runs well, and Chris – quite rightly – is a rebel. Good luck to him. But I was brand new at the time and I thought I'd better do what I was told. And Chris, bless his heart, let me know that there's more to life than following everybody's rules.'

Too Much Gravy was on the air for six months, during which time, she estimates, they rowed every week.

'He made me cry once. Just because I was scared shitless of what was going on.'

Even so, Lucy remains indebted to him for showing her the ropes of pop radio, and stresses that he would praise as well as criticize. When the series ended he presented her with an antique radio set.

'He just breezed into the studio and said, "Here you are", and handed it to me.'

She took it as a major compliment, a sign 'that I had understood that whatever had happened between us, he had done it all for the best of the show.'

Expanding her analysis of Chris's dissatisfaction with Too Much Gravy, she says: 'I can understand why he wanted things to work, but I mean – he was falling out with Carol at the time . . .' Realizing that she may be speaking out of turn, she stops mid-sentence.

Her reticence, though understandable, is unnecessary, for by May 1992, everyone in the Evans–McGiffin circle knew only too well that they had hit the rocks. There had been marvellous interludes, as Carol's photograph album reveals. They holidayed in Portugal and Florida, and dined out in style. For Chris, however, it was never enough. His eye began to wander and eventually settled upon Brenda Kotzen, an attractive and athletic South African-born primary school teacher who specialized in dance and worked part-time behind the bar at the Lingfield Health Club.

'Brenda thought Chris was charming,' says Maria Costello, then Brenda's flat-mate and operations manager at the Lingfield. 'Although he was a rising star and she was a teacher he told her he wanted to talk to her because she was a real person and his life was boring.'

He invited her out for drinks and 'flattered her by showing her a lot of attention,' says Maria. Although Brenda felt uneasy about seeing a married man, she found herself falling for him.

'I don't know how long it lasted or exactly what happened,' says Maria, 'but they were very close'

No one can be certain how far their liaison progressed, for after a while Brenda – like so many who have loved Evans – was frozen out. No warning, no goodbye, Chris just stopped calling. 'She was very hurt and very disappointed,' adds Maria.

In March 1994, aged thirty-one, Brenda died of a heart-attack. Chris has never discussed his feelings, but his reaction to the news speaks volumes. After opening a new swimming pool in Derby, he left instructions for his £1,000 fee to be donated to St Mary's Primary School, in Haringay, North London, where Brenda had taught. The money was spent on a new stereo system. A tree was also planted in the school grounds in her memory.

It is difficult to believe that Carol was unaware of Chris's feelings for Brenda, for he made little attempt to disguise them. Furthermore, Maria says: 'He always made a point of including her in things when he was with Carol and other people.'

But there were worse indignities to be endured. 'He is very manipulative,' says Carol, particularly when it came to their love life. 'He had this nasty way of trying to get you to do things. He would say that such and such an old girlfriend had done such and such, "So why won't you?"'

According to Grundy, Evans also had a penchant for boasting about his more adventurous bedroom exploits. One story he related to Grundy allegedly involved voyeuristic sex in the garden of a grand stately home, where he was attending a ball. However, when Chris spoke like this, Grundy says, it was sometimes difficult to separate truth from fiction.

At this stage, with both his professional and personal lives in chaos, it was clear that Chris needed to stop and search for the root-cause of his problems. Clear, that is, to everyone except Chris. It was not until the following March, in 1993, that he was able to look back and reflect.

'Over the past five years, I've spent three of them annoying people and the other two apologizing,' he told the *News of the World*'s Sunday magazine. 'I'd got so passionate about things that everyone I knew hated me. Even my best friend [Andy Bird] wasn't speaking to me. There was something going wrong but I didn't know what it was . . . I'd got too big for my boots and very arrogant. I just wasn't nice to be around.'

His hypochondria was by now chronic, too. 'I'd get an itch or a scratch and ring the doctor. It sounds silly, but I got bumps on my leg and I thought I was going to die. It went on intensively for about six months. I was literally worrying myself sick over every bump, lump and graze.'

At least some of the bumps were not imaginary. They were caused by phlebitis, a condition he has suffered from. Usually caused through infection, or injury, it inflames and roughens the veins, disturbing the blood-flow. It is generally confined to the legs, causing tenderness and red, hard-core swellings, treatable by ointment, painkillers and sometimes antibiotics. The danger is that it can lead to blood-poisoning or clotting, but this is very rare and only about one of every thousand reported cases proves fatal.

This was small consolation to Chris. Morbidly obsessed with meeting his end far earlier even than his father, who lived to fifty-seven, his reaction was to run even faster. Like some out-of-control juggernaut hurtling down hill, he raced from meeting to meeting, hunting down potential new projects to supplement his radio work. Before long the one he had waited for materialized.

The failure, in ratings terms, of the broadsheet-style breakfast news magazine *Channel 4 Daily*, meant that the station's 7–9 a.m. slot was up for grabs. Planet 24, a Docklands-based production company run by two whizzkid business partners, Waheed Ali and Charlie Parsons, had entered the bidding for its £10 million franchise. In Bob Geldof they already had a charismatic spearhead and they were beginning to assemble an impressive young backroom team, too. What they needed

to ice their cake was a brilliant, yet fresh-to-the-scene presenter. Someone to kick the stuffing out of established, 'comfy
sofa' breakfast TV on the main network channels.

'It was meant to be very much like a radio show and Chris
was simply the funniest, most talented DJ we happened upon,'
says Sebastian Scott, editor of what was to become *The Big
Breakfast*. 'As we did the pilots, it was further and further
adapted to his ideas and personality.'

The first *Big Breakfast* was served up in September 1992,
but the pilots were shot some four months beforehand, in
Lewisham, south-east London. Still fronting Round At Chris's
and Too Much Gravy, Evans had no time to recover from
the weekend. On Monday morning he was inching his way
through rush-hour traffic to link up with Danielle Lux, a
dusky beauty in the Bianca Jagger mould, who hoped to
co-present with him. The trials were conducted over four
days, in a for-sale house, with nearby residents providing the
audience.

'On the last day, we all had a champagne barbecue in the
rather public garden and people stood round and stared,'
recalls Anna Paolozzi, who became the show's head of make-
up. 'That was very Planet 24.'

Though there were reservations over Danielle – brilliant
behind the cameras but inexperienced in front of them – there
were no such doubts about Evans. Hundreds of hours of
'practice' before zero-rated audiences at BSB made him
appear a seasoned veteran. Soon he was being introduced as
the coming man to Geldof and his then wife Paula Yates,
who both planned to conduct interviews on the programme
– his serious, hers frothy – and other key members of the
Planet 24 team.

And where was Carol amid all this fevered activity? Outside it all. Eight months after the Camden Register Office
fiasco, she walked out for the first time and moved in with
friends.

Outwardly their break-up seemed to affect Chris little.

'There was just this period on Round At Chris's where
Carol wasn't there,' says Miles Mendoza. 'It lasted a few

months, but it was never referred to, Chris got another of the team, Cecile, to stand in for her.'

Inwardly, however, his split from Carol was proving to be a catalyst. In rare moments of privacy he began to reflect on his behaviour and the chaos it was causing; an activity that had always been anathema to him. For all his success, he viewed himself as a failure. He had failed to maintain important friendships, failed to keep his marriage together. Failed, despite all his best efforts, to escape from his past. Like so many tragic comedians – Hancock, Milligan, Sellers – it had reached the stage where he only felt fulfilled when he was working. He didn't want it to be like that. After a silence of four months, he called Carol. He wanted to give it another try, he said. He knew he had been impossible to live with, but he was willing to get help. He picked up the *Yellow Pages* and flicked through to the letter 'P', for psychotherapist.

Evans attended his Friday evening session with Claire Chappell for about ten weeks, undergoing some twenty hours of intense retrospective self-evaluation. According to experts this might have been sufficient time in which to tackle some specific problem – failing to attend his father's funeral, or being bullied, for example. It is unlikely, however, to have allowed him to embark on a lengthy emotional journey encompassing all his childhood-oriented problems. Nonetheless, Evans has said in several interviews that he believes therapy helped him profoundly.

'As I talked to my therapist I started to realize how scared I was of dying,' he said less than year afterwards. 'The first stage is fear, and hypochondria can be next. I would go to therapy every Friday night because I thought it would be a good end to the week. But it's like going through five traumas an hour. I'd come out exhausted. You have to open your mind to get rid of all these things. It's painful – but my therapist was brilliant. All these memories just came cascading back to me. She was helping to turn the keys in my mind.'

Behind the unlocked door he found himself face to face with his father, possibly for the first time since he was thirteen.

'Looking back, my immediate reaction to his death was, "Right, you've got to get on with things now",' he says. 'My mum was devoted to him and although I didn't think about it much then, I think I blamed myself. I started running to get on with my life with such a sense of urgency I was too scared to stop. My mum was fantastic at the time. But it was then that I developed a huge fear of death, because ever since I've done nothing but work.'

After the sessions, he says, he was able 'to think about my dad with a huge amount of affection. And I can get upset, which before I never did ... there's a fine line between unloading your problems and passing on your guilt. And I'm coming to terms with slowing down.' He had started to play tennis and work out in the gym, he said. It also 'meant I was all the more determined to get my marriage sorted out. The advice that I give to myself now is, "Take part in the race but as you pass each spectator, have a good look. Remember what they're like and, for heaven's sake, don't miss out on what's around you".'

An impressive philosophy to guide anyone towards a more contented and balanced existence. And, for a while, it did precisely that for Evans. Altogether more affable and capable of rational argument, Chris asked Carol to return. She agreed and it was as if their courtship had newly begun.

'In the summer before he worked on *The Big Breakfast* we travelled as much as possible and we were extremely happy,' she recalls, bringing out the photographs once more. They depict a couple meandering across the country, apparently at peace with themselves and the world. Chris acquired a beautifully maintained old green Jaguar 340 automatic and whenever they had a spare day or two they hit the road. Down in Weymouth they fished from the pier, giggling like teenagers at their ineptitude and catching not a solitary fish. They motored north to the Lancashire resort of Morecambe – omitting to turn off at Warrington – where they ate sticks of rock and posed for a snap beside the now-demolished Central Pier. Their next stopping-off point was the Lake District, where he booked them into one the finest hotels. He ordered – and devoured – a 21 lb steak, and the photographs reveal that happiness is making him fatter.

'He did put on weight – his weight goes up and down,' says Carol. But he didn't care – he was living for the moment and for the day. 'When we were on our own, away from everyone, and there were no pressures we got along fantastic-ally,' she says. 'We didn't argue at all.'

Determined that they should not regress, Chris – with not a trace of irony – suggested that starting a family might cement the bond. His tone was hardly reassuring, however.

'He did say, a couple times, "If you want to have kids you can have kids",' says Carol. 'But there was no real conviction, and anyway I didn't want that at all. I'm not cut out for kids. I find the whole notion of giving birth repulsive. I'm glad now that I didn't. It would have been a hundred times worse. The only difference,' she adds wryly, 'is that I would have got more money after we split up.'

One plan that *was* followed through was swapping the cramped studio flat for a much bigger house that would osten-sibly give them more breathing space. Chris let his flat and, while house-hunting, they moved temporarily to a rented house in north London's Parliament Hill. The following year they would take residence in a secluded, £350,000 executive home in Highgate, on the fringes of Hampstead Heath, where the Jaguar and Chris's new snow-white Porsche sat behind high iron gates in the drive.

'But I thought we needed more than a change of address,' Chris told the *Sunday Mirror*, 'and one day I secretly snuck off to the travel agent and booked a one-week cruise around the Caribbean for the two of us. Carol knew nothing about the holiday until we got to Heathrow and boarded the flight to Miami. Her face was a picture.' Not even a chance meeting with Eamonn Holmes, Chris's new rival on GMTV, who was filming on location, could spoil the romantic break. 'I'm all right and Carol's all right,' he said, 'and that's all that really matters.'

The change did not go unnoticed at *The Big Breakfast*, either.

'He's nice to work with now,' Paula Yates remarked when confronted with stories about his temper. 'In fact, he nearly kills himself trying not to upset people.'

To emphasize that she not only valued him as a colleague but considered him extremely sexy, she invented yet another name for him: Mr Throbby Love Gussett.

'All my girlfriends think he's gorgeous,' she proclaimed, and it wasn't long before the popular newspapers warmed to her theme. As *The Big Breakfast*'s audience soared from 600,000 in week one to more than 1.5 million, making it the television success story of 1993/1994, Chris Evans, the puniest, geekiest carrot-head ever to walk the streets of Orford, was transformed into the unlikeliest sex-symbol the country had ever seen.

'Every Girl's Favourite Turn-On', ran the headline on one tabloid supplement, and suddenly his fanciability was being analysed and debated by Fleet Street's top feature writers and columnists. Limelight of this burning intensity was what he had craved, the ultimate reward for his relentless effort. The question was, how would the supposedly mellower, more emotionally mature Chris Evans handle it?

CHAPTER SEVENTEEN

'I don't think success will change him. I knew him
when he was an arrogant sod, and he can't get any
worse than that.'

JOHN REVELL, Evans's close friend and business
colleague, *The Independent Magazine*, January 1993

Revell is as well qualified as anyone to assess Evans, and for
a few months his prediction held good. Swept up on a tide
of euphoria at landing his dream job and greeted every morning by the most enthusiastic, diligent and upbeat family team
he had yet worked with, Chris won popularity among his *Big
Breakfast* colleagues.

'The emphasis is on happy,' he chirped to one interviewer.
'The presenters are happy, the crew are happy – rarely do we
fake that. Sometimes we do, 'cause we have rows and stuff
during taped items. But generally we're genuinely happy.'

By the summer of 1993 he might have agreed that 'pig-sick'
more accurately described the atmosphere around the *Big
Breakfast* table.

Producer Courtney Gibson, who worked on the show from
October to December 1992, then took a six-month break in
her native Australia, couldn't believe how Evans's demeanour
had changed when she returned.

'I noticed a remarkable Jekyll and Hyde-style transformation,' she says. 'I left this infectiously excitable, disarmingly

Freak or Unique? ☆ 219

delightful maverick presenter who kept rubbing his hands like a little boy in a sweet-shop and saying, "I can't believe they're paying me to do this." And I returned to find an aggressive, rude, mean-spirited malcontent with a profound lack of humanity and the shortest wick in showbusiness. He had become this didactic monster from hell. It was just a totally different atmosphere. I thought, where was that lovely boy who was so thrilled to be here?'

What could have brought about such a drastic change?

'I don't know. Maybe it was achieving fame, maybe it was the ridiculous hours and the strain of producing a show day in and day out.'

Even for a turbo-charged workaholic, Evans's schedule was draining. Dragging himself away from the warmth of Carol, and bed, Chris would leave home with military discipline at 4 a.m. Fifteen minutes later his Porsche pulled up beside the *Big Breakfast* studio – a trio of knocked-through lockside cottages near the River Lea, in Bow, East London. The scene that confronted him at that unearthly hour was straight from a science fiction movie. An eerie green-yellow halogen light shone from the cottage windows, illuminating the hens that hopped between the surrounding yard and the door. Inside, on the Cath Pater-Lancucki-designed set, the walls were covered with giant fried-eggs and flowers. The backdrop was a day-glo pastiche of shrieking colours: turquoise, pea-green, poisoned Marigold and candy-floss pink. The overall impression was that of a children's pop-up storybook, with Evans and his co-presenter Gaby Roslin the heroes.

Roslin, then twenty-eight, had been drafted in as a replacement for Danielle Lux just four days before the launch date, but she and Evans struck up an immediate rapport. On air she adopted the role of Chris's 'screen wife', or perhaps big sister, yanking him back by the arm when he strayed too close to the precipice of good taste; putting him in place when he grew too uppity. A perfect barometer for his humour, she knew instinctively when to giggle along and when to frown disdainfully; when to interrupt and when to stay silent. Their chemistry was not manufactured for television, nor could it have been, and when the cameras stopped rolling, Gaby was one woman Chris never criticized to her face.

'He and Gaby got along brilliantly,' says Anna Paolozzi, the show's head of make-up. 'In all the time he was there I never heard them have a cross word. I think it was because he respected her so highly.'

Chris's first daily task was to attend a 5 a.m. conference, at which he and Gaby assessed the ideas for that day's show, written through the small hours by his five-strong production team. It was an ordeal that Courtney came to dread.

'When he was in a mood, or didn't like something he would say, "My producer thinks this is funny." Then he would make you look a complete fuck-wit by reading it out in a dead-pan voice, making it sound as boring as possible. And you were dog-tired, and this was something you had been slaving all night to produce. I think he would only be happy if he could write, produce, film, edit and present the show himself, then he would be the only one to blame if it went wrong.'

After the conference, Chris scoured the tabloids for amusing stories to spark off, and then, around 6 a.m., he went upstairs to the dingy cottage bathroom, where he soaked in the chipped old enamel tub, cleaned his teeth and washed his hair.

'That was his way of relaxing, getting into the mood to perform,' says Anna. Yet so obsessive was his perfectionism that even his ritual bath was subject to scrutiny. 'It had to be a certain temperature and just the right depth, or His Nibs would have a fit,' says Courtney. 'This is how mad he would drive people.'

About half-an-hour later, wearing an orange and blue vertical striped towelling dressing-gown that frequently gaped open, exposing his nakedness to embarrassed passers-by, he summoned Anna to do his make-up.

'He didn't care who copped an eyeful of his dick,' says Courtney. 'There was no sense of decorum at all.'

Averting her gaze, Paolozzi's instruction was to apply 'a bit of tan, nothing else really'. But even this ostensibly simple task could be a nightmare. 'You should have tried getting it on,' she says. 'He never sits still for a second, because he's hyperactive, and it would be like trying to hit a moving target.' Every so often he also asked her to polish his glasses. 'He always wore the same pair,' she adds.

Make-up artists are often privy to a performer's innermost thoughts, and Anna gained a rare insight into Chris's. He confided in her that he was undergoing psychotherapy, and that his marriage was in difficulty. And, while she says he never became nervous before appearing on television, he was 'completely insecure'.

'I think he's quite a sad guy. Intrinsically, he's quite lonely, even though he's surrounded by lots of people.'

Why did she suppose this?

'It's just there, I feel it. I knew him very well. I think his whole life is work, and he's fantastic at throwing parties, making people laugh. But he's not one of these people who likes being on his own.'

The immediate reaction to *The Big Breakfast* was mixed. While the viewing figures were climbing steadily, critics used to a diet of news and light interviews panned it as frothy, puerile and trite. By early 1993, however, the penny seemed to have dropped. Triviality was precisely what younger viewers wanted to buoy their humour before another mundane day in the office or at school. And although Evans gave a passable impression of a lunatic leading an uprising in the asylum, *The Big Breakfast* was in fact one of the most cleverly-orchestrated live shows yet seen on television.

The praise was perhaps phrased most eloquently by James Saynor, writing in *The Independent* magazine, on 23 January 1993. He compares Evans with the legendary Fred de Cordova, who produced Johnny Carson's *Tonight Show* in the seventies and eighties. Semaphoring signals to Carson from just off camera, de Cordova was the master of orchestrating the mood and rhythm of talk television. Evans, declared Saynor, had the same gift.

'He knows how to draw out and compress the seaside taffy of the broadcast stream into an infinite number of gimcrack shapes, from seven to nine each morning, five days a week.'

The eulogy continues:

'Geeky and ginger-haired, like a young Woody Allen, Evans is a fill artist of consummate nerve and invention. He talks a mile a minute in tones packed with incredulity, his on-screen routine a carefully patterned mix of gags, wind-ups, up-your-jumper whoopery and occasional sullenness (reminiscent of Eric Morecambe or Basil Brush). He has a profound understanding of the meaningless chaffing of young people, but also incarnates the more ancient values of good old British 'cheek', tickling people's fancies across the generations. Although *Big Breakfast* appears to have evolved out of youth television, there's little that's demographically excluding. To moppets, Evans is a teasing older brother; to young adults, he's the office wag; to those with wrinkles he's a chirpy, hormonal nephew.

'The viewer is served up a Ready-Brek of useless and/ or facetious information – sex advice from a pair of Tantrists, news analysis from two psychics, warmed-over tales of kiss'n'tell, barking budgies, featherweight news summaries from ITN . . . At the centre of it is Evans, daft as a bottle of crisps. Notwithstanding the virtues of Gaby Roslin, the show's torrentially cheerful female anchor . . . *The Big Breakfast* has been largely built around Evans's on-air persona, which is that of a hyper-active child at the back of the class. His favourite word is 'fan-tas-tic', stressed through his snaggly teeth with a little sideways snake of the head; among his favourite phrases are, 'Don't try this at home – it's just for fun', and 'Try this at home – it works a treat!'' '

In Saynor's interwoven interview, however, Evans betrays the strain of achieving and maintaining such a high level of performance, morning after morning.

'I don't find it easy,' he says. 'You've got to stay on top of it all the time. And I am on top of it all the time – and concentrate absolutely one hundred per cent. Even then, there are things I overlook. Because I do make a lot of mistakes. I make ten or fifteen mistakes every day. Little mistakes, mistakes in my mind.'

If his own errors were a source of irritation, the errors of others were intolerable. At first he logged them painstakingly during the show, on blue cards measuring six inches by four: 'NO FOLDBACK SPEAKER', read one. Another, held up like a schoolmaster before the embarrassed camera crew, said: 'LITTLE BOY NOT FACING CAMERA.'

Before very long the blue cards were accompanied by blue language. In September 1993, on the show's first anniversary, Evans earnestly told the *Sun*'s Piers Morgan that he was 'a lot calmer now', and that he realized it was 'not clever to shout at people'. But his words were greeted with disbelief by colleagues who suffered his temper, which was back with all the bile and ferocity of his worst days at BSB. On such days, Paula Yates would say he was 'wearing his grumpy trousers', but her euphemism masks the serious distress he could cause.

It is difficult to imagine how a make-up artist who performs the same function each day can do too much wrong, but even Anna Paolozzi was targeted. Why?

She laughs: 'You haven't worked with him. He's a perfectionist and if things weren't perfect he used to get upset. I don't think he liked my make-up very much. He used to say I wasn't very good. "You haven't done a good job today." Just like that. He shouted at me, but I would argue back. We rowed quite a lot and when that happened he would say we were "having a little domestic".'

Others among the production team were less sanguine, notably Courtney Gibson.

One of her tasks was to fetch readers' faxes from the phone-room, a thirty-second dash from the studio, and give them to Chris to read out. She always did this promptly, but one morning he began shouting at her, "Get the faxes, get the fucking faxes!"

'I said there was plenty of time and everyone looked at me as if to say, "You spoke back!" I was actually warned by an executive not to do it again, they were so scared of upsetting him.'

'Another time he had me in tears for days. I was the whipping boy for the day and he was just completely horrid to me. After the show he came up and said it was nothing. I said, "If it was nothing then don't dare to scream at me on the air again." I went to see Charlie Parsons and he must have said something to Chris, even though I asked him not to. Because a few minutes later my phone extension went and there was little quiet voice: "Courtney, this is Christopher."'

Evans only refers to himself as Christopher when he is feeling contrite.

'I said, "Christopher who?"' she continues. 'He said, "Christopher Evans. I heard you've been crying. I'm so sorry". At the end he was all teary about being bad-tempered and *I* ended up consoling *him*. Kind of absurd. You see, I think he genuinely cares what people think about him. When he knows other people hate him, especially people he regards as friends, he does feel bad.'

To the oppressed staff revenge was sweet, even though it was necessarily conducted guerrilla-style.

'I know one person who used to spit in his coffee and another who regularly gobbed in his bath,' says Courtney. 'It was just the sheer satisfaction of seeing him drinking, or swimming in, their sputum.'

They also had unsubtle nicknames for him: The Ginger Cunt, The Ginger Monster, The Ginger Minge. Later, when she was producing Channel 4's *The Girlie Show*, Courtney was able to hit back more openly. At her suggestion, Evans was featured as Wanker of the Week.

'I heard that that really shit him up. He felt betrayed because we were on the same channel,' she smiles.

Another harassed female executive came to question Evans's mental stability. Speaking on guarantee of anonymity, she said: 'He's the most unhinged person I've come across. I stood up to him once, and pinned him against the wall and screamed and yelled in his face. He was such a bully, and I refused to let him bully me. I should have lost my job over it because I was actually in the wrong.' Evans evidently does not bear grudges, for she added: 'We got on very well after that. He can be a most engaging and loving person.'

She likened Evans to the manic depressive Peter Sellers and went on: 'I left before the shit hit the fan ... it was pretty easy to see that it was going to. Because, you know, he got bored. He's got a very low threshold of boredom.'

She particularly disliked it when he bawled at the runners. 'He would stop it if no one was watching. He's like a child who has to be noticed. He is also a divide-and-rule person. He puts people against people, that's how he controls. He wanted us all to go down to the pub at lunch times and Lisa Clark [who later married Evans's Radio One soundman Dan McGrath] was the only one who would stick with him. Lisa was the one he loved. But I think he has a time span of how long he loves people. He is very, very clever, and very, very clever people are easily bored, and it's all a bit of a game.'

In fact there were others in the *Big Breakfast* team who would 'stick with him'. They included a resourceful and unflappable young researcher named Will Macdonald. No matter how much flak came his way, Will, a softly-spoken Berkshire boy, would soak it all up and conduct his duties with quiet efficiency. Evans mentally noted this down. He was also intrigued to learn that Will was an Oxford zoology graduate and Old Etonian.

'That was perfect for Chris,' says the anonymous source. 'It wasn't about control. It was more to do with a working-class northern boy being accepted by what he saw as the establishment. But Will is bright, a slow-burner, and he obviously writes well, because Chris doesn't suffer a fool.'

Equipped with these qualities, Will was to take on a role previously played by Gates, Palin, Daley, the two Andys – Davies and Bird – so many different people: that of sorcerer's apprentice.

'He started off in the early days always being the butt of Chris's jokes,' says Fiona Cotter-Craig, ex-series editor of *The Big Breakfast* and now vice president of a Middle Eastern satellite broadcasting company. 'I don't know if that's progressed much.'

Among the apprentices, however, Will is the longest survivor. More than that, his loyalty has earned him a place in nineties youth consciousness. Today, five years on, he is 'Weee-eeel', Chris's much put-upon foil on *TFI Friday*.

Macdonald, now thirty, appears comfortable with his part and denies that he is a fall guy.

'Yes, I get those accusations, and I have had some letters that aren't very nice,' he says evenly. 'I do think I sometimes appear to be a bit of a whipping boy but I am not a cap-doffing sycophant. I shout back.'

What is the dynamic between him and Evans?

'I want the ability to be rude to people at the right time, and maybe he wants my knowledge . . .' he begins, then reconsiders. 'No, wait. That sounds too pompous. Chris wants to be a middle-class bore, and I want to be a scallywag from Warrington.'

Will, Lisa and others in Evans's chosen group would be invited back to his house to play cards or board games, or listen to music. Outsiders were treated rather like courtiers who had incurred the wrath of a despotic king. Fiona Cotter-Craig, then thirty-six, was among those who fell out of favour. Her punishment was to be spitefully and publicly humiliated.

'He used to tease me,' she says, 'and one day, after the show, I was sitting down on a sort of sleeper, thinking, "Thank God that's over" – it was a Friday. And he came up in front of me and got his dick out. It was very unpleasant. It was at eye-level, inches away from my face. This is honestly true. And he said, "I bet you haven't seen one of those for a while".

'I said. "For God's sake put it away", and walked off. This was behind the set, outside the house in the garden in the back. I'm sure other people must have seen it. It was hardly quiet. Imagine what a shock it was for me. I certainly would have told people immediately afterwards, but the awful thing was you became inured to all of that. It's only afterwards when you think, "Jesus, I could have made more of a fuss."

That's the awful thing about psychological warfare. You get so used to it, you think, "Oh, well, that was it." It's not until you have time to stand back that you ask yourself, "Why, in God's name, did I allow myself to be put through this?" It's a bit like the syndrome where you make friends with your kidnapper.'

Now able to distance herself from the incident, she adds scathingly: 'Chris thinks his dick's fantastic, but actually it is a tragic little stubby, uncircumcised red knob. Hideous. But I do remember veiny blue balls. And for his information, I had seen a penis rather more recently than he imagined – but the point was, it had nothing to do with him. It wasn't a great moment in my life.'

Although Evans's exhibitionism was never again so directly and personally insulting, another woman who worked on *The Big Breakfast* says: 'We all got flashed at all the time. In other working environments it would be classified as sexual harassment.' Sexual terrorism might not be too strong a phrase. 'It crossed my mind that if there was a new researcher, or someone who wasn't mature enough to handle it, they might get a bit intimidated.'

By repeatedly displaying his manhood, Evans was being disinhibited, according to the forensic psychologist Dr Bryan Tully.

'To be disinhibited you just have to be less sensitive to what people think. In fact, it really helps if you are not too concerned what they feel, other than that they approve of you. There is a narcissistic aspect here, which doesn't just mean that someone feels they're the bee's knees, but that theirs is the only view of the world that is tolerable. It means they are entitled to approval and entitled to behave any way they like, and they are just as important as others. It is a requirement of a condition like that that you are not tuned in to how people think and feel.'

In general terms, he adds, a man who displays such traits 'could very easily be classified as either someone with a personality disorder or a personality problem approaching a personality disorder'.

'Central to this disorder is his detriment – not being able to control what goes on in his life, says Dr Tully 'Sudden loss comes into that. Being humiliated by other people, too. He did discover one kind of way to salvage his self-esteem, though: his humour, which can be razor-sharp. I have no doubt he hit back with that in some ways. But of course, that type of hitting back requires an audience – you can only humiliate a bully if someone is listening and laughs. I have met a number of people like this. Their way of handling things has some pay-offs. Unfortunately these people think they are the only ones that exist.

'This sort of person is very good at the engagement process. They are wittier than the rest of us ... if you cross them or kick them, or let them down, the only way they can handle that – the way of not being treated the way they see themselves – is by employing a severe, even vengeful way of putting people down. Re-establishing in their mind the difference between themselves and others. They see the others just as turds, not worthy. And in that sense they have to put them in their place. They can't live with the fact that people haven't behaved towards them as if they were as wonderful as they think they are – which is what most of us have to go through.

'If I was using extreme terms to describe this character-type, psychopathic and narcissistic would be appropriate. They are people whose way of behaving works for them, and gets other people to accept what they are saying must be right, through what appears their extreme self-confidence and their willingness to cross boundaries of social behaviour. The one thing about gaining acceptance and success in the media is that you can be accepted for what you are. No broadcasting organization is going to be wrecked because a DJ or presenter has a particular role. But there are people like this in other professions who can wreak havoc because of the way they attribute the success, or failure, of everything to themselves: "This enterprise would be nothing without me." These people will sometimes give a disastrously misleading picture to a board of directors, or a boss, which might make a very important decision on that basis. But they can always find new supporters to back them.'

Evans and the cultured Cotter-Craig clashed from their first meeting, some two years earlier, when she was asked by his then agent, Noel Gay, to assess a tape of *TV-Mayhem*.

'I thought it was very funny, very innovative but very laddish'.

When she gave Chris her opinion he 'went ballistic'. With heavy irony he asked whether she thought he should include something on women 'as tokenism'. She replied that, no, he should just write in some good female-oriented material, whereupon he glared furiously at her and stormed out of the meeting.

When they met again on *The Big Breakfast* he never mentioned the row and for a while, she says, she could do no wrong in his eyes.

'He was charm personified. He was sweet. He was thinking, "This is so exciting, big career break for all of us – aren't we lucky, all one big happy family. It's gonna be great!"'

But when his exuberance died down she must have committed some perceived sin, for they resumed battle.

'He treated me like a complete idiot, so I didn't awfully enjoy that, and, you know, he's brilliant. His mind works in a different way from most people's and he's able to channel that. Very unforgiving. Very rude. The best story I can give you to illustrate how difficult I found working with him . . .

'My job was basically to approve everything that happened. And as it was a live show if he decided to do something there was very little I could do about it. One day he said he wanted to do this thing which involved the difference between tangerines and satsumas. I said I didn't think we could do justice to it on that day. It might be better if we waited, thought more about it.'

There was, she digresses, never any point in asking Evans why he wanted to carry an item like this. 'He'd just get a fixation about something, and . . . nothing would stand in his way. You'd just think, "Oh fuck it, let him get on with it." If

I had said absolutely don't, there would have been a horrible screaming match. So he did it and afterwards he said, "What did you think, Fi?" I said I didn't really think it had worked and I wished he hadn't done it, at which point he went purple in the face.

' "What do you mean?" he yelled. I said "I'm entitled to my opinion", whereupon he said – and I direct quote: "You can't have an opinion about that!" I said I could have an opinion about anything I wanted. It was that kind of thing that if you disagreed with him you were just so far out of the picture it didn't make sense.'

She regarded Evans as a bully and 'a brat who wants fame without any of the responsibility that goes with it. When God was handing out the component parts that make up a decent human being, He left Chris out. We had to work the most appalling hours . . . and he'd just come in and one morning he'd think something was the funniest thing he'd ever seen, the next he'd think you were the biggest pile of shit, and you're all useless and you're all cunts and, "I hate you all, why have you got jobs? I'm going to get you fired." The feeling to begin with was that we were all doing something fun and different, and then it went horribly wrong.

'Living in dread is the most accurate way of describing it. It was like constantly waiting for the Gestapo to come and knock on your door in Jewish Berlin between 1923 and 1945. It really was hideous.'

But there was nothing anyone could do.

'Chris was the most important thing in the show and he knew it. If you went in to Charlie Parsons and said, "It's him or me", it was, "Well, goodbye then, off you go." In part the channel controllers are to blame. We create these people, tell them they're wonderful, and therefore we lose our critical faculties.'

As his 'grumpy trousers' days became more frequent, even Gaby Roslin was not immune.

'She worked so well with him, she was the one person in the world he was never openly nasty to,' says one source on the set. 'But he could be very, very rude about her behind her back. Not to her face because he was bright enough to know that would have ruined the whole chemistry between them.'

Roslin's serious sofa interview slot was referred to by the crew as 'of the moment' and usually involved her questioning someone in the news.

'Gaby was incredibly proud of them and thought she did them well,' says the source. 'And Chris would be very nice to her about them but in fact the reality was that he was vile, and he would say they were rubbish and we shouldn't have them in the programme. But it kept Gaby happy. He certainly said it to me and I would imagine he said it to other people as well.'

From his treatment of her, Gaby would never have guessed that Chris was decrying her work. Courtney Gibson remembers the day that Evans presented Gaby with a luxury car. 'He didn't need a special occasion,' she says. 'Chris loved doing that – being able to be the philanthropist. He's special like that.'

What might you make of a man who buys extravagant gifts for someone, then derides them behind their back? Dr Bryan Tully says such duplicity is not uncommon in people of Evans's personality type.

'Even though, from time to time, there is an ostentatious show of generosity – a gift given now and again – this does not necessarily indicate a generosity of spirit. Other acts, like loyalty and being there when people need you, for example, are much more substantial than that.'

Roslin certainly fulfils those criteria for a meaningful friendship, and she has never uttered a bad word about Evans.

'When we're not doing *The Big Breakfast* I miss him so badly that I have to call him in the evening,' she said on the eve of his first *Toothbrush* show. 'When I first saw him on *TV-Mayhem* I used to giggle and dream of how much I'd love to work with him. Honesty is his best policy. He's totally real, what you see is what you get. He's funny, very sensitive and extremely kind. I'd never say any of this to his face – I'm very much in love with my boyfriend. But we do adore each other, we're great friends. He's given me tons of confidence and we have great respect for each other.'

She might have added that Chris brought out a side of Roslin that none of her viewers knew she had. Two *Big Breakfast* out-take tapes, hitherto seen only by select crew members, reveal the shockingly explicit banter with which she and Chris amused themselves, and the team, when the audience weren't watching. Their humour is both lavatorial and sexual, and at one point a giggling Gaby straddles Chris for simulated intercourse. The tapes, shot in 1993 and 1994, also feature Paula Yates's famous on-the-bed celebrity interviews with the likes of Patrick Stewart, David Cassidy and Phil Collins. They frequently have to be re-shot because they degenerate into lewdness.

Other sequences depict the unbridled *joie de vivre* Evans can generate. Childlike, he swats an imaginary fly on Paula's head with a rolled-up newspaper, then cuddles her better. He is gripped by such an uncontrollable laughing fit during a song with the puppets Zig and Zag that tears roll down his cheeks and the take drags on endlessly. Yet when he is peppered with snowballs by the crew as he sings 'White Christmas' he reacts like a petulant kid: 'Okay,' he snaps, after being struck in the eye, 'I'm not doing this. I'm going inside – because there was no need for that.' The fun mood abruptly grows sombre – Mr Grumpy Trousers isn't laughing.

One man who gave as good as he got from Chris was Sebastian Scott, the show's brilliant young Millfield and Bristol University-educated editor, as inventive and clever as Chris was. Their 'artistic differences' led to a series of heated exchanges which would ultimately end in a parting of ways. Anna Paolozzi says it was a case of 'Sebastian being a megalomaniac and wanting to do things his way . . . Sebastian can't accept someone disagreeing with him.'

One argument, she recalls vaguely, occurred after Chris had 'been on the razzle' and wanted a morning off. Fiona Cotter-Craig describes Scott as 'the cleverest man I've ever dealt with in television'. He was, she says, 'the only one of us who could come up with better ideas than Chris on a regular basis, and Chris hated that.' The two men 'had a very young stag-like relationship. Sebastian was the one person who could make him do stuff because, at the beginning, Chris respected and admired him. But in the end Chris's ego just got too much and he thought, "Fuck it, I don't need anyone to tell me what to do, I'll just do it all myself."'

But, of course, he couldn't do it all himself, and, under pressure, he regressed. Cotter-Craig says his phlebitis recurred and he suffered appalling hay-fever. Able to see only a few inches in front of his nose without glasses, this would make his vision more blurred and his temper worse.

'He'd come in and say he wasn't feeling well, but he's a hypochondriac. He worried about his phlebitis.' It made his leg go bluey-purple and 'swell from the bottom of the calf to his ankle, there wasn't much definition; just straight down and it didn't look very nice. He wouldn't necessarily talk about it a lot but he would let you know his concerns, which are pretty major. And he certainly said to me he didn't think he'd live till he was very old.'

The stress intensified until, at around 2 a.m. one morning – just five hours before he was due on air – he woke Cotter-Craig at home and, weeping, told her that he was not mentally fit to present that day's show. He had called Fiona because Charlie Parsons was abroad and she was in charge of the programme that day.

Evans, she says, was 'incoherent, sobbing and crying . . . I think the pressure of everything was getting to him. It was while he was doing *Toothbrush* as well, and he just couldn't cope with it. He rang up, and I had to find somebody else to do it. There was no question that he was going to come in. I can't remember if the stand-in was Paul Ross or Mark Little, but I had to ring one of them . . . pick them up at two in the morning.'

Had Evans apologized for causing such disruption?

'No, he was just sobbing, saying, "Poor me, I'm completely cracking up. I don't know what's wrong with me. I can't face it any more. But he was honestly crying. That comes as no surprise because he used to cry very easily . . . he'd cry if you asked him about his dad.'

But why would he be discussing his father, of whom he rarely spoke, even to his wife, with Fiona? Perhaps the therapy had removed a blockage, for she says he would do so, in passing, either before or after the show. He told her the Blackpool Illuminations switch-on story, for example, and would become tearful.

Around this time, according to Courtney Gibson, Evans' raw and entangled emotions were such a cause for concern that Waheed Ali – one of the few men whose counsel he accepted – advised him to 'sort himself out'. As a result, she believes, he went back into psychotherapy.

'Maybe Waheed suggested it . . . he was riding a real emotional roller-coaster. He has got this bastard exterior, but things really get to him. God knows why, but I found myself worrying about him. There was this feeling that something awful might happen.'

Suicide?

'Yes.'

Chris's last *Big Breakfast* was seen on 29 September 1994, and after his departure Lock-keeper's Cottages resembled a Mid-West town in the aftermath of a tornado. Everyone had different feelings, but no one had been left untouched. Fiona Cotter-Craig says she wept 'tears of joy, I can assure you', adding: 'No, I did feel quite sad in a way . . . I knew it would never be as good again. The brilliant thing about him is that he does push people to produce their best. There is a benefit to his viciousness.'

For others, a damp-eyed Gaby Roslin most prominent among them, the outpouring of sorrow was heartfelt and genuine. Even if Chris did gloat unfairly that he didn't know how she would manage because he had 'nicked all the best staff for *Toothbrush* and left you with the dross'.

Whatever their opinion of him, no one will forget the incredible party he organized to say farewell. The staff were instructed to assemble in the studio car-park, where two coaches were waiting to collect them. The drivers were under strict orders not to reveal their destination, and some ninety minutes later they arrived in a sumptuous hotel in deepest Berkshire. Chris, who acted as DJ, handed each person an envelope containing £20 and gave them a choice. They could either keep it or swap if for another, holding a bingo ticket.

'The bingo prize was £1500 of Chris's own cash, and it was nice because a security girl who didn't earn that much won it,' says Anna Paolozzi. 'Chris loved that. He was really very generous.'

Courtney Gibson cannot comment on the event because she was among a group who boycotted it. 'I don't suppose he noticed,' she says, 'but it was my small protest at the way that we'd been treated.'

A few days after our interview Courtney faxed me from her home in Darlinghurst, New South Wales, with her considered appraisal of Chris and her time at *The Big Breakfast*. It provides such a rich insight into the Evans psyche that it is reproduced here virtually in full:

'Like I explained on the phone, we were never friends. I regarded him as one would regard a herd of bull-elephants; they're fascinating to observe, but it's something you want to do from a safe distance. He is absolutely the last person on earth I'd want to be stuck in a lift with, and I wager you'll find many former colleagues who say the same.

'He just seemed so dangerous to me, and I always worried for friends who got involved with him, not necessarily on a romantic level – just on a social level. People would suddenly be caught up in this centrifuge, spending all their time with him. It was like some tragic cult – probably still is – and I always heard too many stories of too many former friends he'd turned into bitter and twisted emotional wrecks. I don't even think it's necessarily malicious, I just think Chris isn't like the rest of us. He doesn't see himself as a small part of a bigger picture. To be at the centre of your own existence is normal, but to regard yourself as absolutely pivotal in the lives of the many people around you, as he seems to, indicates the most rapacious ego and childish naiveté of mind ... I used to get terribly upset by him and hated him with a passion.

'He was certainly a prankster – always holding a lighter to the bottom of the cameraman shooting an interview Gaby or Paula might be doing. It's hard to hold a camera steady when your bottom's about to catch fire. Sean, the cameraman, would probably tell you a tale or two ...

'He was, and still is, just so clever and gifted and brilliant, but what's the good of being brilliant if you're a complete bastard who fills the people around you with self-doubt, fear and unhappiness? The problem with television is that even the most simple programme is a collaborative effort. A show like *The Big Breakfast* is a huge operation and Chris doesn't work well with a large, disparate group of people. The current Chris coterie is a very talented one – it's the same one that has surrounded him since he started *Toothbrush* – but in order to reap the many benefits of working with him one has to be sycophantic to the point of obsequiousness and say, "Yes Chris, you're absolutely right" four hundred times a day, when you'd often rather say, "Why don't we try it this way instead?"

'Despite the bastardry, I'm still convinced that somewhere within Chris lurks this big sweet kid who just can't believe his luck. After all, he was the geek with glasses and ginger hair who wound up wooing his teenage pin-up girl, Kim Wilde. He has been given virtual carte-blanche to make exactly the kinds of TV and radio programmes he likes. He makes so much money he can give friends the most extravagant gifts, and he loves doing that. It's almost cyclical – he'll be really awful to someone one minute and next thing you know he's giving someone else a car. His mood swings are so swift and profound you never know how you'll find him. Will he be jolly or will he be satanic? It's like talking to Sally Field in *Sybil*: the different sides of his nature are constantly jockeying for position . . .'

CHAPTER EIGHTEEN

Towards the end of his two year stint on *The Big Breakfast* Chris's love life had become a topic of such fevered speculation that it had created a cottage industry for the tabloid press. Headline-writers dreamed up such gems as 'Ginger's Blonde At Brown's', 'Good Evans: Can This Really Be God's Gift To Women?' and 'Don't Forget Your Girlfriend's Name'. One paper's graphics department even devised a chart showing how he changed his woman every time he changed his job. Something of an exaggeration – although he does buy a new car whenever he starts a new show. The newspaper stories, usually written in tones of grudging admiration, do not convey the emotional havoc that his romantic wanderlust caused: not only to himself but more often to his increasingly long-legged consorts. Perhaps these blondes from the superficial worlds of showbusiness, modelling and media might have held his attention for longer had they adopted the same attitude towards Evans as Alison Ward's.

Alison is one woman who refuses to be browbeaten by Chris and, soon after he had become a household name through the *Breakfast*, she resisted a blatant and cynical attempt by him to manipulate her.

In February 1993, hungry for any juicy morsel about Evans, journalists learned that he had a 'secret love-child'. As Alison tells it, Jade's existence was uncovered by fluke.

'I had been sitting in a pub, talking to the landlord about Jade, and a reporter from the *Warrington Guardian* overheard me. A friend came over and asked for my address and the next thing I knew the *Daily Star* were on the phone. I refused to talk to them, but the editor said he would print the story anyway, so I went to *The Sun* to ask if they could do it. You know what I'm like – gullible. The reporter I spoke to said he would sort it all out and they printed the story and photo. At least it was accurate. I got £500.'

The resulting article, published in *The Sun* on 13 February and tagged exclusive, revealed that Evans had not seen Jade for two years. Worse, Alison disclosed, not unreasonably, that she was being hard done by.

'He'll be on a few thousand a week, a lot more than the £72 benefits I get,' she said. 'He has sent £150 a month for Jade since we split.'

It was pointed out that, only the previous week, Chris had been offered a £1.1 million three-year deal by Channel 4. He is widely reported to have accepted £1.5 million.

When Chris was approached for a comment he was rattled. Any unfavourable publicity, particularly that which highlighted his past indiscretions, could damage the loveable-loon image he was then keen to propagate. His publicist Matthew Freud – brother of Emma, Chris's one time radio producer – made a statement saying that Chris had never denied Jade's existence and that he and Alison were 'on amicable terms'. But evidently this was not considered enough. As other newspapers made follow-up inquiries, Alison received a phone-call from Chris, who had been conspicuously silent for quite some time. In retrospect she realizes that he needed something from her: his voice was soft, his tone seductive.

'He said that the papers had been on about me and Jade, and, basically, he wanted to bring us down to London and play happy families with him,' she says. 'He wanted us to do an article for the *Daily Mail*, saying that we were all very good friends and that he saw me and Jade regularly. It was all for the publicity. He wanted it all out in the open to keep his clean image.

'I said, "No, sod off, because it's not true, and you know it's not." Yes, we spoke, but he didn't send Christmas or birthday cards for Jade, never mind come and see her. Why should I make him out to be this great person?'

Evans, by this stage accustomed to getting his own way, was, for once, lost for words.

'Oh, er . . . right,' he mumbled, crestfallen. 'I'll ring you back.'

If he thought Alison would soften he was disappointed. When he called again the phone was answered by her then long-term boyfriend.

'He said, "Is Alison there, please?", in his little uppity way, and he got a real mouthful. My boyfriend told him straight, "It's not bloody right, I'm here looking after Jade, not you." He said Chris didn't know what he was missing, not seeing Jade. And when Chris started saying something back he called Chris an arsehole and put the phone down.'

Evans has not called since. Alison is not sorry for herself, but she is fiercely protective of her daughter – now a predictably bubbly and sharp-witted ten-year-old whose thick copper hair and cheeky grin make her a mirror-image of her father, the more so when, for a laugh, Jade dons her granny's thick-rimmed glasses. Her cheerful nature does her great credit, for life as a superstar's neglected daughter has not always been easy.

'We have never hidden the fact that Chris is her dad, but other kids sometimes say things,' says Alison. 'Jade's brilliant at handling it, though. When she started a new school she walked in on the first day and stopped any gossip before it could start. She just stood up in front of the class and said, "Yes, I am Chris Evans's daughter." No one said anything after that.'

Jade occasionally watches Chris on television and Alison has told her that, should she wish to be reunited with her father, a meeting might be arranged.

'She's never pushed it, and I don't think she's ready,' her mother adds.

Alison's greatest sadness is that Jade no longer sees her paternal grandmother.

'We used to go round regularly and Minnie thought the world of Jade,' says Alison. 'Then, when she was going on two, Chris phoned me up and said, "My mum doesn't want you to take Jade down any more." I couldn't believe it and asked him why. He said: "She's scared that if you get into another relationship, or marry, you'll stop Jade going round and she'll be the one who gets hurt." I told him he knew me better than that, and that it would never happen. But that was it. Jade hasn't seen her since. When it all came out about us in the papers I went to see Minnie on my own, and she cried. She said, "There isn't a day goes by that I don't think of Jade." I don't really know who made the decision. But, knowing Chris's mum, she knows her own mind.'

While all Evans's chickens were coming home to roost in Warrington, his personal life in London was fast disintegrating. A grand new house and bold promises could not paper over the cracks in his marriage, which widened in April 1993 after he reluctantly quit GLR and signed for Richard Branson's new national radio station, Virgin – lured by an offer of £60,000 a year for just one weekly show. This may have taken his total income to a reported £8,000 per week but, to Carol, money counted for little. Chris's new job meant that he would no longer be working with her at a time when she was seeing less of him anyway. His departure from the studios in Marylebone Road also signalled the end of a golden and groundbreaking era in radio, one that Chris would never be able to recapture.

'When he left GLR he held a big leaving party and he was in floods,' says Miles Mendoza. 'He thanked everyone who'd been with him and said it was the best job he'd had by a long way. He was obviously devastated to be leaving, but each time he had turned Virgin down they kept upping the offer. It reached the stage where he would have been mad to say no.'

Bold new ventures now came thick and fast. Determined to be his own man, and earn accordingly, on 17 May 1993,

Evans formed Ginger Television Productions Ltd, the first arm of his Ginger group. Carol offered to come out of 'retirement' and help run the new company – a reasonable suggestion since she was an experienced broadcasting Miss Fixit and had been running Chris's affairs so efficiently.

'But he wouldn't have it,' she says. 'He just said he wanted to keep his professional and private lives separate.'

Given that every one of Chris's subsequent relationships has emanated from his work, Carol now views this excuse as ironic. But he was adamant. Nor would he entertain the idea of her working on *Don't Forget Your Toothbrush*, the first and most lucrative of Ginger's in-house productions.

'When he was spending all his time at work, I said that if I couldn't get involved we really didn't have a life together,' Carol told the *Daily Express*. 'Internally I could see it was time to move on.'

Their rows frequently resulted in one or the other staying with friends. 'I was never scared of Chris, but towards the end, once we knew it wasn't going to work, there was a definite sense of walking on egg-shells. We should have talked more, but I guess we didn't want to enough.'

Evans might have taken some consolation if his Saturday slot for Virgin had been a success. But although he claims never to have made a career mistake – 'only mistakes while on the actual stepping stone' – in truth The Big Red Mug Show was not vintage Evans.

'It was sponsored by Nescafe, and Chris and sponsors don't make the ideal mix,' says Miles Mendoza. 'If he was talking about vibrators that might not be good for their image and they would be asking him to tone it down. And he would say, "Fuck off, I'm not toning it down."'

The show also suffered, he says, for two other reasons: Evans was forced to squeeze his gags between incongruous classic rock tracks, and there was no studio audience.

It is worth recording that the boss in the invidious position of relaying Nescafe's reservations about Chris's humour was John Revell, then Virgin Radio's joint-programme director. According to Mendoza, there was a time when Evans and

Revell weren't really talking. Any falling-out, however, was short-lived. Revell would later achieve renown as Johnny Boy on Evans's Radio One breakfast show. More importantly, he also became Ginger's pinstripe-suited managing director – the man responsible for pulling together the company's big-money deals.

On 30 June 1993, however, after just weeks on the air Evans announced that he was quitting Virgin. Friends at first blamed his punishing *Big Breakfast* schedule, but he later claimed that this was a last-ditch effort to keep his marriage together. If so, it was in vain. By the following August, with pre-production work on *Toothbrush* forging ahead, the largely neglected Carol decided they should part for what proved to be the last time.

'It was me who made the suggestion that we should break up,' she told one journalist, 'but it was simply a matter of who was going to say it. We just went through a bad patch and didn't talk about it. I don't really know why we broke up. There could be lots of reasons. I could guess at anything, and I used to spend hours thinking, "Well, it was this", or, "It was that." But it just went horribly wrong and I don't know the real reason. I wasn't as confident during the later stages of my marriage, but I think that probably had something to do with not working. Chris was doing really well – and I don't begrudge him any of that – but I think I may have felt a bit of a spare part . . . his job was so demanding and so important to him. I just made his job important to me as well.

'I always knew Chris wanted fame and when we were together I wanted him to achieve that because he wanted it so much. But in some ways I always thought we could remain as we were. That his feet would stay firmly on the ground. But fame is a drug. Some people are ambitious for fame and I can't really understand that. It's so awful when you know they are worried about how they will cope when the fame comes to an end.'

Carol remained in the Highgate house – and eventually kept it by way of settlement – and her husband began a new bachelor life. Severing the umbilical cord with his beloved Haverstock Arms and NW3, he moved first to a rented company flat in Docklands that had been used by the creators of *Big Breakfast* puppets Zig and Zag, and later to a penthouse apartment nestling beside Tower Bridge, in Shad Thames. It was only twenty minutes away, in his new £48,000 Ferrari, from Belsize Park, but for a while Chris was hardly ever seen in his old stamping ground.

'He just cut off his friends when he left the area,' says his former personal assistant Maria Costello. 'It was as though they didn't exist. He's very faddish like that. It's all or nothing with him. People and places are either in, in which case he's never away, or they're cut out of his life.'

With a change of address came a new girlfriend. Blessed with regular good looks, slender figure and golden blonde hair she was called Rachel Tatton-Brown. If lording it over Old Etonian Will Macdonald accentuated his sense of superiority in the studio, Rachel fulfilled a similar function when she was seen, clinging to his arm, in fashionable clubs and restaurants. The daughter of a wealthy Westlands engineer from Cobham, at the heart of Surrey's gin-and-tonic belt, Rachel was the ultimate trophy girlfriend for a council estate kid like Chris. Everything about her spoke of an impeccable pedigree. Size eight feet and 'Bugs Bunny teeth' notwithstanding, she first appeared on the fashion pages of the *Daily Mail* in 1988. A year later, aged twenty, she was named British Super Model of the Year – the kind of girl who made Nigel Dempster's Diary. She won a place at Swansea University, where she intended to read chemistry, but in time-honoured fashion she postponed her studies to take a secretarial course and strut the catwalk, after which the attractions of academe dimmed.

What was a nice girl like Rachel doing with a guy like Chris? The papers would have it that they met while she was a production assistant on *The Big Breakfast*, but that tells only half the story. Their first introduction was, in fact, at GLR, where Rachel, and her elder siblings, Duncan and Claire, were studio guests.

'Chris thought they were really funny and he couldn't stop remarking on Rachel's looks,' says a GLR source. Both the Tatton-Brown girls were later given jobs on *The Big Breakfast*. Evans denies engineering their recruitment.

'I know it's hard for people to believe but I had nothing to do with Rachel joining,' he says.

According to Jules Fuller, the way Rachel and Chris subsequently began dating was entirely consistent with his modus operandi.

'Chris was never really a womaniser, despite all the hype. He wasn't a blatant, go-out-and-chat-'em-up type of bloke. Everybody he has been involved with has been work-related, or he has met through acquaintances,' says Fuller, echoing Carol McGiffin.

'He's not the sort of person who's like, "Right, I'm on the pull tonight." He's a very dynamic man when you meet him, and in a way he's always chatting people up, coming on to people. But not in a sexual way. It doesn't matter whether they are male or female or animal, he's just very in-your-face.'

By the time she was taken on at *The Big Breakfast*, Rachel had already won the admiration of footballing legend Paul Gascoigne, who asked for her photo to pin on his bedroom wall. Not to be Gazz-umped, Chris began showering her with attention and found it reciprocated.

'When he first started going out with Rachel he was like a puppy-dog around the place,' said an insider on *The Big Breakfast* 'His mood lifted, and for a while it was like having the old Chris back.'

The tabloids first began floating stories about their budding relationship in late September 1993. 'The Blonde And The Breakfast Star' ran a restrained headline in the *Daily Mail*, while the *Daily Star* was less subtle. The front page belched: 'What TV Mr Ugly Has For Brekky!' Juxtaposed alongside the text were photographs of a pouting Rachel poured into a silver body-suit and a dishevelled Chris. Rachel was portrayed as 'a shoulder to cry on' after his marriage collapse.

Witnessing all this from Orford's Greenwood Crescent, Minnie Evans was said to be less than pleased, and was keen for Chris to reconcile his marriage. But anyone who believed there was a chance of that did not know Carol, who felt humiliated by almost daily new revelations about her husband's affair with the 'six-foot stunner'.

She says: 'It was a shock. Other people split up and don't know what [their estranged partners] are doing. I watch this every day in the newspapers.'

It can hardly have helped when an article was written, comparing Rachel – all legs and plunging necklines – with a bespectacled Carol, wearing jeans and her dog-walking coat.

The romance crackled along until November, interrupted only when Chris flew to Los Angeles with Will Macdonald, who he had co-opted to help him devise early formulae for *Toothbrush*. The pair were photographed relaxing by the pool together.

'That was the first time my nipple appeared on page three of a national newspaper,' Will quipped to *The Sunday Times*'s *Style* section. He was slightly less chipper when journalist Anna Pasternak mentioned that he and Chris had shared a hotel bedroom.

'But not the same bed,' responded the blushing Weee-eeel, who lives with his girlfriend. He added: 'Of course there were insinuations that we were gay.'

Any such speculation quickly evaporated soon after Chris's return, for within a month he had landed the ultimate prize: his boyhood fantasy Kim Wilde. His feelings were transparent on the day they first met, when she was standing in for Gaby Roslin on *The Big Breakfast*.

'Chris said that as a kid he had wet dreams about Kim and that he plastered her photograph over his wall,' says Courtney Gibson. 'He was almost salivating at the sight of her, and he kept making "Cor – gorgeous!" faces behind her back.'

The admiration was mutual, particularly as Chris helped Kim over an eleventh-hour bout of anxiety which almost stopped her appearing.

'After I agreed to do it I became petrified,' she recalled in an interview. 'I couldn't cope with presenting a live programme.

Fortunately, my mum talked me round . . . from the moment I arrived on the set, the team – and especially Chris – were fantastic. He helped me through it all.'

Kim's boyfriend for the past twelve months, Rupert Kenyon, took one look at the show and knew his romance with Kim was over.

'As a psychology student I could see that their body language was giving them away,' he said. 'Kim said she wanted to see him and that it was over between us.'

Chris and Kim were pictured together at a Sylvester Stallone movie premiere party, but it was difficult to be sure whether stories of a relationship were being hyped. The more so when Evans's spokesman told *The Sun*: 'Chris is a Wilde – spelt W-I-L-D-E – and crazy guy. He doesn't want us to say any more than that.'

By 16 December, however, Chris was telling everyone of his 'amazing love' for Kim. She had confided in him, he said, that she had only accepted the presenter's stint because she wanted to trap him.

'We got on very well,' he said. 'What I didn't know then, but know now, is that Kim decided I was going to be the man for her. She made up her mind then to have a bit of fun and play the field before pulling me into her clutches. And it worked. As soon as she started *The Big Breakfast* I fell for her and we are having a completely wild, wonderful romance. Kim's just the most amazing, beautiful, sexy, intelligent girl. This is the real thing, I am head-over-heels in love. We literally can't take our hands off each other!'

The infatuation lasted approximately eight weeks, during which time Chris ticked off yet another poignant childhood ambition.

'He told us that he had always wanted to say, since he was little, that he had eaten his Christmas dinner with Kim Wilde,' discloses Fiona Cotter-Craig. 'Gaby Roslin held a Christmas party every year, and that year Chris and Kim went together.' They may not have sat down to roast turkey, but afterwards he would say he had achieved his aim.

Still starry-eyed, Chris went on Jools Holland's Hogmanay

show and predicted that he and Kim would marry in 1994 (a pronouncement that surprised Carol, with whom he had not even discussed a divorce). Then, seven days later, it was all over. Both Kim and Chris were clearly upset, so much so that Evans phoned *The Big Breakfast*'s duty editor to say he was sick and would not be appearing that day.

Everyone has a different theory as to why they parted. Some say Evans was gripped by the irrational jealousy which manifested itself so disturbingly when Carol booked a Caribbean holiday with her old school friend. Kim is fiercely private, self-contained and family-minded, and – to borrow a phrase from psychologist Bryan Tully – he couldn't tolerate other 'suns in his solar system'. Others are of the opinion that, once the initial excitement wore off, Chris and Kim simply had very little – apart from stardom – in common.

Chris himself has refused to explain. But he added to the intrigue by saying: 'Mad is the only word to describe what happened between me and Kim. It started madly, it ended madly, and what happened in between was equally crazy. If the story behind our splitting up should ever be told, it shouldn't be told by me.'

This seemed to be an open invitation to Kim, but almost two years elapsed before she guardedly accepted it. 'What I really like about Chris is that he's very down-to-earth,' she told a national newspaper. 'But our relationship became very public. I've never been comfortable with the public side of my life and being with Chris made it worse . . . with Chris there was a certain craziness about the whole thing, which I didn't like. And I was working a lot, too. I'm not a great girlfriend. I'm very independent and don't like having my wings clipped. Anyone would have to take all that on if he stayed with me.'

Kim refused to belittle their time together.

'There was always a good feeling between us and always will be,' she added. 'Chris is very special. He was very important to me. We've kept in touch but it doesn't necessarily mean we'll be together. We're good friends now, and that means more to me than anything.'

The third possible reason why the Wilde–Evans dream ticket was ripped in half is that Chris refused to stop seeing Rachel during his brief romance with Kim. Her nextdoor neighbour in west London's Acton reportedly spied Chris entering her flat while still ensconced with Kim, and 'after Christmas Day he was parked outside for four days'. Questioned about this the following February, however, Chris emphatically denied there was any overlap between Rachel and Kim. Furthermore, he suggested that his romance with Rachel only began after his split with Kim.

'Rachel was a friend for a long while before things developed,' he told Andy Coulson. 'We were spending so much time together [working] that in the end we thought, "Well, why not?" The amount of work we have on means we spend far more time talking than snogging. Rachel is a great friend and good company. It's a very relaxed thing. It's just nice to be with someone who likes me for who I am. Just lately I have grown used to drawing the attentions of women who are only interested in Chris Evans the star.'

He quipped: 'I suppose I could go out with a different bimbo every night, but Rachel has suggested I stick to just the one.'

The reason that Chris and Rachel had been seeing so much of one another was that he had lured her away from her lowly job at *The Big Breakfast* to help present *Don't Forget Your Toothbrush*, the first episode of which was shown on Channel 4 on 12 February 1994. By the year's end the show would make him financially secure for life, but the first pilot, costing £200,000, had been an unmitigated disaster. Although the core idea – audience arrives with suitcase and passport hoping to win exotic trip – was catchy, the format was ill-conceived.

'It was all over the place,' Evans admitted less than a month before the series began. 'We just didn't know what it was about.' He pledged to iron out the faults. 'We will do another pilot, and another and another . . . I ain't going to do it until it is right. If it's not something I would want to watch, I will say no.'

The cigar-chomping Michael Grade, then Channel 4's Controller, made it clear that he would save Evans the decision. 'Fucking amateur hour, this,' he pronounced, the threat implicit in his voice.

Evans was not accustomed to failure, and he was shaken. Before another trial show he surprised the studio audience by warning them to laugh at his jokes.

'If any one of you fuck this up for me I will drag you up and humiliate you so much you'll wish you had never come,' he snarled.

'I was shocked by his comments,' said audience member, Andrew Cromie. '[We were] slave-driven all night. Chris Evans seemed so worried about the show. When he told us to laugh he really said it quite viciously.'

The main problem, Chris perceived, was that while he was attempting to create a conventional game show, he wanted to present it in a camped-up, unconventional way. Bruce Forsyth meets Pee-wee Herman: but they just weren't gelling. Casting around for someone to blame, he homed in on ex-*Big Breakfast* colleague Sebastian Scott, now the new show's producer. Scott was not scapegoat material, however, and, amid ear-shattering rows said to have surpassed anything witnessed at Lock Keeper's Cottages, he left.

Scott plays down the clash. 'I did the pilot and then I went back to *The Big Breakfast*,' he says, deadpan. 'It was very difficult to do both. All the ideas originated from the pilot. There is tension on most pilots. *Toothbrush* became the most successful British format game show of all time; that speaks for itself. I just didn't want to do it any more.'

Evans, he adds, was 'no more difficult than any other presenter I've worked with . . . obviously you are not going to agree, eye to eye, on everything. He never lost his temper with me; we had a very good working relationship. People talk about him having raging furies but that puts things out of perspective. In general he was fantastically good to work with.'

Jules Fuller, who received a frantic 'drop everything and work for me' call from Chris, offers a different perspective.

'There was a clash of egos,' he says. 'Chris and Sebastian was not a marriage made in heaven.'

It was now, in his desperation, that Evans plunged a white-gloved hand into the top-hat and brought out a rabbit. Scott's replacement, he announced, would be none other than the veteran quiz master William G. Stewart – a man whose impressive track record includes *The Price Is Right* and Channel 4's quiz show *Fifteen To One*, but who hardly sat easily among radical young turks like Will Macdonald and Lisa Clark.

'It seemed a bizarre choice, but it turned out to be an inspired one,' says Fuller. 'Chris treated William Stewart with huge respect. Whatever William suggested, he would go along with. I have never seen him like that with anyone before. William was older, much more experienced, and he certainly brought the show into line: took out some of the bullshit. He kept the commercial element and put on whacky stuff over the top of it.'

On the first show, almost adulatory appreciation of bygone stars inspired Evans to enlist bare-footed sixties chart-topper Sandie Shaw to sing her old hit 'Always Something There To Remind Me'. Then, unashamedly filching his own Person or Personality? idea from Round At Chris's, Sandie engaged a Norwegian in a quiz on her own career. Apparently more personality than person, Sandie lost – unable to recall her own birthplace or maiden name. In another whacky game, a woman named Hannah Cox was invited to indulge in a thirty-second kiss – worth £1,000 – with either an old flame, her boss, or a total stranger. As she contemplated the choice, a python was pulled from her suitcase.

But it was largely thanks to Stewart that when, after an unprecedented four pilots, *Toothbrush* was finally aired, the reviews were lavish with praise.

'If Evans's looks, gestures and frequent "whey-heys" are reminiscent of [Eric] Morecambe, then his warmth and ease with people suggest Michael Barrymore, while his mastery of a tricky format conjures Brucie to mind,' wrote the *Evening Standard*'s television critic Matthew Norman, reminding us

252 ☆ *Freak or Unique?*

that a humiliating fiasco had been expected. 'Extravagant comparisons these may be,' he continued, 'but consider that where those three geniuses spent years in the clubs honing their craft and timing, Evans is still twenty-seven and had, until Saturday, neither hosted a show on his own nor worked with a large audience; and that it was live; and that he invented and wrote the show himself. Consider this, and it would be churlish to sidestep the obvious conclusion that Chris Evans may well be something of a genius himself.'

Norman's eloquent critique contains excusable inaccuracies. Evans credits John Revell with inventing the show. And he had manoevred big audiences in Warrington's pubs and clubs, and while helping to run Piccadilly Radio's roadshow. He was also professional enough to have kept his hand in more recently. He had appeared as a guest artist at an Islington comedy club where, Miles Mendoza recalls, the hippest of crowds found themselves playing Take A Tenner Or Take A Chance On A Chicken.

'You either took £10 or stuck your hand up the arse of these frozen chickens hanging from a clothes peg,' says Mendoza. 'Some had £50 inside.'

Nonetheless, the message was unequivocal: by demonstrating the ability to switch from breakfast crackpot to Saturday evening quiz-king, Chris Evans had proved himself the most versatile broadcasting star of his generation, bar none. More than that, Evans had something over the legends whose ranks he was joining – a business brain that, in generations gone by, might have been pitted against Tommy Drew, king of Warrington's backstreet bookies. When exchanging contracts for *Toothbrush* with Channel 4, he clinched one of the smartest deals in British TV history. It reportedly gave his company, Ginger, a fifty per cent share of all *Toothbrush*'s foreign sales.

Where overseas television companies struggled to replicate the show – which won the coveted Golden Rose first prize – Evans supplied idiot-proof instructions via Lisa Clark. It was another masterstroke. The Swedes bought the formula and introduced topless women; the Germans and Danes both unearthed Chris Evans lookalikes as frontmen, while in

Portugal one in five prime-time viewers were soon tuning in.

'Some of the countries even copied *Toothbrush* so closely they put in our mistakes, and there weren't very many of those,' says Clark. 'When Chris couldn't find the right person in the audience and whispered to the floor manager for help, the French thought that was all part of the show and put it in.'

Although only twenty-six programmes were screened in Britain, Evans's foresight had again come up trumps, but this time the stakes were far higher than they had been when he made *TV-Mayhem*.

'Much later, Chris rang me and offered a third of everything he made from selling the programme abroad,' recalls Revell. 'It was very generous of him.'

So it was, but Evans could well afford such largesse. Today – thanks largely to that one deal – Ginger and its various offshoots are conservatively worth £20 million.

CHAPTER NINETEEN

The antique wooden table was steeped in character and came with eight elegant chairs. It caught Chris's eye as soon as he entered the furniture shop and, by the time he walked out, he had become its proud new owner. "That'll look perfect back in the flat," he thought. But as he steered his red Ferrari back home to Shad Thames, his pleasure gave way to a sadder reality. Richer, now, than he had ever thought possible, he could easily afford to splash out a four-figure sum on the table of his choice. But where was the sense in buying a dining table that accommodated eight people when he didn't have seven friends to sit around it with him?

It was a thought that depressed him for days afterwards, unsurprisingly since it said so much about his personal values and the choices he had made. If he was isolated, who else but himself was to blame, when he had placed his ambition before his relationships and severed so many close ties? If he stared long and hard at the polished surface of his prized new table, he might have glimpsed some familiar faces: Mike Gates, Tim Grundy, Ian Daley, Alison Ward, Trevor Palin, Dave Whittaker, Mike Hollington, Carol McGiffin, Andy Davies, Andy Bird . . . loyal friends who would have gladly shared supper with him.

Several of the northern crowd had tried to contact him when they saw him on TV – just to say well done, he'd made them proud. The reaction was always the same. His personal assistant would take their names, the line would go dead for a few moments, then she would trot out the PA's killer phrase: 'I'm sorry but Chris is unavailable.'

'It's as though he's afraid of his past,' Ian Daley says. 'He probably wants to make a new life, shut the door on the last one. But he can't. His past will always be part of him.'

Talking to a journalist, Evans confirmed his former pal's words. Asked whether he enjoyed returning to Warrington he said, 'I get scared to be honest. It's all so foreign to me now.'

With his table empty, 1994 – the year that he entered the superstar bracket – was the loneliest he had ever encountered. Weekdays were bearable enough because then he had company. When *Toothbrush* kicked off he reduced his appearances on *The Big Breakfast* to three per week, and on those days his routine remained the same. On his non-*Breakfast* days he would stay at home until gone 9 a.m. Then, leaving the Ferrari, the £23,000 Cherokee Jeep and the 1956 MGA safely in the garage, he cycled for twenty minutes to reach Ginger's headquarters, close to Canary Wharf, at the heart of Docklands. On arriving he would be greeted with cheerful obsequiousness by his bubbly, bright and very young team.

'Hey, Chris, how's it going?'

'Great, how's you?'

'Jeez, my fucking head, on the piss last night . . .'

The banter rarely rose beyond this gossipy, banal level for the ten or twelve hours he was in his office.

As the year progressed, and the initial problems surrounding *Toothbrush* were overcome, then at least his mood was sufficiently equable for him to feel like joshing along. For the first few months, however, particularly in the studio, staff were best advised to keep their eyes lowered when the carrot-top hove into view.

'His nerves showed in that he would have a go at everybody,' recalls Jules Fuller, who worked on the first series of *Toothbrush*. 'It was the old thing. The pressure was on and he would start shouting and screaming. Cue cards were the classic thing. Instead of holding them in the right place next to the camera, some kid doing it for the first time would do it wrong. Instead of saying, "Listen, mate, you've got to hold the cue cards up", he would go berserk. "Fucking ridiculous! I can't work like this!" Or sometimes he would say nothing, and just stop and throw his hands up in the air, which was almost worse than being shouted at. It meant, "This person is crap", and it was harmful to their sanity, health and self-esteem.

'He did it to me once. We'd taken the whole audience to EuroDisney over night, and I'd filmed the piece, and it was being run in next week's show. The script had just been finished and he got hold of it, and said, "Who the fuck wrote this script? It's crap. Jules! This script is crap!" I was in the gallery and I stopped myself [from saying anything back] because, at the end of the day, he's the guy out there in front of everybody. But he'd actually written the script himself and I'd only changed two or three words. He had clearly forgotten, so I went down and quietly told him, "If the script is crap, it's because you wrote it that way." He just looked at me and laughed. It was gone then, and he moved on. I don't think he holds massive grudges.'

Given his treatment of stoical colleagues like Fuller it was small wonder that Chris's evenings and weekdays were often so empty. Fuller numbers himself among those potential close friends who spotted the pitfalls early and chose to stay one step removed.

'It's always a huge pleasure to see him, especially when it's not work-related,' he says cautiously. But his message is clear when he adds: 'I would hate to bump into him at a social function when he's on show.

'I was never one of his cronies, but he is an insecure artist and he needs his sidekick, his batman around him all the time. John Revell is not in that category because I think he is more of a steering influence, but I saw three people go through that with him: Will Macdonald, Gary Monaghan and Andy Davies. Dan McGrath went through it for a while, too. Round [at Chris's] every night and he doesn't do anything without you. [Chris] is a hugely entertaining person to be with. He makes them feel like they are the other fifty per cent of what's going out on air. He's like George Michael needing his Andrew Ridgely. I'm sure Ridgely had a lot more to do with Wham! than anyone knows. But Chris needs longevity out of someone – and if Will is fulfilling that need now, then brilliant for both of them.

'They had a particular way of working together which excluded everyone else. They would have a long meeting and go through ideas, and then Will would re-write, re-write, re-write. I'm sure Will has been with Chris long enough now to have a very steady hand on what he's doing. But I did see people fall by the wayside – Andy Davies suddenly out of favour, then Gary, Dan through *The Big Breakfast*. I'm sure it starts out as fun, but then it just becomes hard. I didn't want to get involved in the whole cliquey process, so I don't feel as though I have been dropped.'

Back in 1994, Chris was seeking to recreate the sense of security he had found in the Haverstock with Carol, Gary and the two Andys.

'I realized that apart from the people I work with I haven't actually got any friends,' he found himself musing to Robert Crampton of *The Times Magazine*. 'Well, a couple. But I haven't got a network of friends. Most people set up a network of friends, and then they get a job that sustains their life. What I've done is, I've got a job that sustains my life but I haven't really got a life out of work. So I'm having to do it the wrong way round and it's quite difficult.

'What used to happen to me,' he continued, apparently using the interview as a form of self-purgation or therapy, 'was, in the week, life was a breeze. Friday night I'd get home and literally – and I'm not joking – the phone wouldn't ring until Monday morning. I thought, "I can't do this any more" ... I do like going out on my own. What I did for a while was go for a ride in my car on my own or go down to the Pont de la Tour on my own with a book.'

The thought of Chris Evans reading alone, night after night, in one of London's busiest and trendiest restaurants would soften the heart of his most put-upon runner. Unconcerned that he might be derided for self-pity, however, he continued in the same vein.

'See,' he told Crampton, 'when I used to live over at Haverstock Hill, my local was the Haverstock Arms. I had a great time. I lived in the pub for two years, doing GLR and *The Breakfast*. I had loads of friends there. Then me and Carol split up and I had to come over here. And when you order a beer here, they're so polite, but you don't get a decent conversation. None of it's real, is it?'

At the hub of the new 'network' he was trying to create were Revell, Will, Dan and Lisa Clark. On the periphery were people like Jules Fuller. Evans began by inviting them for drinks at Shad Thames, or taking them out for after-work supper. But, says Fuller, 'There was no wild party scene. Like any comedian, he didn't want to smile all the time. He would say he was bored shitless from smiling. "I'm going to have to smile for two hours, let me miserable till I get to the studio." He was a bit Tony Hancock-ish. If you scratch not too deeply there's quite a few parallels. I don't think he's a manic depressive, but there is that constant striving for the next thing and, at times, he would just look at he was doing and say, "Why am I doing it, this is boring, this is crap."'

Underlying this angst was his growing sense of mistrust. In the old Haverstock days no one was rich and no one was poor, and everyone stood their round. Now he was a millionaire, and that set him apart.

'You got the impression that he never knew whether he should be picking up the tab for everyone or making them stand his round,' says one source then at Ginger. 'I always felt he didn't know whether he was being taken advantage of. And because he was so intent that this shouldn't happen, he sometimes went the other way, so he could be quite mean when you didn't expect it.'

But Evans's suspicions were not solely materialistic.

'He was also uncertain about who genuinely liked him and who was befriending him because he was Chris Evans, mega-star', the source added.

Alone in his apartment, he may have agonized similarly over Rachel Tatton-Brown. Would the statuesque beauty really have fallen for him if he was still selling shirts in the Warrington branch of Top Man? The question remained relevant only until the autumn, when their flickering romance died. Some in their circle were surprised that it lasted that long, claiming that Rachel didn't always appear to be on Chris's wavelength.

'I'm not sure whether she understood when he was taking the piss out of her or not,' says Fuller, who sometimes shared after-work drinks with them. 'She's bright, don't get me wrong. But you got the feeling that it was going to be hard to keep up with Chris. The rapier wit kicked in now and again.'

Despite working so closely with him, however, in the studio she was spared his fierce temper.

'His rages came out on everybody but never on Rachel,' Fuller adds.

During the early spring and summer months of 1994 they appeared to have a future together. Making a foursome with Dan and Lisa, in April they packed Chris's Cherokee and beetled down to the West Country village of Stogursey, where they stayed in a remote twelfth-century castle. Hankering, perhaps, for his car-boot sale mornings, Chris went bargain hunting at a school auction and emerged with a 50p box of wind-up toys. In May they were spotted looking at houses, and the following month an exclusive story in *The Mirror* trumpeted glad tidings: 'TV Chris To Wed Rachel'. She did move into the Docklands flat, but living together exposed their incompatibility. By September he was ranting again, and after one tongue-lashing Rachel stormed off to stay with her sister in West London. When she returned Chris told her he didn't want her back. She was replaced on *Toothbrush* by another model, Jadene Doran, and although she and Chris were dating again in November, their reunion did not last.

Still bitter, Carol McGiffin was quick to take her revenge.

'I'm not surprised they split up,' she snapped, when approached for comment by *The Sunday Mirror*. 'She's a numskull. I saw most of the shows and I wasn't impressed by her. I thought perhaps she'd improve as the series went on, but I don't think she did.'

In the same article, Carol considerately answered the question that may have bothering Chris at night.

'She wouldn't have looked at him twice if he was a dustman. Women who wouldn't have given him a second glance before he appeared on the telly approach him now because he's got fame and money. It's a big problem for Chris and I hope he realizes it.'

However, even as Carol fired off this well-aimed parting salvo, another of Chris's glamorous subordinates was casting admiring glances in his direction. Like Rachel, she was tall, pencil-slim, blonde and vivacious. And like Rachel her parents were wealthy – her father having recently retired as a company director. They lived in Banstead, another affluent Surrey village not far from Rachel's former home in Cobham. Her name was Suzi Aplin, and after working with Michael Aspel on *This Is Your Life* she had moved to the *The Big Breakfast* as a celebrity booker, fixing Paula Yates's star interviews and other guest appearances.

Had she been Courtney Gibson or Fiona Cotter-Craig, Suzi's first brush with Chris would have soured her opinion of him ever after.

'He took the mickey out of my crooked teeth . . . in front of everyone,' she told a friend. 'I felt completely humiliated and burst into tears. Chris was so sweet when he realized how upset he had made me. He handed me a red rose, apologized for being a complete idiot and offered to give me a lift home in his Porsche.'

Suzi forgave him immediately. Moreover, as the lifts became more regular she developed a monumental fixation on Evans, but kept her feelings well hidden. One of the few people she felt able to trust was his make-up artist Anna Paolozzi.

'She had a crush on him for ages before they went out,' reveals Anna. 'She told me she just adored him. She would say she loved him and she didn't know what she could do.'

The other woman she confided in was Rachel, who reassured her that she and Chris appeared 'made for each other'. Imagine, then, her sense of betrayal when Rachel went out with him herself. 'I was really hurt,' she told her friend.

Suzi was left licking her wounds until the spring of 1995, when Chris phoned her out of the blue to suggest dinner. By this time she had left *The Big Breakfast* to work as an assistant producer on a forthcoming BBC television show presented by Steve Wright. Coincidentally, Evans had just taken over Wright's slot on the Radio One breakfast show.

During the intermission between Rachel and Suzi, Chris's loneliness returned with a vengeance. Briefly entertained by diversions like hosting the Brit Awards, he spent long hours alone in melancholic contemplation. Neighbours were alarmed to see television's brightest young talent shuffling miserably along the road to the fish and chip shop for his supper, or browsing over the videos in his local rental store. 'All I know is that he was a bit of a sad git,' said one woman who lived in the same building. 'He always seemed to be on his own – you never saw him bringing friends back.'

He bought ingredients from the local supermarket and taught himself to cook more exotic dishes than bacon off-cuts. Italian sauces became a speciality, but there was rarely anyone to sample them. And when loneliness threatened to engulf him he started to read books, something he had never considered before because he dismissed it as too passive. His choice reflected his twin pre-occupations: *The Bridges of Madison County*, a tale of true love and heartbreak; and *The Late Shift*, chronicling the intrigue-filled ratings war between rival American TV presenters David Letterman and Jay Leno. He also thumbed through the biography of Michael Caine – another working-class boy made good – who was soon to become a business associate.

Bleak solitude and emptiness permeated almost every interview he gave in 1994.

'It hit me the Sunday morning after the first *Toothbrush*,' he told Matthew Norman of the London *Evening Standard*, 'that all I ever wanted was the ten o'clock Saturday night slot on Channel 4, and now I'd achieved my life ambition at twenty-seven. So what do I do next? It's not as if I can bask in it because there's no emotion at all. There's no sense of achievement, no sense of adulation, no sense of anything. You can compare it to climbing Everest. You climb Everest, and what do you do then? Climb the north face? Okay, but so what? And then? Climb the north face with a grand piano over your shoulder? There has to be more to life.'

He also spoke vaguely about taking off in different directions: writing a book, perhaps, or acting, or lecturing media students. Pondering future possibilities was something he tended to do in forlorn moments. It was almost as if he was back at Padgate High School, dreaming of becoming a rugged, all-action fireman – a dream that was thwarted just because he was short sighted. Carol McGiffin recalls how, when the pressure hit home, he would fantasize about running a sandwich bar somewhere.

Jules Fuller says: 'I remember sitting on a balcony with him while we were doing *Toothbrush*, and he was saying he'd like to give it up in a few years time and open a school for kids to learn how to present TV.

'"By the time I'm thirty-five I want to jack the whole thing in and open a cottage school in the country because I never got taught how to do it – had to claw myself up. I'd like to give some kid the chance to get up there." That was really nice.'

In a desperate attempt to raise his black moods, Chris – who was never previously interested in money or the luxuries it buys – began spending at random. Strictly a cash or cheque buyer – his parents had advised him never to ask for credit – he acquired unusual gadgets, properties, vehicles and other rich men's extravagances. He bought a model helicopter and a replica plane, but then hardly ever flew them. He assembled a small fleet of cars but seldom drove them. He moved from the penthouse apartment to the flat directly underneath just for a change of scene. Soon he would switch his attention to fine houses, perusing a French chateau one week, a Scottish castle the next. But when he called his mother and offered to buy her a nice new house away from the Greenwood estate, she was unimpressed. At sixty-nine, she said, she was far too old to leave her friends and neighbours. She thanked him and resolutely stayed put.

Carol McGiffin – kept informed of Chris's progress through mutual friends – recognized his latest behavioural syndrome only too well.

'He is always thinking about the next house, the next car, the next girlfriend,' she told the *Daily Express*. 'He loves acquiring things but doesn't like keeping them. He can't stand permanence. He gives the impression that he's happy and he's having a great time but he's not. He's never satisfied. He believes that happiness lies just around the corner.'

In the geographical sense, it once had: in Belsize Park. Hankering after its familiarity, over the winter of in 1994–95, Chris began drifting back there after an absence of almost two years. From the moment that he first burst through the blue-painted doors of the Haverstock Arms and shouted for a pint of lager, it was as though he had never been away. The stoutly-built Irish landlord Andrew Carey – now famed as the barman on *TFI Friday* – greeted him warmly, like a returning soldier. So, too, did his favourite regulars: actor Ronnie Fraser, Tony Ashton, from the seventies rock band *Ashton, Gardner and Dyke*, and his wife Sandra, Chris Gillett, the manager of the Lingfield Health Club, and Mel Galley, from the heavy metal band *Whitesnake*. By the end of his first marathon session back at the Havvie, he was already pondering where in NW3 he might make his new home. He was so excited by the prospect of a permanent return that, before long, he abandoned the Docklands flat and took temporary residence in the Posthouse Forte Hotel, just up the hill from the Havvie, in Hampstead.

Around this time, crossing Haverstock Hill one afternoon, he bumped into Maria Costello from the Lingfield, and the pair struck up a conversation. When Chris inquired whether she was still in her old job, Maria said no, that since their last meeting she had qualified as a masseuse.

'Great,' said Chris, 'you've just got a new client.'

On the first Monday that he visited her, Maria discovered how stress had devastated him. It was difficult to discern whether the damage was physical, emotional, or a combination of the two.

'He told me he had been seeing a Harley Street doctor because he was suffering terrible problems with his back,' she recalls. 'He had this hypersensitive condition which would send his back into spasm and went right round to his stomach. The doctor said it was likely to be sensitive nerves, and even if you just tickled that area with your fingers he could seize right up in agony. He said the massage helped.'

He was still in this precarious state of health when, as he prepared to leave home one day to rehearse *Toothbrush* at London Weekend Television's South Bank studios, the phone rang. It was his old boss at GLR, Matthew Bannister, who was by now Controller of Radio One.

'I've got a job that I think you might be interested in,' he told Evans, who promptly invited him round for a meeting.

Part of the Birt revolution at the BBC, Bannister had been trying to lure Chris back to the station since 1993, when he unceremoniously booted out the old guard of DLT, Simon Bates, Whispering Bob Harris, Johnnie Walker and Alan 'Fluff' Freeman. But the breakfast show was all that interested Chris. And, despite falling audience figures, even the ruthless Bannister considered its host, Steve Wright, to be sacrosanct. When Wright told Bannister he was moving on to television, Bannister was secretly delighted, for now he was free to offer radio's most coveted slot to Chris.

'I had a chat with Matthew just after he appointed Evans to the breakfast show, when they had seen the first listening figures and they were really good,' said a radio industry source. 'Matthew said they had got really lucky. Steve Wright was going nowhere, down-hill fast, and they had tried to get him to re-invent himself but he had failed. But who was going to fire Steve Wright? He was a legend. When Steve solved the problem for him by quitting, Matthew had to pinch himself.'

Chris affected nonchalance when Bannister made his approach but he, too, was pinching himself. The position he had yearned for since retreating to his bedroom with the wireless after lessons at Boteler Grammar was now his for the taking. What was more, as Ginger was an independent service provider, free – as he saw it – from the stifling constraints of BBC bureaucracy, he could dictate the terms. The deal was sealed as a tracksuited Chris and Bannister sipped cups of canteen coffee on the veranda outside LWT. Conveniently, a press photographer with a long lens happened to be on hand to capture the moment that Chris said yes to an arrangement under which his company, Ginger Air Ltd, would receive around £1 million to produce the show for an initial eight-month period. It was, unquestionably, the most lucrative contract in the history of British radio.

Two months before he took Wright's mantel, however, Evans gave Bannister a taste of the nightmare to come. He granted an interview to his favourite newspaper, *The Sun*, and its lengthy headline told the Controller all he needed to know: 'If my friends had found out I was joining Radio One they would have locked me up in an asylum.'

In case Bannister had missed the message, Evans reminded him that he did not need the job, and had been close to signing a TV deal that would have 'set me up for life'. He spoke of the huge career gamble he was taking by 'joining a station with serious problems'. He aired concerns about the atmosphere at Radio One, and the type of show he would be able to produce.

'I said to [Bannister]: "If I'm going to have to take a risk, so are you",' Evans said self-importantly. '"You are going to have to be totally committed to the show."'

He had taken the job solely because it was a challenge, he added. His aim? 'To help make the station great again.' Coupled with his vastly inflated salary, such a grandiose statement of intent was guaranteed to set the critics sharpening their knives, but Chris was oblivious to the danger. He was so confident of amassing a new following that at 6.30 a.m. on 24 April 1995, he began by serenading his new Radio One audience with Peters and Lee's ballad 'Welcome Home'.

In a way, Chris had gone home, too. To Orford, where as

a sixteen-year-old he had bombarded Tom McLoughlin's ears with the greats of 'Wonderful Radio One'. At first there appeared every chance that he would, as promised, single-handedly recreate that golden age of radio. So what if some of the apparently brilliant new ideas were resurrected from GLR – The Kids Are All Right But Only If They're Wrong and Honk Your Horn, for example. Those who noticed did not care. So what if the jokes were near the knuckle: 'I know Hugh Grant is going to be listening this morning. What I want to know is whether he likes to get up Hurley.' Bannister could stomach a little smuttiness if he generated this much excitement. At 9 a.m. – when his inaugural show reached its raucous finale – he rushed into the studio to congratulate Evans and his team.

One or two dissenters apart, the Controller's praise was echoed by the media – even its least likely quarters.

'A saviour is in our midst,' wrote Marcus Berkmann in the *Daily Mail*, a bastion of conservative Middle England. 'He has carroty red hair, National Health specs and rather more teeth than are entirely seemly ... Whereas Steve Wright was the calm in the eye of the storm, Evans is a maelstrom of early morning energy, constantly provoking, prodding, making stupid jokes and embarking on giant conceits that you can't help laughing at ... this is the sort of wild arrogance Radio One desperately needs.'

But the honeymoon period was to be pitifully brief. How could it be otherwise when Chris – in the job of his dreams despite all his bravado – seemed intent on blowing himself sky high?

CHAPTER TWENTY

'Radio One is bigger than any personality. It's not a dictatorship or a vehicle for the stars ... it's a creative community.'

MATTHEW BANNISTER talking to the *Daily Mail*, 20 April 1995

'The DJs aren't promoted like they used to be. They should all be larger than life.'

CHRIS EVANS talking to *The Sun*, 24 February 1995

Unlikely though it may seem, by the summer of 1996, Chris Evans – the product of decent, hard-working, everyday folk – had become a subject for national debate. You either loved him, in which case you arrived at work or school still tittering at his effrontery and pirated his risqué gags and catchphrases for the rest of the day; or you loathed him so passionately that you wrote letters of complaint to the BBC and joined Michael Gates's wife in banning his name from your home. The argument was so heated that there were no in-betweens. Surprisingly, given the level of interest, no reliable opinion polls were conducted on the matter, but the camps were roughly divided along lines of age and sensibilities. Evans's detractors tended to be middle-aged or older members of the chattering classes who feared that his humour – lavatorial, crude and frequently sexist – was dangerously subverting the morality of the younger generation. It followed, therefore, that his supporters were largely, though not exclusively, youthful and disinclined to take life too seriously.

If Evans appeared to revel in his new-found notoriety, who could blame him? All publicity is good publicity, and statistics did not lie. More than 600,000 new listeners tuned into his show in the first week, a figure that had swelled to one million by the end of 1995. Yet as the anti-Chris Evans lobby became more strident – championed by *The Daily Mail*, which branded him 'the most hated man in radio' – he would not back off. Conversely, his antics grew more outrageous, almost daily. Not content with cracking risqué jokes and inviting women readers to 'fax us yer breasts', he began seriously to abuse his position. He publicly shamed his young researcher, Justin Bradley, for fiddling his expenses by £20; threatened to expose the name of a plumbing firm for alleged shoddy workmanship at his new house; then alienated his hard-working fans by boasting that the house, in Kensington Park Road, Notting Hill, cost £600,000 ('That's £560,000 plus the agent's commission'). He scoffed at accepted convention by slagging off other broadcasters, most notably Anthea Turner. 'How about we get together while I kick you in the mouth,' he taunted her over the air waves, after savagely attacking her TV show *All You Need Is Love*.

How could he square his man-of-the-people image with threatening women and parading his wealth? More pertinently, as the criticism spread beyond the frowning middle-classes to encompass large elements of the social group that spawned him, why did he continue to destroy himself? Perhaps it was this simple: perhaps he was awakening to the awful realization that attaining the number one job in radio could never obliterate the pain of a bullied childhood, nor fill the void that had been within him since his father's death in April 1979.

'Career success is often pursued remorselessly by people who suffered in childhood,' says the psychologist Dr Bryan Tully. 'They use it as a substitute for what they have lost. It's like having a bigger penis – a sign of power, prestige, something that can be flaunted. It goes with the search for a seemingly better woman, a fancier car, a bigger deal, a more luxurious home. In reality, of course, these things can never compensate for the loss that has been suffered.'

Whatever was driving him, he confounded Matthew Bannister. The smooth-operating law graduate remembered the days when a Bermuda-shorted Evans had roller-skated down the corridors at GLR, so he was prepared for a few fireworks. Yet as the months passed, he saw – often to his personal embarrassment – how mischievous eccentricity had degenerated into nihilism. During the period ending September 1995, a relatively modest three complaints against Evans's show were upheld by the Broadcasting Standards Council, all centring on sexual innuendo. But between noon on Wednesday 21 December and dawn the following day – a period that has passed into Ginger's history – the pattern was set for the coming year.

The debacle began when Evans invited his Breakfast Show gang, plus some of Ginger's staff, to Christmas lunch at fashionable Trader Vic's restaurant in Park Lane. From the moment the diners were assembled, sports journalist Clare Balding says that it was clear Evans had planned something more than turkey and crackers.

'He had gone out and bought these beautiful presents. Holly got a pair of leather trousers laced down the side, like chaps. He got Tina Ritchie [the newsreader] a beautiful velvet jacket; another girl called Stash [the Breakfast Show's booker and researcher] is quite an awkward shape, and he had stopped a woman with a similar figure on the street to make sure her jacket would fit. He loved buying people presents – he was like a kid. He bought me a pair of silly pyjamas because he said I never went out with them at night. I have never known such generosity.'

But this was only the beginning. After lunch, the boozing continued long into the afternoon, whereupon the chosen people were led on a West End pub crawl which ended – so far as anyone can remember – at Evans's club, the Groucho in Soho, watering hole of the media glitterati. Clare found that Evans had booked no less than six rooms for use by his entourage. He told his them he had done so 'in case anyone wanted a shave or a nap because we had been up so early'. But the suspicion persists that Chris had planned – or at least anticipated – the all-night session that followed, and prepared accordingly. If so, Clare was not in on the little jape.

'When I left, at around 12.15 a.m., they weren't that pissed and I thought no more about it,' she says.

The only team member who made it in to the studio on the morning of 22 December was Holly Samos, and by the time she arrived, just fifteen minutes of the Breakfast Show remained. Evans was carpeted and fined £7,000 for dereliction of duty and predictably joked about it on the radio the following morning.

'I don't think they went to bed at all,' says Clare. 'I think they stayed at the Groucho and, about 3 or 4 a.m., they just decided they weren't going to go in. Holly had gone home, and they rang her to say they weren't going in. But where Chris had been very good was that he hadn't rung Tina or me and told us. We were the BBC's employees, not Ginger's, and he knew it would be a lot worse for us if we didn't turn up.'

It was only when she arrived for work, at 7 a.m. next morning, that she discovered that DJ Dave Pearce had been asked to stand in for the paralytic Evans. Yet although he attempted to make it sound like every honest drinking boy's impromptu festive season bender, Clare's story paints a somewhat different picture.

Jules Fuller adds an interesting post-script.

'The last time I saw him was just after the Groucho incident,' he says. 'He said, "Look at the press – it was all deliberate. We got more press out of that than anything else." He was saying to me that it was half worked out, that they'd done it as a big press story, but I didn't believe it. It didn't hold true."

Pre-planned or spontaneous, the attitude of Evans's shipmates that night might be seen to exemplify the way they unwittingly colluded in his downfall at Radio One. None of them steered the skipper back on course. Not his first officer, John Revell, thirty-eight years old and supposedly more mature, nor Dan 'The Man' McGrath, nor Holly, and certainly not the two young deck-hands, Jamie 'The Student' Broadbent and Justin Bradley.

'I don't think he has anyone around him who will say, "Chris, you're in an irrational mood at the moment and I'm not going to act on it," ' says Maria Costello. 'I feel he is surrounded by people who don't stand up to him, and the one who is in the best position to, but doesn't, is John Revell. He is the managing director and he has been with Chris the longest, but he will keep Chris happy and he won't argue too much, especially on behalf of the staff.'

Maria replaced Kim Vendryes as Chris's PA in April 1996. The previous September, Evans had publicly pronounced Kim as 'friggin' great'. But, such are the fluctuating fortunes of Evans's employees, that Kim was told that Suzi was now to look after most of Chris's affairs, so there was no job for her.

'Which was rubbish,' says Maria. 'She wasn't one to suck up to him, and she felt out of favour, so she was half expecting it. But she was very upset.'

Five traumatic months later, Maria would suffer a similar fate. Before dismissing her indictment of life at Ginger as vexatious, however, witness the following abridged dialogue, recorded by a *New Musical Express* journalist in September, around the time she was dismissed:

Revell: 'He's so famous that when we went out on the Roadshow he had to have four minders with him, whereas me and Dan can stand at the bar having a quiet pint and no one will know who the fuck we are. Chris has got all these girls jumping on him . . . bastard! But I think he likes to surround himself with normal people.'

Holly: 'He will still go down the high street shopping on his own. Y'know, he'll go to Top Man, it's not like he's suddenly become a Harvey Nics man. He still does normal things . . .'

Jamie: 'So that's official! Chris Evans is normal!'

Justin: 'No, he is. We go down the pub all the time . . . he's quite a simple soul, really.'

Jamie: 'Life's so good that you never have time to stop and think about it. I just go with it. I love it.'

Mancunian Jamie Broadbent, in his early twenties, who landed his job after winning a work experience place at Ginger, is then asked how people react to him in his role as 'court-jester'.

'People are very sympathetic,' he replies with heavy irony.

'Especially the birds,' another of the team harps up.

'He's a fanny magnet.'

'Yeah, a shag-happy fanny-magnet . . .'

The Breakfast Show crew snigger in unison.

Evans, of course, was not blind to such sycophancy. Indeed he has said that he sometimes feels like Elvis Presley, always surrounded by his entourage. But better to sup with hangers-on who laugh at your jokes than sit alone at an eight-seater table.

Well-versed in manipulating such circles after his days at GLR, *The Big Breakfast* and *Toothbrush*, he perfected the art on returning to television with his own pop-chat-and-gimmickry show, *TFI Friday*, which was first aired on 9 February 1996. With the exception of Revell, who was appointed executive producer, the *TFI* personnel – including Will Macdonald and girlfriend Suzi Aplin – was totally different from that on the Breakfast Show. Moreover, in Egton House, where Ginger rented office space from the BBC before moving to its own HQ in Great Titchfield Street, the two staffs were separated by three storeys. Ginger Television Productions was in the basement, while Ginger Air was on the top floor.

Chris made little secret of the fact the he regarded his hand-picked radio crowd as his A-team, but he would flit between the floors, playing off the two groups against one another.

'At one party, one of the girls from TV got really drunk and just collared him and said, "You think we're all shit",' says Maria. 'He said she was absolutely right. He didn't take much notice of the TV lot. The TV people were strangers when he first began. But he's got so much power and he would be so arrogant about it. On his thirtieth birthday he held a party at Langhams and a couple of his favourite TV people were invited – Clare Barton [the production manager on *TFI*], Will, and David Granger [a co-producer], for example. But quite a few were left off the list and felt excluded.'

This divide-and-rule policy hardly fostered a good team spirit.

'He would invite people out for lunch sometimes, or drinks in the evening, and we were always watching nervously to see who was "in",' Maria says.

Those who were 'out' were either sent to Coventry or subjected to a tongue-lashing, sometimes without ever being told how they had sinned.

'When I first started he always said hello when he passed, then suddenly would completely blank me,' she says. Nor were Revell and Suzi exempt from his moods. 'He'd go into John's office, which was by my desk, and he'd be screaming and shouting,' she says. 'You'd suddenly hear this "No! No! No!" He used to shout at Suzi because she would dither about things. And he hated it when she was on the phone. It was "Suzi! Get off that fucking phone!"'

Shortly before she started at Ginger, Maria had bumped into Carol McGiffin, and Chris's estranged wife had issued a warning: 'You wouldn't believe a person could get so angry.' She hadn't been exaggerating.

But he employed more subtle controlling tactics, too.

'When *TFI* began he called a staff meeting in the board-room to explain what the show was about,' says Maria. 'Chris should have been at the top of the table. But he didn't come in, he stayed outside doing something else and his seat was left empty. John Revell was left to give the address. Everyone took it that Chris couldn't give a damn.'

Sometimes he was lavish with his praise, at others he acted as though 'thanks' was an alien word.

'I oversaw the entire move from Egton House to Titchfield Street; bought all the furniture from IKEA, made sure the computers were set up properly, everything,' Maria says. 'He didn't say one word.'

Evans can be spontaneously kind, buying lunches and drinks, or deliberately tight-fisted. On her thirty-sixth birthday, Maria – who virtually ran Evans's life at that time – was presented by Suzi with an £8.99 sun top. How did she know the price?

'The tag was left on.'

His emotions also fluctuated wildly, so that he was either laughing maniacally, or melancholic.

'I once saw him burst into tears at a party, just looking across at one of the old regulars from the Haverstock. He drunk too much and found it terribly sad.'

Maria attributed his mood-swings to an almost tangible loneliness.

'He has to have people around him all the time. I remember when he had a week's holiday and he kept turning up at the office every day. He would get people to drink with him. He said he just couldn't bear to be at home.'

As the year wore on, and he juggled his time between radio and television, his behaviour deteriorated. Browsing through his timetable, one understands why. Every weekday began at 4.30 a.m. with a wake-up call for the Breakfast Show. By the time he handed over to Simon Mayo at 9 a.m. he had completed more than half the average person's working day, yet his was only beginning. On Monday, still high on Breakfast Show adrenaline, he would preside over the dreaded inquest on the previous Friday's *TFI*.

'He was always particularly grumpy on Mondays,' Maria says.

Rollockings duly handed out, he might record a voice-over for one of the products he endorsed; Del Monte, for example. Since his first take was usually perfect – earning him thousands of pounds in repeat fees for a few minutes' work – he regarded this as money for old rope. Where possible, Tuesday was reserved for socializing and his great love, golf. On Wednesday he convened *TFI*'s creative team – Will, Danny Baker, David Granger and sometimes Revell – to write that week's script. On Thursday, the TV show's pre-recorded inserts, such as stunts and interviews, were shot. But Friday was the real killer. Vanishing at 9 a.m. prompt from Egton House, he would reappear, Houdini-like, half an hour later at the Riverside Studios in Hammersmith to begin the ten-hour marathon of producing and presenting that evening's *TFI*.

This fails to take into account his celebrity appearances and carousing. Days that started to the tinkling of milk-floats frequently reached their boozy anti-climax as the next dawn broke. Thick-headed and foul-breathed, Evans would then chuckle over his latest *faux-pas*, as reported in the tabloids, always abetted by Johnny Boy, Dan The Man, Holly and the rest. By the middle of 1996, barely a newspaper was published without reference to Evans, who occupied more column inches than any one person, with the possible exceptions of Diana, Princess of Wales and the then Prime Minister, John Major.

One eight-day period, commencing on 7 May 1996, epitomizes the madness of the time. First Evans was roundly criticized for refusing to accept a prestigious Best Broadcaster award from Sony because he had not won the Best Breakfast Show, too.

'So you're saying I'm the best broadcaster but my breakfast show isn't the best,' he raged, adding that the honour was 'pointless and meaningless'.

The fall-out had barely settled when Chris, by now investigated thirty-one times by broadcasting standards watchdogs, read out a listener's faxed joke about oral sex. The following day it was reported that the BBC had shelved plans to buy *Toothbrush* for fear that its host was too hot to handle.

The next anti-Evans story highlighted an incident in which Chris smashed a plant-pot belonging to his neighbour, whose crime was to have played music too loud. Glen Cardno, a 6ft 3ins tall, but mild-mannered and middle aged scriptwriter, lives in the basement flat directly below Chris's in Belsize Park. When Chris and Suzy moved in he had welcomed them with champagne. In relating their subsequent argument, he portrays a man apparently close to the edge.

'It was about 11.15 at night and I was with a girl who's a friend,' he says. 'We were listening to some music she had written and sung, semi-pop I suppose you'd call it. Because of Chris's lifestyle you never knew whether he was in, but he came banging on the door and shouted, "Turn that fucking music down!" What was particularly galling was that three weeks before he had done a TV show from his flat, and they kept me awake, rigging cables, till two or three in the morning.

'The girl I was with came out and explained that I was sampling music she had written. Chris just looked at her and said, "Well, if you wrote that, it's shit." She told him to sod off. I asked him to calm down and reminded him that he woke me up when he went to work every morning. I tried to reason, suggesting, "Let's both get something out of this." Evans refused to listen and suddenly picked up a terracotta pot on the window-ledge and hurled it to the ground. He then stormed off. Cardno took the advice of a solicitor and reported the matter to the police, but he did not wish to take action.

Cardno and Evans have since become good friends. The catalyst was their mutual affection for the actor Ronnie Fraser, their drinking mate at the Haverstock. Fraser died after suffering a stomach haemorrhage and, at his funeral, Chris was a pallbearer while Cardno was an usher.

'The day before we buried Ronnie, Chris came up to me and said, "I think we should make up, don't you?",' says Cardno. 'It takes a big man, who's a millionaire, to say sorry and for him to come over in front of all his friends was a hell of a thing to do. He said later that it had been so hard that he had looked up and said to himself, "Hey, Ronnie, you've got to give me a hand here. I can't do this on my own." He loved Ronnie dearly and he had given his career a new lease of life. In the years before he died, Ronnie couldn't get parts and Chris re-invented him as The Lord of Love, who read poems on *TFI*.'

In Cardno's view, Fraser's death had a profound effect on Chris.

'You could see by the way he was sobbing when he carried the coffin, and from what he said afterwards, that there must be a strong link between his father dying and Ronnie's death. They both died quite young, and I know Chris looked on Ronnie as something of a father figure. He felt cheated as a kid, and here it was all happening again. Since then he has changed completely. Think about it. You are on a freefall, your dad has died and you can do what you want. Then someone very close to you dies and it brings back memories of when you lost your father. And you suddenly think, 'What am I doing? I am horrible to everyone. I have reached the top of my career and it is time to take stock. Oh, fuck it, let's start being nice. Life's too short.''

'I think he has taken stock and got himself together. That's to be applauded and someone should say something about it. Chris has made an effort. His priorities have changed. He loves his golf, Suzi, his mum. Those are the things that he values most.'

Before this apparent transformation, Evans also fell foul of his neighbours in Nettlestead, a picturesque Kent village, where the previous year he had purchased a £350,000 white-walled mansion, The Old Rectory, intending to use it as a weekend retreat. His attitude towards the local residents would have brought wry smiles to the faces of Palin, Daley, Whittaker and co.

'When he arrived he threw a big party and we did the catering,' says Carole Apperley, landlady of the nearby Hop Pole pub.

'He had all his friends: Timmy Mallett, Ronnie Fraser and the rest. After that he and Suzi and the crowd would be in here most weekends, or he would ask us down to his garden for drinks. They were all over us, really. He always had time for everybody, especially youngsters. He gave them autographs, made them laugh.'

Chris shared his gossip with Carole and the Hop Pole regulars. When he took in a mongrel from the local dog rescue centre, then had to get rid of it because it chewed all his antique doors and window frames, they were the first to know. He sealed his place in the local community by giving the Bible reading at Carole's daughter, Jo-anne's wedding. But then, as suddenly as he had arrived, he cut Nettlestead and its people out of his life.

'The last time I saw him was just before Christmas, 1995,' says Carole. 'He had a drink and said he would see us after the holiday and we've never seen him since. It's a shame. I can't understand it. I can only think he's the sort of person who picks you up and drops you like a ton of bricks.'

Yet this apparent contempt for anyone outside his clan was nothing compared to that which emerged in August 1996. Claiming that London's pollution was making him ill, he cranked up huge publicity by donning a kilt and removing the Breakfast Show to the Scottish Highlands. What should have been a fun little ruse developed into a fiasco of epic proportions. Superstars rarely pitch base-camp in Inverness, and the townsfolk afforded Chris and his acolytes a genuinely warm Scottish welcome. Instead of accepting their out-stretched hands graciously, however, he behaved like a colonial overlord deigning to venture into the boondocks. Not content with mocking the 'clockwork studios', mimicking the local accent and leering at 'tartan tottie', he attempted to ridicule Moray Firth Radio's £13,500 a year breakfast DJ, Kevin 'Tich McCooey'. Tich's salary, he gloated on air, was '£12,500 less than Jamie's, who answers the phones for us.'

It was a gratuitous cheap-shot at a popular, unashamedly small-time local broadcaster, and in its own way it surpassed anything meted out to him in his Orford schooldays. The reaction was outrage.

'Not since Butcher Cumberland laid waste to Bonnie Prince Charlie's forces at Culloden 250 years ago has an Englishman excited such Highland wrath,' one commentator fulminated.

The *Daily Mail*'s Edward Verity asked rhetorically: 'Has radio's most revolting man finally gone too far?'

Was Chris chastened? Hardly. When Tich, all of 5ft 7ins tall, went to Evans's hotel to try and make peace, Evans, seven inches taller, rounded on him mercilessly.

'Don't consider that we even do the same job. If you were

any good you would not be on Moray Firth Radio,' he sneered at McCooey. 'You are merely material for my show. If you turn up, we will ignore you. We are successful and you are not.'

Every last punch that bruised the young Chris's face, every wounding insult about his hair, puny physique and glasses, might have been stored up for years, ready to be unleashed in that one unerringly savage reposte.

The humiliation of Tich can never be justified, but behind the scenes lay mitigating factors. For one thing, Suzi had not accompanied him to Scotland. Chris asked her to oversee the refurbishment at the Old Rectory in Nettlestead, and their separation caused constant friction. Confronted with his dis-interest when she phoned with plans for the now-neglected country house, Suzi was also hearing reports of the wild time he was having without her.

'Finally she told him she wished he would take as much interest in Kent as he was in Scotland,' recalls Maria Costello. When Suzi repeated the remark on his return it would lead to one of several temporary break-ups.

More disturbing still, the past just would not go away. Determined that her daughter should reap due benefit from Chris's fortune, Alison Ward was seeking to increase the £600 a month she received from him towards Jade's upkeep.

'He's a millionaire but Jade has never even had a holiday,' she says. 'She wants to learn the drums, but we can't afford a kit or lessons. She deserves to live in a house with a garden until she's eighteen, go out in a car, and have some decent clothes.'

Her mother Maureen adds, 'Chris has been where Alison and Jade are now but he won't help them out of it. You don't forget your roots.'

Their sense of injustice intensified when they learned that Chris, in a typically surreal whimsy, was paying Carol McGif-fin £150 a month for the upkeep of their greyhound bitch, Angelina.

The court application for a maintenance top-up has dragged on for so long that, on going to press, it has still to be settled. But on 2 August 1996, at the height of the Scottish debacle, Chris quietly sloped off to the office of Frank Tindal Milne, solicitor and notary public, in High Street, Nairn, Highland. There he swore an affidavit pressingly needed for submission in case 94 CP 521, Alison Ward versus Christopher Evans, filed at Warrington County Court.

For legal reasons, the details of his statement must remain confidential. However, it is understood that Evans attested to his personal assets, plus those of Ginger TV Productions Ltd and Ginger Air Ltd. Although the figures are likely to date back to the previous accounting year, totalled together they are believed to have placed him in the millionaire bracket.

In the intervening two years his fortune has mushroomed. He has formed at lest four more companies, Ginger Roots Ltd, Ginger Services Ltd, Ginger Radio Ltd and Tired Ltd. He owned – at the last count – two elegant houses in Notting Hill, together worth well over £1 million, plus the Belsize Park Gardens flat and the Nettlestead country residence. This summer he was also rumoured to be interested in buying a golfing retreat at Turnberry, and hotels as far apart as Torquay and Kenya. His fleet of cars ranges from a majestic, racing green Bentley Brooklands to a Matchbox-style bright blue Morris van, built more than thirty years ago but restored to mint condition.

To a single mother living in a council flat and working in a sewing-machine factory, such wealth is almost beyond comprehension.

But who was the happier, Chris or Alison? Charting his journey via press reports and grapevine gossip, his old friends knew the answer. As the year rolled on, Tim Grundy and Jules Fuller, to name but two, began to harbour dark thoughts that refuse to go away.

'I just have this secret fear,' says Grundy, 'I wouldn't like anything to happen to him. It's been a tremendously dramatic life, and quite often tremendously dramatic lives have tremendously dramatic endings. I was thinking something along the lines of James Dean,' says Grundy.

Fuller echoes: 'I just don't think you can keep going at that pace without bursting a blood vessel or getting so many ulcers your body gives up. Or he might just think, "What the fuck? I've done it all. What's the ultimate gag?" Killing yourself, that's what.'

Up in Scotland and later in August, on the Radio One Roadshow, Evans's emotional well-being appeared to concern him little. Those who watched *Six Go Mad In Somerset*, a Roadshow travelogue made for the for BBC TV (by Ginger, of course) might conclude that he was too intoxicated – either by fame, power or alcohol – to care. The fly-on-the-wall documentary, shot in Weston-Super-Mare, is revelatory in more ways than one. It perfectly illustrates Chris's own Elvis analogy. Evans swaggers through the seaside town like some messianic rock icon, with The Breakfast Show team as backing musicians.

'John! Joo-hn!' he snaps at Revell after buying a bag of chips, 'Can you pay, please?'

His faithful retainer reaches into his pocket.

In the background, Justin and Jamie posture and preen, signing autographs and checking out the talent. The rock band metaphor is complete during the following day's show when the team take to the stage complete with instruments to belt out an *Oasis* number.

Scrape away the sycophancy and child-like pranks, however, and the film serves a more serious purpose. It offers a fascinating insight into the way Evans can mesmerize a crowd, a talent honed from his earliest days in the Mersey pub and on Piccadilly's outside broadcasts. Taking the reins in the Stars nightclub he shows himself to be a brilliant dance DJ, but then, next day on the beach, he is equally inspirational in whooping up a vast holiday crowd. Flashbacks to early Roadshow kings, like Ed Stewart and Mike Read pale by comparison. It cannot be a coincidence that it is at these moments, when he is hosting the most happening party around, that Chris Evans looks at his happiest. Indeed, as he bids a sentimental goodbye to Weston-Super-Mare he resembles a schoolboy who realizes he's living an all-too-fleeting dream. The lyrics of his Roadshow signing-off tune, 'The Weekend Song', tell us how the little boy must have felt:

'I want to live in a castle,
I want the ocean as a pond,
I want a Jumbo jet just to get to work,
'Cos it always takes me far too long,
I want Spielberg to focus my camera . . .
Always look on the bright side of life.'

If there was a lump in Chris's throat when he led the communal singing, perhaps it was because he remembered his own family's seaside holidays. Perhaps he knew, too, that he would never feel this elation again: a few months later he announced that he would not be doing the Roadshow next year.

'I'm too old,' he said. 'I can't do all those wey-heys any more.'

On his return to London the champagne summer abruptly turned flat. The prospect of another gruelling winter, stretched to breaking-point between television and radio, was too much to contemplate. No amount of soothing office stress massages from Suzi – who cooingly refers to Chris as 'ba-bee' – could placate him.

'He sacked a lot of people,' says Teresa George, a props buyer who left Ginger voluntarily in October. 'He would just sack them on the spot. If he shouts at you and you answer back you get fired. He got angry every week. He always had to shout at someone.'

Teresa was not among his victims. On the contrary, in a not uncommon act of generosity, he allowed her – an aspiring singer – to use the TFI set for concerts without charge.

Maria Costello, however, was treated less benevolently. Castigated for allegedly contributing to one or two administrative mix-ups, she was finally sacked over a trivial incident. Seeking to shave time off the tedious Friday morning car journey from the West End to Hammersmith, Chris decided to buy a motor-scooter and gave Maria less than twenty-four-hours to arrange delivery.

'Don't forget to ask for a crash-helmet,' he told her, and she is adamant she did not.

However, when, the following morning, the blue Piaggio scooter arrived, minus the helmet and covered in the vendor's promotional stickers, Maria's fate was sealed.

'Chris didn't even tell me himself, he got someone else to do it. The following morning he left a meek-sounding message on my answer-machine. "Maria, it's Christopher, can you ring me please?" I didn't ring back because I know how charming he is and how easy it would have been for him to say he was sorry.'

The following Monday, when Maria switched on The Breakfast Show, she was sickened to hear Evans and his crew making light of her dismissal.

But there was levity, too, after Chris was again hauled over the coals for gratuitous offensiveness by Matthew Bannister.

'Yesterday we were talking to the boss, the Fat Controller of Radio One, Two, Three and Four – Mr Matthew Bannister,' Evans told his seven million listeners. 'Look, how ungrateful is this guy? We saved his job because, frankly, before we joined he was slipping *down* the bannister – he was out on his ear. We turned this station round ... and yesterday, after eighteen months of doing the show he decides to give us a pep talk all of a sudden.'

For once a member of the team corrected and soothed him. It had only been 'a bit of a chat', said Dan The Man.

'Well,' said Evans, 'he's never done it before.'

In pushing Bannister to the brink, Chris was betraying a man who had always protected him from his critics. These included no less a figure than the BBC chairman Sir Christopher Bland, who admitted that he sometimes 'winced' when he and his twelve-year-old son listened to The Breakfast Show on the morning drive to school. Evans was also behaving with uncharacteristic naïvity, for he well understood the monolithic inner workings of the British Broadcasting Corporation.

Ginger's huge production fee had created major waves at a time when competition for funds had been thrown wide open, bringing BBC Radio into direct competition with BBC Television. Chris was aware of the simmering resentment, but fuelled the flames with gasoline. He alienated Trevor Dann, then Radio One's Head of Production, by gleefully ignoring his record play-list. Instead he introduced a string of talented new bands – which was at least a boost for the often overlooked independent music industry. Worse, he then ridiculed Dann – who had spoken in praise of his talent at his GLR leaving party – on air.

'We unreservedly loathe the man,' he said.

No Radio One DJ, however popular, would have escaped with this under the old regime. But Evans felt immune. He answered only to Bannister . . . if he felt like it.

The Evans backlash spread through the BBC like cancer. Chris thought himself above carrying a security pass, but one morning, when he tried to enter Broadcasting House he was blocked by a guard.

'How do I know who you are?' the guard asked, staring at the country's most instantly recognizable star.

A cursing Evans suggested he look in the lobby, where his portrait hung on the wall.

'Matthew then got a letter from the Head of Security reminding him to instruct presenters to carry security passes at all times,' reveals the ex-Radio One deputy head Paul Robinson. 'Matthew was furious, but there were all sorts of incidents like that. I would have made sure the security guard got a good bollocking.'

But Bannister was growing weary of championing his own tormentor. In late October, Evans returned from a seven-day break and immediately demanded another week off, complaining of fatigue. His gums began to bleed and he lost his appetite, hastening the return of his hypochondria. Behind the semi-jocular radio banter about his poor health, privately he feared some terrible affliction. Tranquillisers and sleeping pills were among the drugs prescribed.

During the 1 November edition of *TFI*, even his entourage

were alarmed. Parading a smorgasbord of pills before the cameras, Chris began to ramble.

'I'm here against doctor's orders,' he said. 'I am medically unsound and shouldn't be on the radio [sic], and if you don't believe me, look at these. This is not a joke, it's true . . . no one believes me and my bosses won't give me any time off but I am mentally unwell.'

Four different drugs were preserving his sanity, he continued. 'One helps me sleep, one calms me down and one, in the words of my doctor, brings me down an octave.'

A close-up of his extended tongue revealed that it was covered in ulcers. And later, while interviewing the actress Helen Mirren, his concentration – normally pin-sharp – deserted him.

'I'm completely out of kilter and I don't know what I'm doing any more,' he told her.

'Evans: I Am Going Mad', ran the front-page headline in the following day's *Mirror*. A few days later, the *Daily Telegraph*'s showbusiness reporter Alison Boshoff recorded a bizarre encounter with Evans at 2 a.m. at the British Comedy Awards.

'He was,' she wrote euphemistically, 'slightly the worse for wear. I said hello and he looked at me with glassy eyes. "Open wide, I want to see if your gums are healthy or not", he said, then drifted off.'

Set against this background, the only surprising aspect of Evans's departure from Radio One was that everyone was so surprised. His programme by now reduced to a daily bulletin on his own perceived misfortune, on 17 January he reported the news to a stunned nation.

'We have no choice, we are being forced out,' he said, as though he were Chamberlain relaying the message that Hitler had refused to withdraw from Poland. The reason: Bannister had refused to allow him to work a four-day week, leaving Fridays for *TFI*.

'I don't want people to think that I planned all of this,' he said later. 'But the truth is, I love doing the show for Radio One and I didn't want to resign. They paid me well . . . but the money means absolutely nothing. I could earn ten times from TV what I earned on radio. I don't even look at the pay cheque from Radio One. But I wanted Friday off because I simply could not go on with the workload. I'd been asking to work a four-day week since last year and Matthew always said no.'

In another interview he said he had resigned 'to keep my sanity'.

In the view of Paul Robinson, well-acquainted with the intricacies of BBC Radio politics, Bannister had been left with little option but to 'make a sacrificial lamb' of Evans.

'People high up at the BBC were saying he hadn't got control of Radio One and Evans. He was now the Controller of all BBC Radio, not just Radio One, and he had to show he had a grip of his own house. I think he also thought that he had got so much out of Chris Evans that he could afford to let him go. The greater objective was to demonstrate he was in charge.'

He added: 'Matthew and Chris are close professionally but not close friends. He looked after him as best as he could but Chris got increasingly demanding. He pushes and pushes. Having said all that, he is a brilliant talent and I still think Matthew was wrong to let Chris go.'

Evans had initially agreed to stay on until 27 March so that a replacement could be found. But when – just thirty-six hours after the announcement – he defiantly played a round of golf with Revell rather than host the show, Bannister must have been pleased he wouldn't be working his notice. The prospect of having his authority, and the station's reputation, undermined for two more months cannot have been appealing. By nice irony, Mark Radcliffe, the man who saved White And Two Sugars from the sack after he wiped Tim Grundy's Geldof tape, was rewarded with Chris's old job.

In the aftermath of his departure from the BBC, Chris made a brave attempt to disguise the blow. Drawing on reserves of chutzpah built up during his busking and Tarzan-o-gram days, he resolutely put himself about. He engineered a Concorde trip to New York with Richard Branson, ensuring journalists were on the flight to witness their back-of-a-napkin negotiations. He was reportedly close to signing a £20 million contract to turn *TFI* into a thrice-weekly show; Channel 5 were said to have offered him £42 million contract. None of these deals came to anything, and reeked very strongly of hype. The speculation ended on 22 March. Grinning like a Ginger Tom who'd got the cream, Chris put his signature to a £15 million renewal agreement that keeps him at Channel 4 until the end of 1998. The moment was captured by the *TFI* cameras, naturally.

It was good money, all right, but the second the credits rolled, Chris stopped smiling.

'Hey, Mike. Mike? What was it that Oscar Wilde said about ambition?'

'On the face of it you have a very successful,
likeable, interesting, almost happy-go-lucky
character. Whereas in reality you have a
fundamentally unhappy man, who has been
frighteningly single-minded in his determination to
succeed; who has used and abused those around
him; has left a trail of devastation in his wake, and
hasn't finished in his endless quest for power and
glory. I really hope I am wrong, but it will probably
all end in tears.'

TIM GRUNDY, Summer 1997

Summer 1997. At 11.15 a.m. on a light, breezy morning a
taxi pulls up beside the Riverside Studios, overlooking the
Thames by Hammersmith Bridge. The tall figure who emerges
immediately makes you smile. He is wearing a floppy, white
Flowerpot Man hat, pulled down so low that it covers the
black upper-rim of his glasses. The spindliness of his ginger-
flecked legs is exaggerated by baggy Bermuda shorts and
black-and-red Manchester United football socks, rolled low
around his ankles. The overall impression is that of a Gang
Show actor who took a wrong turning on the way to the
seaside pier theatre and ended up in Crisp Street, W6. Amusing as his outfit appears, however, as Chris Evans reaches
into a cavernous pocket to find his cab fare, his demeanour
betrays tension and irritability.

Thank Fuck It's Friday?

'I'll only thank fuck when Friday's finished,' his face seems to say.

As Evans disappears into 19 Chancellor's Street, the small mews-style house opposite the studio, where the *TFI* team plans the show, the day slowly begins to take shape. A baseball-hatted Danny Baker finishes off his fry-up in the Odd Spot – immortal venue for Cedric's Comment From The Cafe. Sauntering off to join the gaffer, he sings: 'It's your letters, it's your leee-eetters . . .' *TFI*'s catchy postbag jingle. Ten minutes pass before a distinctly sheepish Will Macdonald – late, perhaps? – becomes the next key man to arrive. All this time small huddles of star-gazers and autograph hunters have been gathering opposite the studio's glass frontage.

'Wee-eel,' they hiss, pointing at Macdonald. 'Weeeee-eeeel.'

Andrew Carey, the Haverstock Arms landlord and *TFI*'s barman, seems to crave similar adulation. Hours before he is due on the set he struts about the street with a wire running from his ear to a gadget hidden beneath his crisp white apron. But the crowds are not here for Carey.

Peroxide blondes in mini skirts, leather and leopardskin; blue-rinse mums revisiting their youth; cool young boys with trendy haircuts and uncool ones in anoraks and no-name jeans, they mill about waiting for the bands, and for Chris, or Chrissy Baby, as he is also known to some female fans.

The tedium is momentarily alleviated when Gary from security drops his jeans and moons for the paparazzi. Then finally, at 1.50 p.m., still flowerpotted, Chrissy Baby re-emerges. Smiling now.

'All right, luv?' 'Hi, how are ya?' 'Great to see ya!'

He sounds as though he means it. He poses willingly beside a girl who has travelled up from Bristol and her mother takes an album snap. Scribbles his name on proffered books and scraps of paper, sometimes adding a little message.

'He's a lot taller than I thought,' someone says.

There have been stories recently about a stalker who is out

to remove the quirky grin from Evans's face, and all the time his gaze is shifting, clocking everyone and everything around him. Perhaps the fear that another Shaver Browne might be out there – fists cocked, bladder full – is making him edgy. He certainly doesn't resemble the relaxed, transformed character Glen Cardno described after Ronnie Fraser's funeral.

What's eating Chris? The temptation is to ask The Man Who Knows What's Going On, now twirling his handlebar moustache over a cuppa in the Odd Spot. But *TFI*'s all-seeing sage appears too lost in thought to be disturbed. Less so Cedric, the show's cotton-wool bearded, Venezuelan-Guyanan muse. Waiting for Chris or Danny to inform him what this week's Comment From The Cafe is to be, he lets us in on one or two closely-guarded *TFI* secrets.

Actually, he confides, the greasy-spoon isn't his. It belongs to an Irish woman and he just pretends to be the proprietor on Fridays. Chris gave him the role after remembering his character-filled face from the audience of *Toothbrush*.

'I don't decide what I say on the show,' he adds glumly. 'I read it all from a board. They decide everything. Sometimes I don't even know what it will be until a few minutes before I do my piece.'

Never mind. At least this week's assortment of Freaks look happy. Or Uniques, depending how you see it.

Remembering some of the all-time greats – the Girl Who Can Cry Milk, the Woman Called Bear Who Makes A Noise Like A Lamb, The Man Who Can Stick A Coat-hanger Through His Nose, The Man Who Can Make His Stomach Resemble An Elephant and The Incredibly Tall Old Lady (who never did get picked) – an intriguing thought comes to mind. Perhaps the motley assortment of Freaks, Fat Looka-likes and Ugly Blokes who at once amuse and repel us on *TFI Friday* offer the best possible clue about Chris Evans's view of himself. Imagine him in the kitchen at Greenwood Crescent, close to tears after another day's torment at school. One can almost hear Minnie Evans consoling her son: 'Your not a freak, Chris. You're unique.'

Accepting this possibility, and coupling it with the untimely death of his father, everything Chris has done in his thirty-one years begins to drop into place. Indeed, in the months following his departure from Radio One, his determination to confirm his 'uniqueness' has continued unabated. What Ordinary Bloke could go on a bender with Gazza; name the time and the place for a *Vogue* cover interview with the beautiful Mariella Frostrup; zoom off in a river launch with Sir Paul McCartney? What Ordinary Bloke spends the first part of his winter weeks playing golf in Portugal and acquires London properties as though he were playing Monopoly? What Ordinary Bloke drinks himself into oblivion for nine consecutive days to celebrate the end of *TFI Friday*'s latest series, then wakes up in a Scottish hotel with a Bloody Mary by the bed, wondering where he is?

Our last sighting of him was on Saturday 12 July. At lunch time he bowled into the Haverstock Arms with a slender, blonde lap-dancer from Stringfellows – where else? The pub's regulars have grown accustomed to his drunken eccentricities, but even they were shocked by what happened next.

'Chris and the girl disappeared into the loo and re-emerged wearing each other's clothes,' one onlooker said. 'He was prancing around in her cat suit, and she kept saying, 'Chris! Chris! Where's me fuckin' shoes?'

Later that evening, Evans arrived at a party at the Lingfield healthclub with a different blonde, this one the hostess of a sex programme on cable TV.

Such behaviour would finish most long-term relationships, but thus far Suzi Aplin has accepted it. Why? Some say she simply buys Evans's explanations, that it keeps their partnership fresh. According to others, however, there is a more hard-headed reason.

'Suzi knows that Chris only does these things to keep his name in the papers,' one says. 'He says he doesn't want things to cool off over the summer, when he isn't on TV.'

This theory became more compelling when, a few days after his lost Saturday, Evans was spotted out on the town with the *Sun*'s hottest Page 3 girl, Melinda Messenger. A lust for blondes or shameless hype? Either way, it doesn't suggest a secure man, at peace with himself.

So, in his never-ending quest for extra-ordinariness, is Evans as fundamentally unhappy as Tim Grundy suggests?

Back at the Riverside studios, it is 4.15 p.m., and rehearsals for another show are now over. Evans is holding court beneath the dartboard in the Chancellor's pub opposite the studios, where, inevitably, he is surrounded by Will, Danny, Carey and one or two others. Budweiser bottle in one hand, cigarette in the other, he leaps around like a demented Jack-in-the-Box, as incapable of sitting still now as he was when he once trampolined on Maureen Ward's couch. Though perpetually in motion, Chris dominates the banter, which centres on the drinking exploits of Gazza.

'He doesn't drink glasses, he drinks bowls of beer,' he marvels.

'Bowls of gin,' interjects Baker. 'No bowl must be brooked.'

'More than Jimmy Five Bellies,' Evans rejoins, lifting an imaginary bowl to his lips and pretending to quaff like Gazza's best friend.

'Hey, Danny,' he says, his mime over. 'I'm going to put a pair of running shoes in your bowl of gin. I've always wanted to spike your drink.'

Will and the crew laugh on cue but, before their mirth has subsided, Chris has already moved on. Now he is distractedly drumming his fingers on the table, eyes darting around the room.

'I'm so bored,' he is saying to no one in particular. 'I'm bored, I'm bored, I'm bored . . .'

The author and publishers wish to thank the following for use of copyright photographic material:

The Evans's council home in Greenwood Crescent; Newsheet, the newsagents where Chris had one of his first tastes of working life (© David Cairns Photo)

Chris in mid-flight with his Tarzan-o-gram money spinner (Courtesy of Karen Welch)

An early PR portrait, circa 1985/6 (Piccadilly Radio)

Trevor Palin at Piccadilly Radio (Courtesy of Trevor Palin)

Minnie Evans plays a 'Fairy Over Forty' at Orford Hall (Courtesy of Pat Daley)

Chris Brewing tea for his pregnant girlfriend, Alison Ward (Courtesy of *Manchester Evening News*)

Jade Lois Ward (Courtesy of Alison Ward)

Alison and Jade Ward (Courtesy of *The Sun*)

Chris in happier times, with wife Carol McGiffin; Chris begins work at the Radio One Breakfast Show; with Michael Grade after signing a lucrative new contract with Channel 4 (Solo Syndication Ltd)

The author and publishers have made every effort to trace copyright holders. All copyright holders who have not for any reason been contacted are invited to write to the publishers so that a full acknowledgment may be made in subsequent editions of this work.